MEN

AND

MOLECULES

Second Series

MEN

AND

MOLECULES

NORMAN METZGER

Based on the radio series sponsored by the
AMERICAN CHEMICAL SOCIETY

Introduction by Isaac Asimov

CROWN PUBLISHERS, INC., NEW YORK

for benjamin jacob metzger

574.192
M56m
82803
apr.1973

Designed by Ruth Smerechniak

PRINTED IN THE UNITED STATES OF AMERICA

Published simultaneously in Canada
by General Publishing Company Limited

ACKNOWLEDGMENTS

Many people provided the knowledge that made this book possible. Scientific research is by nature contentious, and not all of those who helped me will agree with the way their contribution is presented. However, I am deeply grateful to all of them, and I would like to acknowledge them by name: Leland Allen, Princeton University; John N. Bahcall, California Institute of Technology; Jake Bello, Roswell Park Memorial Institute, Buffalo, New York; Johan Bjorksten, Bjorksten Research Foundation, Madison, Wisconsin; H. Marshall Blann, University of Rochester; Justin L. Bloom, United States Atomic Energy Commission, Germantown, Maryland; Murray Blum, University of Georgia; Vaughan T. Bowen, Woods Hole Oceanographic Institution; Robert H. Brill, Corning Museum of Glass, Corning, New York; S. Barry Brummer, Tyco Laboratories, Waltham, Massachusetts; David Buhl, National Radio Astronomy Observatory, Green Bank, West Virginia; R. H. Burris, University of Wisconsin; Joseph Chatt, University of Sussex; Eugene F. Corcoran, University of Miami; Howard Curtis, Brookhaven National Laboratory, Upton, New York; Raymond Davis, Jr., Brookhaven National Laboratory; Robert E. Davis, Purdue University; Robert DeMars, University of Wisconsin; Robert G. Denkewalter, Merck Sharp & Dohme Research Laboratories, Rahway, New Jersey; Bertram Donn, Goddard Space Flight Center, National Aeronautics and Space Administration; Robert L. Fleischer, General Electric Research and Development Center, Schenectady, New York; Frederick Fowkes, Lehigh University; Nelson Fuller, Scripps Institution of Oceanography, University of California; Albert Ghiorso, Lawrence Radiation Laboratory, University of California; Edward Goldberg, Scripps Institution of Oceanography, University of California, R. W. F. Hardy, The Du Pont Company, Wilmington, Delaware; David Harker, Roswell Park Memorial Institute, Buffalo, New York; Denham Harman, College of Medicine, University of Nebraska; Leonard Hayflick, Stanford University; Robert L. Herrmann, Boston University School of Medicine; Ralph F. Hirschmann, Merck, Sharp & Dohme Research Laboratories, Rahway, New Jersey; Ralph Albert Horne, Woods Hole Oceanographic Institution; Icko Iben, Massachusetts Institute of Technology; Barclay Kamb, California Institute of Technology; Gobinath Kartha, Roswell Park Memorial Institute, Buffalo, New York; William Klemperer, Harvard University; Robert R. Kohn, Case-Western Reserve Medical School; Michael Lesch, Peter Bent Brigham Hospital, Boston, Massachusetts; Ellis Lippincott, University of Maryland; R. Bruce Merrifield, Rockefeller University; Leonard E. Mortenson, Purdue University; William L. Nyhan, University of California, San Diego; Karl A. Piez, National Institute of Dental Research; P. Buford Price, University of California, Berkeley; Sherman W. Rabideau, Los Alamos Scientific Laboratory, University of California; Wendell Roelofs, Cornell University; Denis L. Rousseau, Bell Telephone Laboratories, Murray Hill, New Jersey; Edward V. Sayre, Brookhaven National Laboratory, Upton, New York; Robert L. Scranton, University of Chicago; Glenn T. Seaborg, University of California at Berkeley; Douglas B. Seba, University of Miami; J. Edwin Seegmiller, University of California, San Diego; Nathan W. Shock, Gerontology Research Center, National Institutes of Health, Baltimore, Maryland; John B. Siddall, Zoecon Corporation, Palo Alto, California; F. Marott Sinex, Boston University School of Medicine; Lewis Snyder, University of Virginia; Philip Solomon, Columbia University; Aloys Tappel, University of California, Davis; Stanley Thompson, Lawrence Radiation Laboratory, University of California; Daniel Wilkes, Lawrence Radiation Laboratory, University of California; Carroll M. Williams, Harvard University; E. O. Wilson, Harvard University; Richard Wolfgang, Yale University; Eugene E. van Tamelen, Stanford University.

Grateful acknowledgment is made to the publisher for permission to use excerpts from the poem "The Neutrino and Mr. Brinsley," from the *Asbestos Phoenix*, by Ramon Guthrie published by Funk & Wagnalls. © 1968 by Ramon Guthrie.

CONTENTS

PREFACE

Chemistry, a British wit said, is like gin: dull on its own but a wonderful mixer. Like most witticisms, it harbors only a measure of the truth. Chemistry (here mixed with astronomy, genetics, nuclear physics, archaeology, etc.) is an exciting, active science, dramatic on its own, capable of generating its own peculiar theatrics—as in the "weird water" controversy—and serving as a mediating force in such other tangled fields as research on aging.

The diversity of the topics covered in this book demonstrates the scope of chemistry. But whether men are creating new atoms, seeking clues to a bizarre genetic disease, probing the mysteries of the sun, or simply trying to satisfy their curiosity about insects, there is always the unifying principle: understanding the interactions and transformations of atoms and molecules.

My aim in writing *Men and Molecules* is to present a broad snapshot of chemical research in the seventies and hopefully to convey an insight into the nature of scientific research. Science has been called a constantly changing set of approximations, and many of the areas covered here demonstrate—sometimes frustratingly!—just such changing "truth." What really is the truth on aging? Who was right in the polywater matter? How do the molecules of space form, and what is their message, if any? What is the best way to assess the status of the oceans?

This book is the product of many interviews with outstanding scientists who sat in front of a microphone—pointed at them like a gun—patiently, sometimes nervously, explaining their work. The tapings were for the radio series *Men and Molecules*, supported by the American Chemical Society as part of its efforts to inform the general public of the true nature of chemical research.

I am grateful to Mrs. Gloria E. Thompson and Mrs. Jacqueline P. Early for typing the manuscript, often against great cryptographic odds. My thanks also go to Miss Judy Bitting for her fine line drawings. The Society's executive director, Dr. Frederick T. Wall, supported the preparation of this book, while Mr. Roy Avery and Mr. James H. Stack were tolerant to the extreme of my lengthy disappearances during office hours while "working on the book."

Finally, I am most grateful to the members of the American Chemical Society, who made it possible for me to visit their laboratories to find out what they were up to.

NORMAN METZGER
Washington, D.C.

INTRODUCTION:
THE GROWING
EDGE OF SCIENCE

For a little better than four centuries now, science has been expanding at an increasing rate. It is a sphere of light and knowledge, growing and biting in every direction into the limitless ocean of the dark unknown.

It began in 1543 with Andreas Vesalius revolutionizing the world of biology by describing the human body as it is—through the revolutionary technique of looking at it. And now the human brain is striving mightily to understand itself, and we are on the verge of being able to redesign the human body Vesalius looked at and to remold it nearer (we hope) to our hearts' desire.

It began, again in 1543, with Nicolas Copernicus revolutionizing astronomy by going to the trouble of calculating planetary positions on the basis of a sun-centered universe rather than an earth-centered one and showing that everything suddenly made much more sense. And now, the human brain gazes outward some nine billion light-years to a distant quasar and backward for eons to an exploding cosmic egg and forward for eons to— what? Another cosmic egg forming?

It was a great discovery once to look through a lens and see whole forms of life so small as to find a universe in a drop of water. Now we probe protons and neutrons, to which an invisible fragment of that drop of water would be a universe, and we wonder—is there something smaller yet?

It was a great discovery once to find out that air, a colorless, odorless, tasteless gas, so insubstantial as to appear nothing, was actually a mixture of two gases, equally colorless, odorless, tasteless, and equally insubstantial—but so different. Now the atomic architects of the laboratory take molecules of incredible complexity, pull them apart into their ultimate parts, and put them together again—or put together new compounds that never yet had existed, but designed to perform tasks that need doing.

At every stage of its growth, science has affected the individual and society—whether for good or ill—to such an extent that life now would be unbearable and unrecognizable without it.

And always it is the growing edge of science that is of the greatest importance. It is that surface of the steadily expanding sphere of light that wins from the surrounding darkness the today-discovery that will change tomorrow-man and tomorrow-society; that will make us all over; save us, if properly handled; destroy us, perhaps, otherwise.

Knowledge can strike the enemies of mankind or ourselves depending on how it is wielded. It can destroy poverty and sickness, or it can make wars more terrible; it can renovate the environment, or poison it.

The more of us there are who know and understand what is going on at the growing edge right now, the greater the chance that we will know enough to direct the new knowledge it is giving us in proper fashion.

For those who are actually involved in the growing edge of science, life is a constant excitement and adventure. Those not directly involved might envy them that excitement and might wonder what changes lie in store for us all—but they are not totally condemned to unsatisfied curiosity.

They can read *Men and Molecules,* which deals with the vast chemical sector of the growing edge, and, in effect, they can look over the shoulders of the scientists at work and share in the excitement of some of the most thrilling aspects of the growing edge of science.

ISAAC ASIMOV

1

ATTACKING
GENETIC MISTAKES

We're all imperfect. We are all victimized by mistakes that are transmitted when sperm adds its packet of genetic information to the mother's egg and a new life begins.

Happily, most of us pass through life unaware of our shortcomings. However, for a few these genetic miscues at the beginning of life are a disaster. They warp minds, disable muscle, inexorably rip apart the body's interwoven chemistry, and often kill. The consequences of genetic errors may be subtle: both autistic and schizophrenic children may be partial victims of heredity.

Genetic diseases cut into more life years than cancer, heart disease, and stroke—diseases that occur mostly late in life. A geneticist and Nobel Prize winner, Dr. Joshua Lederberg, told a Senate hearing a couple of years ago that a quarter of the hospital beds in the United States are "occupied by persons suffering some degree of genetic disease."

The diseases are as diverse as man himself, including cystic fibrosis, in which a child's lungs are choked by mismade mucus; lethal Tay-Sachs disease that had its origins some five hundred years ago in a village on the Polish-Lithuanian border; Huntington's chorea, one of the most tragic because it stays hidden until the late twenties, striking down its victims in the prime of life.

The list of what can go wrong genetically is almost infinite; there are some forty varieties of genetic deafness alone. But, diverse as they are, these diseases all come together at the genes, where the genetic information we received from our parents is chemically encoded in the molecule deoxyribonucleic acid, or DNA. In conception, the sperm and egg meet, combining their packets of genetic information (DNA).

The genetic information—DNA bundled into genes and distributed on chromosomes—of the fertilized egg (zygote) serves as a blueprint for the manufacture of proteins that will be needed for growth and development. The zygote divides and redivides—128 cells in a week—with each new cell given identical genetic information—the same genes, the same DNA—as the original cell, the zygote. In virtually all cases the sole products of the genes are proteins, such as enzymes. But the particular mix of proteins given a cell—as yet, by a still unknown master plan—decides its role in life, whether it is to be a heart cell, skin cell, a bit of the brain, or part of an eye.

If a gene, a section of DNA, is faulty, then the protein it helps to make will also be faulty. We *all* harbor a few faulty genes, but the few mismade proteins matter little to most people because a second, normal copy of these genes is usually present to ensure an adequate supply of normal proteins. Of course, such sudden genetic changes in the structure of DNA—mutations— are the mechanics of evolution. This is how nature creates new variations and tests them. Some are found wanting and are discarded; others thrive and remain.

Genetic diseases may be the gray zone or margin of error, experiments with new genetic patterns that went astray to produce a new but warped life. Occasionally, hints of good intentions are visible. For instance, those who have an inheritable anemia—sickle-cell anemia—more common in blacks, are unusually resistant to malaria. If they live in malarial zones, their anemia may protect them. Other diseases such as cystic fibrosis may have unsuspected benefits that would explain their survival from generation to generation.

But these rationalizations mean little when the realities of genetic diseases are encountered in full detail. The most arresting of all is the Lesch-Nyhan syndrome.

It affects only boys. Its signs appear in the first few months of life—the head begins to droop, and arms and legs begin to shake uncontrollably, much as they do for a victim of cerebral palsy, often the mistaken diagnosis for the Lesch-Nyhan syndrome. About the third year of life, the children begin compulsively to mutilate themselves. They bite and even amputate their fingers and chew through their lips. They have used braces and the spokes of wheelchairs to destroy their flesh, and when given the chance, have tried to scald themselves with hot water. They do it despite the pain.

"It's quite apparent that they do not want to do this," says J. Edwin Seegmiller, a physician who has worked on the disease. "Often they seek the help of others in restraining their hands so that they cannot get them into their mouths."

This bizarre affliction was identified as a genetic disease in 1963. By 1970 researchers had identified the chemical defect involved and exploited that information to detect affected children in the womb so that they might be aborted. They have learned how to find potential mothers who are Lesch-Nyhan carriers, those who possess the gene at fault but show none of the symptoms of the disease.

The syndrome is named for Dr. Michael Lesch, a second-year medical student at Johns Hopkins when he worked on the disease, and Dr. William L. Nyhan, then associate professor of pediatrics. A four-year-old boy was brought to the emergency room of the Harriet Lane Home in Baltimore, which is the pediatric clinic of Johns Hopkins. The emergency was caused by blood in the boy's urine (hematuria), but other, less-pressing symptoms were obvious: mental retardation, inability to sit up or walk without help, arms and legs that shook uncontrollably— what physicians call choreoathetosis. And the boy's fingertips on the right hand as well as his lower lips were badly mutilated.

There were crystals in the boy's urine which had done enough internal damage to cause bleeding and which examining physicians thought were crystals of cystine, an amino acid. Because Nyhan had the only equipment there that could do a rapid amino-acid analysis, he was sent a urine sample. But the crystals were not cystine or any amino acid; they were uric acid, a normal enough body chemical, except that the little boy was producing three to four times the usual amount.

When Nyhan talked with the boy's parents and found out that the child's eight-year-old brother had similar symptoms— mutilation, retardation, etc.—he suggested to Lesch that they search the literature and find out how to study uric acid metabolism.

The result was a classical study of its kind published in 1964 in the *American Journal of Medicine.* Lesch and Nyhan reported that the two brothers were not only making too much uric acid, but that the entirety of that part of their body chemistry—of which uric acid was the end product, purine metabolism—was over-producing; an assembly line had gone amok, its production outpacing the body's disposal system. The consequences were disastrous but medically fascinating.

"Here," says Dr. Seegmiller, "was a biochemical basis for a stereotyped form of compulsive behavior."

While Lesch and Nyhan were doing a detailed diagnosis of their unusual patients, Dr. Seegmiller was probing the genetic and chemical factors in gouty arthritis a few miles away at the National Institute of Arthritis and Metabolic Diseases, a part of the National Institutes of Health, in Bethesda, Maryland. In gouty arthritis, an adult problem, a chemical made in excess by the body crystallizes as a chalklike material in joints and kidneys. Severe pain, bleeding, and, if untreated, death result. The excessive chemical, of course, is uric acid.

"But we were a bit surprised," Seegmiller recalls, "to find that the patients who produced the most uric acid were not being seen by rheumatologists, but rather were being seen by pediatricians." These were the Lesch-Nyhan children.

Uric acid has a long history. It was named in 1798 when it was found in urinary stones, its high levels in the blood of gout victims pointed out in 1850, and its molecular structure established in 1898 by the German chemist Emil Fischer.

Uric acid is the form in which the human body disposes of purines, a group of body chemicals that have a typically ubiquitous role in life chemistry, the most important (and ironic) being their function as building blocks for the genetic material, DNA.

A standard and successful treatment for gout and gouty arthritis is a drug called allopurinol, originally designed to be an anticancer drug but ineffective as such. However, it did lower the uric acid levels of cancer victims remarkably, and that led to its use in gout and similar diseases where overproduction of uric acid is the problem. Essentially, the drug obstructs the body's formation of uric acid by blocking an enzyme that mediates uric acid's formation from two predecessor purines—guanine and xanthine. When guanine and xanthine therefore accumulate because of the allopurinol, the body reacts in several ways: a portion of the two purines is excreted directly without passing through the uric stage; a portion is "salvaged"; i.e., the body, finding it cannot dispose of waste purines, reverses itself and reuses these blocked purines as building blocks for DNA. Finally, in the most subtle step of all, the body's entire system for making and removing purines is slowed down, which lowers the output of uric acid. In this poorly understood "feedback" mechanism, the pile-up of purines at a critical point signals the body to slow its entire purine chemistry, like a Detroit assembly line where a pile-up of cars at the finish produces a frantic phone call to the other end to hold off on the steering wheels.

This multiple reaction by the body to the blocking of a single chemical step—the creation of uric acid—is what has made allopurinol so effective for gout sufferers, whose problem comes down to the overproduction of uric acid, which then crystallizes in their joints, producing, among other things, that notoriously painful toe that once made it "the disease of kings and the king of diseases."

The point is, it was quite natural for Seegmiller and his colleagues to expect positive results when they gave allopurinol to the Lesch-Nyhan children, who were also making too much uric acid. But while uric acid levels did go down (expected), the purine production rates remained as high as ever (not expected). Moreover, the amounts of xanthine and guanine went up. That meant that the body's ability to salvage these purines for re-use, so useful to victims of adult gout (the Lesch-Nyhan syndrome is often called a juvenile gout), was inoperative, and it was inoperative because the necessary enzyme was either missing or inactive.

Enzymes are proteins and the product of genes. The role of enzymes (explained more fully in the chapter on ribonuclease) is to pace properly the thousands of chemical reactions within the cells. In virtually all genetic diseases, the immediate problem is a missing or faulty enzyme, due, of course, to a missing or faulty gene. The particular piece of body chemistry that the indicted enzyme controls goes awry. Molecules that should have been processed by that enzyme pile up. They crowd the cells, throwing its tightly knit chemistry off balance. As more cells are affected, organs start to misfunction, until finally the signs of disease become obvious. The central problem facing the researcher probing a genetic disease is to find the one enzyme out of thousands whose absence or impotence initiates the disease.

"In order to be scientifically significant," Seegmiller says, "you've got to be able to identify the real biochemistry that is abnormal; which of the thousands of chemical reactions in the body is affected. You must identify which of the enzymes—the protein products of the genes—are abnormal. We've done that in the Lesch-Nyhan syndrome."

The enzyme at fault is called hypoxanthine—guanine phosphoribosyltransferase, mercifully cut to HGPRT. The first two names are purines; the rest tells the enzyme's chemical task. It is the "salvage enzyme" that enables the body to re-use purines such as guanine and xanthine, particularly when their excretion as uric acid is blocked by the drug allopurinol.

How can this insignificant misstep in body chemistry explain the Lesch-Nyhan syndrome, particularly the frightening compulsion of the victims to destroy their flesh?

"The simplest proposal that's been made," says Seegmiller, "is that maybe it's the uric acid that does it. But nature doesn't seem to like having uric acid in the brain, because there is a barrier against its coming into the cerebrospinal fluid." And in fact, the uric acid levels in victims and normal children are the same.

But it is intriguing that in the brain the enzyme implicated in the Lesch-Nyhan syndrome, HGPRT, is highest in the basal ganglia of normal children and completely absent in the victims. Basal ganglia are lumps of gray and white cells scattered about the top of the brain stem that have to do with the muscular control of arms, legs, torso, neck, and so on. Parkinson's disease and similar neurological problems have also been linked to faulty chemistry of the basal ganglia.

William Nyhan is inclined to believe that some sort of purine toxicity is responsible for the compulsive aggression of the Lesch-Nyhan children. The levels of purines such as guanine and xanthine are higher in the spinal fluid of the Lesch-Nyhan children than in normal children. Also, some of Nyhan's students have fed various purines, including caffeine, to rats, rabbits, and mice and gotten a self-mutilating type of behavior similar to what is seen in the children. But Seegmiller isn't too sure that purines per se are what is causing the children to behave in their bizarre fashion. Nyhan and Seegmiller have a chance to debate their ideas at length since they have both relocated to the school of medicine at the University of California at San Diego. Michael Lesch is now at Peter Bent Brigham Hospital, and his interest has shifted to cardiology. However, he closely follows the work on the syndrome to which he lent his name and which he says "had me peaking when I was twenty-four."

Obviously, the line between the biochemical defect (lack of enzyme) and the weird behavior is not at all clear. Part of the problem is that the relevant science, neurochemistry, is still in the data-gathering stage and unable to make the sort of leap that might explain the disfigured children.

The Lesch-Nyhan children are all mentally retarded, although the degree is variable. Early measurements put their I.Q.'s at about 50, but that was due partly to the difficulty of understanding children with mutilated lips. Now, it is agreed that while they may have difficulty expressing themselves, they are very aware of their surroundings and their circumstances.

"I have yet to find a child that didn't keep up with exactly what was going on around him," Seegmiller says. "I've had a fourteen-year-old who commented on his choices in the political elections." And Nyhan, who has seen about one hundred fifty victims of the disease he codiscovered, more than anybody else, remarked of them that ". . . they have really nice smiles, an index of a sense of humor, which in turn is an index of intelligence."

In fact, the Lesch-Nyhan children, in spite of a tendency to grab for eyeglasses and private parts, as well as a free use of Anglo-Saxonisms, often are the favorites of the doctors and nurses in the wards.

It is of more than passing interest that victims of gout often seem to be mentally at opposite poles from the Lesch-Nyhan children, even though they share at least one chemical lapse—too much uric acid. Nyhan and others have pointed out that even though gout is a comparatively rare disease—about two out of a thousand get it on the average—it seems to single out the highly successful. Among the gout victims listed by Nyhan are:

Alexander the Great	Alfred Tennyson
Isaac Newton	Edward Gibbon
Charles Darwin	Samuel Johnson
Martin Luther	Lord Chesterfield
John Milton	Francis Bacon

What to make of this is uncertain. Apparently, purine metabolism is coupled to both behavior and mind, and its defects can produce conditions as variable as the Lesch-Nyhan syndrome and gout. While we're on purines and brains, there is the speculation made by several scientists that the rapid evolution of the brains of man and primate is the reason they excrete uric acid, while all others excrete a simpler chemical, allantoin, which dissolves more easily in blood and urine than uric acid. More crystals appear in the urine of Lesch-Nyhan children when they have a cold and are dehydrated, making it even more difficult for them to dissolve their enormous overproduction of uric acid.

There is no cure for the Lesch-Nyhan syndrome. Victims used to die at or before puberty but now can be managed with therapy and drugs. Nyhan has a patient approaching his twenties and his original patient is doing well, although his older brother died. But survivors' prospects are nevertheless disheartening: a life in the wards or occasionally at home with "strong-willed, long-suffering parents."

An alternative is now available that makes it possible to avoid giving birth to or even conceiving a Lesch-Nyhan child. The skin cells of a woman can now be examined to see if she is a carrier. If she is and if she conceives a child, a search can be made for the Lesch-Nyhan enzyme in the cells of the amniotic fluid that bathes the growing embryo. If found, the child is not a victim. If the enzyme is missing, the child is affected and may be aborted. (To test the amniotic fluid, the physician resorts to amniocentesis. He extracts a tiny amount of the amniotic fluid in which the embryo floats. This fluid, usually taken about the third month of pregnancy, contains cells sloughed off by the growing child.)

That women carrying the Lesch-Nyhan gene can now be found out is due to the fact that the syndrome is sex-linked (only boys get it) and that a woman named Mary Lyon thought about a tortoiseshell cat and realized that the genetic differences between men and women were more real than imagined.

There are probably tens of thousands of genes in a human cell, but nature has grouped them appropriately and placed them on twenty-three "sticks," the chromosomes. A sperm and an egg each contain twenty-three choromosomes, or a total of forty-six when one meets the other. Thus, the fertilized egg contains twenty-three chromosome pairs, and, as it divides, every new cell, by a process called mitosis, is also given the same number. (In a special process, meiosis, the new sperm and egg cells are given half, or twenty-three chromosomes, to keep the genetic accounting in order when the next life begins.)

Twenty-two pairs of these chromosomes found in every body

cell are alike in both sexes. And if any defective genes are located on those—what geneticists call the autosomes—either sex will be equally affected by an autosomal genetic disease. But in the Lesch-Nyhan syndrome, only boys are affected, and the reason is that the same gene defect responsible for the syndrome is located on the twenty-third pair of chromosomes, the sex chromosomes. These are X and Y. An egg waiting to be fertilized has only an X chromosome, while the sperm hurrying to the rendezvous may be carrying an X or Y chromosome. If X meets X, it forms a girl; X and Y result in a boy.

The fact that the female has two X chromosomes helps protect her against genetic diseases where the gene(s) at fault is located on the X chromosome. Two X chromosomes means two sets of identical genes. It is statistically unlikely that a defective gene on one X chromosome will be matched by the defect on the other X chromosome. Therefore, in many cases the bad gene will be masked. But boys, with only one X chromosome, have no matching sets of genes to protect them if given a chromosome with a genetic defect.

In terms of the Lesch-Nyhan syndrome, this means that girls carrying the gene for this disease are protected by a normal gene that can make the missing enzyme. They are carriers. However, boys unable to make the enzyme because they have no substitute genes become victims. So, boys get the disease while girls transmit it. The diagram opposite may be helpful in understanding how the disease is actually transmitted.

It might be noted that the diagram clarifies why 50 percent of boys are likely to be affected, while 50 percent of the girls will be carriers and perpetuate the gene at fault.

We now come to the hypothesis of Dr. Mary Lyon, a British geneticist. "Perhaps she was one of the first to be concerned at the basic level with the supposed inequality of the sexes," Seegmiller says.

The coat of the tortoiseshell cat is a mosaic of yellow and black. Many other cats and, indeed, other animals (all females) also show off-color schemes variously described as mottled, brindled, dappled, and variegated. Mary Lyon suggested in 1961 in *Nature* magazine that these quilted patterns could be ex-

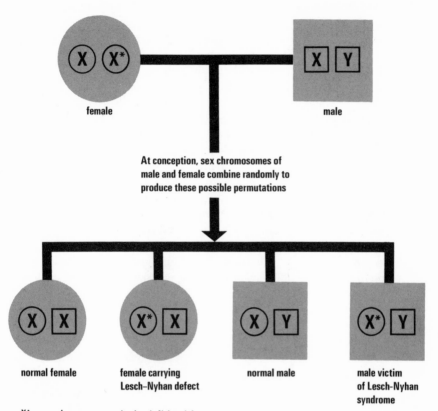

female   male

At conception, sex chromosomes of
male and female combine randomly to
produce these possible permutations

normal female   female carrying   normal male   male victim
                   Lesch–Nyhan defect   of Lesch–Nyhan
                                                            syndrome

X* = sex chromosome carrying Lesch-Nyhan defect

plained by two probabilities: (1) the gene(s) for coat color is
on the X chromosome, and (2) that sometime after conception
(and sex decision) and before birth, one of two X chromosomes
in every body cell of the female was randomly inactivated. Thus,
the tortoiseshell cat is the highly visible and attractive product
of the random inactivation of one of the two X chromosomes
carrying a gene for a coat color—either yellow or black.

"In effect," Seegmiller points out, "she said we're really your
equal because one of the X chromosomes is not working. One of
the consequences of her theory is that if a woman carries a de-

fective gene in one of her chromosomes, she is going to have two kinds of her cells in her body: one showing the defect, the other not, depending on whether the normal or defective X chromosome has been inactivated."

This means that about half the cells of a woman who is a Lesch-Nyhan carrier will have normal amounts of the enzyme HGPRT, completely missing in boys, and half will not. There are two ways to look for the two types of cells in suspected carriers. In both cases, a bit of skin about the size of a match head is placed in a glass dish and given suitable nutrients so it will grow, the tissue-culture technique. In one assay, developed by Seegmiller and his colleagues, the enzyme is found in logical enough fashion by feeding the growing cells a radioactive form of a purine, hypoxanthine. Normal cells with a full complement of enzymes can incorporate the proffered hypoxanthine into their purine chemistry, while cells lacking the enzyme are unable to accept the offer. Which is which is found out simply by placing some unexposed film over the tissue culture. Since the normal cells have taken up all the radioactive purine, while the Lesch-Nyhan cells have none, the only portions of the film to be exposed are over normal cells. The technique is called auto-radiography and is exquisite in its ability to reveal minute chemical differences between cells that are apparently alike.

Seegmiller first used autoradiography to detect a Lesch-Nyhan carrier "when we learned from the mother of one of these children that we had hospitalized for study that her sister's daughter was pregnant in a little town up in Vermont." Her doctor sent a bit of the woman's skin. There were two cell populations. The woman was a carrier.

"Within twenty-four hours," Seegmiller remembers, "we had this frightened young woman who had never left Vermont and who was beside herself that she might be carrying a baby like her aunt's son on a plane to Washington."

A bit of the fluid bathing the embryo and containing sloughed-off cells was examined. "And we told the young lady she was going to have a little girl. But we cultured those cells and found that it was going to be a heterozygous female, a carrier."

That was 1968. About a year later, Dr. Robert DeMars and

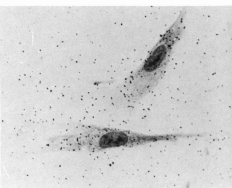

Test for Lesch-Nyhan syndrome. Fetal cells (*left*) have normal complement of enzymes and can incorporate radioactive purine molecules. Lesch-Nyhan cells on right lack the enzyme HGPRT and cannot take up radioactive purine. After washing away excess purines, tissue cultures of both cells are placed against a film sensitive to radioactivity. The normal cells harboring radioactive purines blacken the film, while Lesch-Nyhan cells only darken it slightly. *Courtesy: Theodore Friedmann, University of California at San Diego, and* Scientific American.

his colleagues at the University of Wisconsin Medical School reported detection of an affected boy in the twenty-eighth week of pregnancy. Essentially, the same method for establishing the presence or absence of the enzyme—autoradiography—was used. The fetus was a boy, and it was affected, but the diagnosis came too late to consider a therapeutic abortion. The tragedy was compounded when the "boy" turned out to be boys—identical twins—both of whom had the syndrome.

The first therapeutic abortion of a Lesch-Nyhan fetus was reported in *Science* magazine in 1970 by a combined group from the National Institutes of Health, George Washington University, and the University of California at San Diego, where Seegmiller was then located. A woman already identified as a carrier became pregnant, was asked to come in to have her amniotic fluid checked, but did not show up at the clinic. Only in her last month was Seegmiller able to establish, using a bit of the fetus's blood, that the child was a boy and had the syndrome.

It was a fine looking and apparently healthy baby until about the sixth month "when the head started to droop, and as soon as his lower incisors or teeth came in, he had a groove on the bottom of his tongue where he had started to bite. Eventually, he developed the full syndrome." The same woman became pregnant again, but this time she did show up to have her child tested. It was a boy, again affected, and a therapeutic abortion was done.

Autoradiography, while an effective and powerful tool for studying the chemistry of cells, is expensive and complicated enough to limit its general use. A simpler method to detect both Lesch-Nyhan carriers and affected embryos has been created by scientists at the University of Wisconsin and Johns Hopkins University. The trick here is to feed human cells grown in a dish artificial and poisonous purines that are similar enough to natural purines to be welcomed into the cell's chemistry but dissimilar enough that at some point they block biochemical processes in the cell and kill it. Since only normal cells have all the enzymes needed to take this poison upon themselves, while all the cells of a Lesch-Nyhan victim and half the cells of a carrier lack it, the test is quite simple. "All you're doing is asking a cell whether it can grow or not," says Robert De-Mars, whose group at the University of Wisconsin uses a purine called azaguanine to selectively kill cells. A similar material, thioguanine, is used by the Johns Hopkins group led by Dr. Barbara Migeon.

"Such a system where you throw in something that kills normal cells and allows mutant [defective] cells to survive has a great many potentials," Seegmiller points out.

DeMars has already exploited one: the association of a specific chemical with a specific genetic change or mutation. Chemicals, radiation, and viruses have varying abilities to change the structure of a gene. Since these gene or mutagenic changes are random, the chances of harm are usually much greater than that any good will come out of it. A major problem today is to find and measure the mutagenic powers of new materials, particularly the chemicals that seem to be a necessary part of our culture. Tests ranging from assessing effects on bacteria to counting the litter sizes of treated mice have been devised. Individually, they have drawbacks, although in concert they should offer a fair measure of assurance that we're not playing genetic roulette.

But what is still needed is a test to prove that a particular material is responsible for a particular genetic change and do it in a countable way. Now, DeMars and a colleague, Dr. Richard J. Albertino, offer such a test. The mutagenic agents are low levels of radiation as well as certain chemicals such as nitrosoguanidine. The gene change these produce is apparently identical to the defect found in the Lesch-Nyhan children and can be found in the same way—by feeding the irradiated or chemically treated cells with azaguanine, which kills the unchanged cells while the mutant cells survive.

"One can induce and detect the spontaneous occurrence of mutations in cultured human cells that mimic exactly the mutations found in Lesch-Nyhan," DeMars says. "You can count them because if you start with a million normal human cells, you can find even one mutant cell among them by its ability to form a visible colony of cells in a medium containing azaguanine. So this gives us a way of quantitating mutation rates in human cells."

It is fair to argue that the striking successes in the Lesch-Nyhan syndrome—identification of the defect, tests for carriers and embryonic victims—are due at least partly to its remarkable nature, which attracted some remarkable people.

However, similar inroads have been made in other genetic diseases. The particular enzyme defect in Tay-Sachs disease, an invariably lethal illness limited largely to Jewish children, has been identified by Dr. John O'Brien, a colleague of Nyhan and Seegmiller at the school of medicine of the University of California at San Diego. A number of similar, rare diseases in which the body is unable to properly handle fatty materials, or lipids, have had their chemical defects identified. Parallel work has been done on glycogen-storage diseases in which the body is unable to properly store and use sugars.

Problems remain. Sickle-cell anemia, fairly common as genetic diseases go and limited mostly to blacks, is still intractable to prebirth detection in the uterus, as is phenylketonuria (PKU), in which a child cannot cope with an amino acid, phenylalanine. Cystic fibrosis remains a puzzle. Nevertheless, some thirty-odd genetic diseases are now detectable in the womb. Increasingly, parents who have reason to fear that their future child may be genetically misformed can be offered a perfect choice—an absolute judgment as to whether the child will be normal or defective. "The intrauterine detection of genetic diseases," says a leader in the field, Dr. Henry L. Nadler of Northwestern University, "brings a new dimension and precision to genetic counseling. The physician may now inform the parents that they will have either an affected or a normal child, and the risks are no longer one in four, but one hundred percent or zero."

Obviously, much of the new information now coming in on genetic diseases is of the random, scattered variety. The diseases individually are rare; some two hundred Lesch-Nyhan children have been identified since 1963 when the disease was characterized. Most physicians encounter only a very few if any of the genetic diseases during their professional lives. And the detection methods, where one enzyme out of thousands must be measured, are not simple and often require the supervisory expertise of someone who has actually worked on the particular disease involved. What has happened is that a relatively few genetic disease centers have emerged where blood, urine, amniotic fluid, or skin from a suspected genetic problem can be sent for analysis by physicians from all over the world. These centers are located at the medical schools of the University of California at San Diego, Cornell University, Johns Hopkins, the University of Wisconsin, and a few other places.

Mass screening of newborns for several genetic defects is legally required in many states. Ninety-eight percent of all children born in Massachusetts have their blood tested a few days after birth for several genetic diseases, including PKU and galactosemia in which an enzyme needed to metabolize the sugar galactose is missing.

Detection may be simplified and widened as technology catches up with what researchers have been accomplishing in the laboratories. Kits are now available that enable mothers of suspect children to take and test urine samples. Chemically treated papers are available for spot-checking specific chemical deficiencies. Mass screening for automated analysis of blood and urine are coming into being for genetic diseases. In one technique, blood samples are spotted on filter paper, and small swatches punched out to be sent in proper order through automated analysis systems.

Seegmiller and his colleagues have devised a mass-screening test that finds possible Lesch-Nyhan children by their high levels of uric acid relative to other urine chemicals. "It can be performed," he says, "by automated equipment on a morning urine sample with a hundred percent accuracy so far in identifying these children."

Detection systems may even take a more direct route in the form of specially treated diapers that turn telltale colors. "Perhaps," Seegmiller muses, "have it come out in blue, green, yellow, or purple; see your doctor if there is a metabolic disorder present."

This is the near term. What of the future? What are the prospects for repairing the genetic error that wreaks such havoc in the lives of the Lesch-Nyhan children? This, of course, pulls us into the never-never land of genetic engineering, or gene therapy by some lights. It must be quickly said that as far as the Lesch-Nyhan syndrome is concerned, prospects for genetic repair are not good. Aside from finding a way to do it, it's probable that irreparable damage has been done even before the first symptoms appear. Although it's still debatable whether nerve tissue in these children is actually damaged (a Japanese researcher reportedly has now found that it is), the operation of the nervous system is crippled, most likely beyond repair.

However, the prospects for genetic repair or restoration should not be dismissed out of hand. Work on several fronts—all still in the primitive level—makes it probable that a serious attempt to repair the genetic defect in the Lesch-Nyhan syndrome will at least be made.

What is the exact genetic error that must be repaired? The

answer is suggested by the work of Drs. John A. MacDonald and William N. Kelley of the Duke University Medical Center, who found that the problem of the Lesch-Nyhan children is not the absence of the HGPRT enzyme but the presence of a mismade one. This indicates that the error lies directly in the section of the DNA of a gene that codes the directions for making this enzyme. Perhaps one of the proper building blocks has been substituted for by an incorrect one. Perhaps a building block has simply been omitted. There are more "perhaps," and it is doubtful that we will know very soon what the exact DNA error is that produces the mutilated children in the wards. Our knowledge of the structure of human genes is primitive, and we have yet to map even one.

As for repairing the error, whatever it is, there are two suggestive experiments that point the way—one a case of "metabolic cooperation"; the other, a mutual good turn.

Metabolic cooperation is based on the work of Dr. John H. Subak-Sharpe of the University of Glasgow. He illustrated that if normal and mutant cells (i.e., missing a particular enzyme) from a hamster were mixed in a common "pot," fed properly and allowed to grow, that the normal cells would transmit their ability to make the enzyme, or, less dramatically, give a share of their enzyme to some of the mutant cells that lacked it. Such cellular intimacy was required because only mutant cells that bordered *directly* on the normal ones received any of the enzyme.

Seegmiller and his colleagues, working with Subak-Sharpe, did a parallel experiment with human cells, some supplied by a normal child and the others by a Lesch-Nyhan patient. Wherever there was contact, there was an increase—above the normal amounts—in cells able to take up radioactive hypoxanthine, which meant that some of the mutant cells now had a bit of the enzyme they normally lack. While encouraging, it is too early to say whether this technique can be used to prod the cells of a Lesch-Nyhan child into making the enzyme whose absence has stunted his life.

In a somewhat different approach, two types of cells, each defective, albeit in a different way, have been fused together to form a hybrid cell. The basic idea is that each cell will make up what the other lacks. The idea worked, after a fashion. Cells taken from a Lesch-Nyhan child were fused with those from another child with a different genetic defect. When the hybrid cells were grown in a tissue culture, they produced normal levels of the enzyme that their separate parts had lacked, like two cripples making up for each other's handicaps.

There was an unsuccessful attempt to take this technique—intergenic complementation—one step further. Instead of blending two cells, normal DNA (i.e., the genes) instead of complete cells, was given to the Lesch-Nyhan cells. Intriguingly, the defective cells now made small amounts of the enzyme HGPRT, which indicated that the information for making it was gotten by the defective cells. However, attempts by Seegmiller and his colleagues to have these cells multiply without losing their new-found ability to make the Lesch-Nyhan enzyme were unsuccessful.

Of course, other work is going on, some of which may be applied to the Lesch-Nyhan syndrome. A virus gene has been synthesized at the University of Wisconsin, and others are on the way. Scientists are seeking ways to use viruses, which are essentially DNA (or a similar material, RNA) with a protein overcoat, to deliver genetic information to specific locations within cells. For example, geneticists dream of using viruses to supply diabetics with the genes for making insulin they now lack. It seems probable that within a decade we will begin to see direct repair of genetic defects in a number of diseases, perhaps including the Lesch-Nyhan syndrome.

That this is no idle dream was emphasized by experiments reported late in 1971 by scientists from the National Institute of Mental Health and the National Institutes of of Health. They infected human cells, unable to make an enzyme for metabolizing the sugar galactose, with viruses carrying the directions for making that enzyme. Not only did the missing enzyme appear in the culture of human cells, but the cells were able to divide and still retain their newly won normality.

John O'Brien, who found the Tay-Sachs defect, once pointed out that the current intensive work on genetic diseases "will change the lives of those people who have children with these disorders. If you consider that there are now about a thousand genetic diseases and if you have ever been to a state hospital and have seen the children in the wards, you know that it's a terribly depressing sort of feeling."

Oscar Wilde, who may have won and lost in the genetic lottery and apparently knew it, indicated heredity as "the last of the fates and the most terrible."

He may soon be proved wrong.

2

DISSONANT HARMONY:
THE RIDDLE OF AGING

"There are so many little dyings that it doesn't matter which of
them is death," mourns a poet, Kenneth Patchen. The cruelties
of the "little dyings" mount with the years: a mind that begins
to play tricks, dulled reflexes, a body less able to cope with
disease and injury. These tolls of aging signal the increasing
disorganization within the body, an increasing inability to cope
with change, a slippage in the controls that time the chemical
and physical events that must mesh to sustain life. "Dissonant
harmony," Alex Comfort, British physician, researcher in aging,
a prolific writer on topics ranging from gerontology to the

sexual ignorance of physicians, calls the process. Unfortunately, dissonant harmony is also an apt description for contemporary research on why we age.

"Aging research is at the stage where chemistry was at the time of Lavoisier" is the verdict of Dr. Nathan W. Shock, director of the Gerontology Research Center, a part of the National Institutes of Health, located in Baltimore, Maryland. "Aging," writes a book reviewer in *Science*, "is an underdeveloped biological discipline about which little is known."

But the field is moving, reaching a new and more respectable level of sophistication. Work on the riddle of aging is intensifying, with laboratories in several countries pursuing molecular clues to aging. Drugs—designed to counteract researchers' favorite causes of aging, ranging from genetics to protein alterations—are being tested with interesting, if disputed, results.

Increasingly, aging research is focusing on possible changes in molecules, both inside and outside the body's cells, that may be factors in aging. Outside the cell, researchers look for changes in connective tissue that helps bind cells into their proper patterns. Inside the cell, the work divides several ways: a search for age-changes in the primary genetic material, which controls the division and function of cells by supplying requisite proteins; and, on a subtler plane, a search for changes in the apparatus through which the genetic material executes its commands.

The pursuit of molecular reasons for aging parallels the last two decades of biochemical research, which has reduced many living processes to molecular interactions—the workings of enzymes, the nature and operation of genetic molecules, the complex give-and-take in which molecules exchange energy, and so on. Philosophically, researchers feel that if they understand what happens to molecules during aging, they will understand why cells age and die, and why we grow old.

"But why do cells die?" Shock asks through the years. And there is no answer. Nor is there any idea of what makes a cell old. In fact, aside from the telltale accumulation of age pigments, or cell garbage, in some cells, it is difficult even for a trained pathologist to tell whether individual cells were taken from an octogenarian or a baby. Our allotted life span has changed little in spite of the spectacular growth of science. Our maximum life span approximates only the biblical three score and ten. ("The age of senility today is exactly what it was in the time of Moses," Comfort writes.) No one knows what causes aging, and none of the many theories about it can yet claim to be primary.

With the diverse approaches to the aging riddle, it is not too surprising that the field is split into armed camps, each waving its theoretical banner. Shock calls that a good thing for now, forcing a many-sided attack on what is still a biological black box. Unfortunately, the field has been marred by some questionable research, poorly controlled, typified by dramatic conclusions from flimsy data. "I must admit that many people are not designing experiments as tightly as they should be," says Shock.

With those caveats, current work on aging can be looked at with a view to its possible relevance to those who dislike a fatalistic view of life.

Certainly among the oldest and simplest theories to understand is the possible deterioration of the proteins that prop up the body—the stuff of connective tissue that links bone to muscle, bone to bone, holds the skin together, etc. Proponents of this theory certainly display the greatest bravura. "Conceptually, a mechanism of aging has been found," says Dr. Robert Kohn of the Institute of Pathology at the Case-Western Reserve Medical School in Cleveland. "The only thing needed now is some experimental proof," he adds.

Connective tissue is dominated by two proteins—collagen and elastin. Collagen, the dominant protein in the body, is an extremely tough molecule, difficult to bend and even more difficult to stretch—it takes 10,000 times its own weight to stretch collagen. Elastin, a relatively minor component, is more elastic, as its name implies. The outside ear is largely elastin, whereas collagen is in ligaments, muscle, tendons, cartilage, the cornea of the eye, heart valves, blood vessels, etc.

Biologists, more interested in cells than the material surrounding them, usually regarded collagen as a nuisance. A great deal of what is known of collagen comes from the leather and glue industries; the former tans it, the latter boils it.

A collagen molecule is actually composed of three intertwined chains of amino acids, principally proline, hydroxyproline, and glycine. In a unique arrangement, three collagen molecules twist together, just as a cable is formed from wires, to form a still larger rod-shaped molecule called tropocollagen. Tropocollagen forms a matrix, linking up with other tropocollagen molecules to fashion a strong network of cross-linked fibers. The result is worth the boast of a master builder—a tough, almost inflexible structure that is responsive to the slightest movement of bone, muscle, skin, or limb. A pianist's hands, a typist's fingers, a tennis player's backhand—their skill depends in part on the soundness and inflexibility of their collagen. As we grow, new collagen is formed, which begins to toughen almost as soon as it appears, with the cross-linking peaking in a matter of days or weeks, says Dr. Karl A. Piez, of the National Institute of Dental Research, one of the National Institutes of Health. This network remains with us, barring injury, until death.

Collagen rigidity seems to peak between twenty and forty, declines, and, apparently, picks up again late in life. As young collagen grows, cross-links, from which evolve the above-mentioned matrix, form between vital molecules on adjoining aminoacid chains, with an enzyme apparently playing a vital role in promoting cross-linking. What is responsible for the changes in collagen with age is still a fiercely debated point, and so far no cross-links have been chemically identified in old collagen as they have in young collagen.

Nevertheless, something is happening. Experiments with collagen from rat tails and frog fingers, for example, indicate that the older the collagen, the harder it is to move a weight against it. Or, perhaps the same thing, more heat or chemicals are needed to loosen collagen fibers. Collagen, in virtually all animals tested, becomes stiffer and stronger with age, and harder to dissolve. Much of the initial information in this area comes from the work of Dr. Frederic Verzár of the Institute for Experimental Gerontology in Basel, Switzerland.

Age-changes in collagen are rationalized by cross-links—the same, or similar, cross-links that provide the necessary rigidity in newly made collagen while we're growing up. More cross-links form with age, the idea goes, stiffening collagen, making it harder to stretch, and more difficult to dissolve. It takes more heat to loosen the molecule presumably because more cross-links have to be broken, or melted.

How does that accumulating network of cross-links contribute to aging? Kohn once explained it this way in a book entitled *Radiation and Aging.*

> Diffusion processes would be severely altered in more rigid tissue. But more importantly, tissue deformation would be damped. Blood vessel motility [movement] would become sluggish and inefficient. All of these changes would result in less effective passage of metabolites, antibodies, nutrients, and hormones between cells and blood vessels. . . . Consequences of inadequate diffusion would be precarious states of cell viability and function. Some cell injury and death would be expected.

Unfortunately, while attractive, this picture is more theory than fact.

Some scientists believe that the apparent hardening of collagen with age may be *good* for cells, easing the movement of large molecules in and out of cells when it stiffens enough to open "pores" in cell membranes.

"None of the aging changes found [in aging collagen] have any harmful effects," argues a Swedish scientist. "On the contrary, they contribute to the more precise use of the locomotor system and give it a greater possibility of resisting forces."

Admittedly, there is little evidence that aging collagen interferes with cells, although, Kohn argues, logic alone would dictate that some harm is being done. There is direct experimental evidence, Kohn says, that diffusion of molecules from the air sacs of the lung to blood vessels—as well as in blood vessels of the skin—is impaired. Recently, Dr. Clive Hamlin, a chemist working in Kohn's laboratory, found that there are age differences in the rate an enzyme—collagenase—dissolves cross-links. While the final products are the same, older collagen is less tractable to collagenase treatment than younger collagen.

At the moment, the cross-linking theory, while attractive, has precious little direct evidence to support it. Most scientists—particularly, those favoring other theories—prefer to wait for more returns to come in. Kohn argues for a greater commitment of time, talent, and money to gain meaningful data. "We've got reason to believe that there is a cause-and-effect relationship here. Let's find out if there is."

Why should cross-links form at all? Why not, answers Kohn. Rubber, plastics, and other large molecules form cross-links with age, so why shouldn't collagen? It is all part of a law of thermodynamics that all things—a car, a house, or a life—tend toward random disorder. Everything, if given time, is more likely to fall apart than improve. Collagen, like any protein, is a carefully arranged molecule. Moreover, unlike many proteins, it isn't replaced as it begins to wear out. Rather, it is incubated for decades at 98.6°F., ideal conditions for a chemical reaction. Moreover, several researchers point to a large number of possible chemical agents in the body that could speed cross-linking reactions.

Dr. Johan Bjorksten, the first to suggest cross-linking as an aging factor (Verzár first specified collagen as an aging factor), maintains that there are several dozen possible cross-linkers in the body. These include a variety of agents: organic chemicals such as aldehydes and acids; metals such as iron and manganese; miscellaneous items such as tobacco smoke; physical factors such as radiation; and so on. Bjorksten departs from the mainstream of cross-linking research (if there is one) by asserting that cross-linking occurs not only in collagen and elastin but in a host of other proteins and, more importantly, between strands of the genetic material, deoxyribonucleic acid (DNA). DNA if bridged by one or two cross-links is immobilized, resulting in the destruction of valuable genetic information. Bjorksten summarizes his ideas this way:

"The numerous cross-linking agents known to be normally available in the organism will, by random unencumbered action, slowly immobilize the large molecules in all cells and tissue by cross-linkage."

However, in spite of a great deal of circumstantial evidence gathered by Bjorksten that cross-linking is a widespread process applying equally to DNA, enzymes, collagen, etc., few scientists feel that the case has been proved. Nathan Shock writes: "There is at present no experimental evidence that cross-linking or other molecular changes occur in intracellular proteins."

Bjorksten is a successful industrial chemist who saw a connection between the deliberate cross-linking of proteins for industrial use and fateful changes in the body.

"It is a monument to myopia," he writes, "that it took four years to realize the connection. However, once this was done, previously disconnected facts fitted together with precision and rapidity."

Bjorksten maintains the Bjorksten Research Foundation in Madison, Wisconsin. The Foundation is supported by his own money, by contributions from various private individuals and foundations, and, occasionally, by a government grant.

While cross-linking researchers trace the fate of molecules *after* they are made—how they may deteriorate with time, how their normal performance is crippled, etc.—still others are working on another level. These are examining what might happen to the genetic machinery that (1) produces the molecules, (2) assures the accurate copying of cells, and (3) provides the proper mix of proteins a cell needs to do its job. The level of ideas and work ranges from the somewhat direct to the abstruse. In common, they feed on the day-to-day progressions of molecular biology.

Simpler to grasp, if typically controversial, are the ideas of Dr. Howard Curtis of the Brookhaven National Laboratory, Upton, New York. Curtis, doubly trained as a physicist and physiologist, is senior biologist at Brookhaven. He became an "aging" man in World War II while assigned to the Manhattan Project, which produced the atomic bomb. Nothing was known of the effects of radiation on life, and Curtis was asked to find out. Responding like a good biologist, he exposed mice to various doses of radiation. It was a turning point in Curtis's career that the exposed mice seemed to age faster—a phenomenon now basic to aging research and labeled radiation-induced aging.

"They die sooner on the average than normal mice, and when

you take them apart you find that they die from exactly the same diseases and they go through all the same reactions as a normal mouse does, but they just do it sooner."

Curtis quickly realized that radiation-induced aging could be a valuable probe into the intricacies of aging. "In order to study something, you have to be able to change it somehow," he points out.

The likely target of radiation was the genetic machinery of the cells—the genes, containing DNA and protein, and the chromosomal framework on which they are distributed. This is hurrying the story, because DNA was just identified as the genetic molecule when Curtis found an inverted Fountain of Youth, at least for mice. But it is now known that radiation is capable of damaging DNA, somehow breaking bonds at various points in the molecule.

Curtis linked radiation-induced aging, likely effects on genetic material, and other pieces together to produce his somatic theory of aging, in which genetic material is damaged not enough to kill or inactivate cells but enough to force a change in the patterns of activity—a loss of control, manufacture of badly made proteins, etc. The aberrant molecules misbehave. Cancer, degenerative diseases of the heart and blood vessels, and autoimmune diseases (which destroy somatic cells) such as rheumatoid arthritis may result. Somatic cells are body cells (soma=body) as opposed to germ cells (of eggs and sperm). Somatic cells moulder in the grave; germ cells are transmitted to our children in DNA packets.

Curtis sees aging—at least in part—as a steady accumulation of errors in the chromosomes and, by inference, the DNA of body cells such as those of brain and nerve that are not replaced if lost or injured. These nondividing cells must function with the original set of DNA supplied. Dividing cells—fibroblasts that make collagen, skin cells, bone marrow, etc.—presumably have considerable opportunity for repairing damaged DNA. But Curtis now believes that the damaging changes can also occur in the DNA of dividing cells, based primarily on the experiments of Dr. Leonard Hayflick of Stanford University, described later.

However, logic dictates a greater likelihood that something will go wrong in the genetic components of nondividing cells simply because they cannot correct their mistakes. There is only a measure of truth in this neat theory because researchers now know that damaged DNA can be repaired, albeit imperfectly. There is a molecular apparatus—with the requisite enzymes— that can figuratively snip off damaged portions, cart them away, and substitute the proper replacement parts. This self-functioning molecular patch job is the reason, apparently, why the ultraviolet rays of the sun, which can break DNA bonds, are not lethal to sun worshipers. In xeroderma pigmentosum, a rare form of skin cancer in which a repair enzyme is missing, DNA is not repaired, and the risks of going out into the midday sun are very great indeed.

Curtis's intriguing idea of attributing aging, at least in part, to a steady deterioration in the DNA of cells that don't divide has some experimental support and, like any current aging hypothesis, some telling points against it.

Much of his experimental evidence comes from work with the livers of rats and mice. The liver is an organ whose cells normally don't divide unless damaged. Curtis feeds his animals carbon tetrachloride, a spot-removing chemical that injures their livers. Liver cells respond by dividing and in the process spread out their chromosomes. Curtis freezes and stains them and looks for what he calls chromosomal aberrations—broken chromosomes, joined chromosomes, the wrong number, etc. He reports that the older the animal, the larger the number of chromosomal aberrations, indicating an age-related breakdown of the framework on which genes are distributed. Moreover, he found that a strain of mice that live longer shows fewer aberrations at the same age than short-lived mice. And when he irradiated mice, Curtis found that they aged faster, as expected, and that the number of chromosomal aberrations increased. However, the two effects—aging and aberration—were not proportional, and the number of aberrations went down to normal levels before the effect on aging became apparent. An additional chip in Curtis's pot is that dogs, which live longer than mice, show fewer chromosomal aberrations.

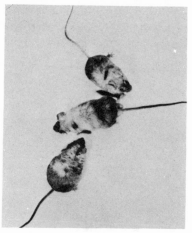

Irradiated (*top*) versus normal mice. Group was irradiated when about eight weeks old. Fourteen months later, many had died, and the remainder showed symptoms of aging. *Courtesy: Howard J. Curtis, Brookhaven National Laboratory*

These changes in the chromosomal framework are regarded by Curtis as a primary factor in the so-called degenerative diseases—cancer, heart diseases, and the like. "The definition of aging I like the best," he explains, "is simply that aging is a phenomenon which causes an increasing susceptibility to one of the degenerative diseases."

Curtis's critics make these points: the chromosome damage produced by radiation levels off to normal levels well before aging effects appear; chemical agents that, like radiation, damage genetic material have no effect on life span; some irradiated mice show an abnormal pattern of disease, indicating other effects aside from aging; 80 percent of a liver's cells may show chromosomal damage and the organ blithely carries on.

Curtis, on the first point, argues that the critical damage is to the DNA itself, and hence not easily detectable. It is this sort of damage, he says, that produces the effects of aging.

However, there is little direct evidence of DNA damage either by aging or radiation. "Mischief is to the nuclear furniture [rather] than to the genes per se," asserts Alex Comfort. As yet, clear-cut changes in DNA with age have not been found, but there may be subtle changes in the proteins to which DNA is bound. More about this later.

These and other criticisms, many acknowledged by Curtis, have produced his "composite theory of aging," in which mutations—chromosomal or DNA changes—are merely one of a series of sequential steps toward cancer, heart disease, autoimmune diseases, etc.

A remaining question in this molecular period of aging research is how can genetic material be altered by radiation, chemicals, and other bodily "brickbats." Granted that Curtis is right, how does radiation induce a fundamental change in the genetic material severe enough to trigger that concatenation of events that introduces premature gray to a mouse. Perhaps, Curtis says, DNA is an inherently unstable molecule, although measurements would seem to discount that. Perhaps, he argues, a host of chemical agents, some of them created by radiation, attack DNA, altering it in some lethal way. Perhaps free radicals are responsible. Free radicals are atoms or molecules that, having an odd rather than the normal even number of electrons, are extremely anxious to react with something. Their lifetime is so fleeting that they had long existed only theoretically before chemists were able to trap them.

To test the free radical hypothesis, Curtis did a joint experiment with the acknowledged leader of the free radical movement, Dr. Denham Harman of the College of Medicine at the University of Nebraska. Harman, Ph.D. and M.D., is professor of biochemistry and professor of medicine. "Free radical reactions are unidirectional, random, and deleterious," says Dr. Harman. "You would expect them to be a sort of noise that accumulates with time."

An atom or group of atoms with an odd number of electrons is common, and, being extremely reactive, generally plows into the nearest available molecule. Familiar products of free radical reactions listed by Harman in his papers include the explosive meeting of gasoline and oxygen in cars, rancid butter, smog, and dried linseed oil paints. Harman believes that when free radicals appear in the body their chemical hyperactivity can cripple the operations of cells.

Free radicals—if formed in the body—could attack enzymes, collagen and elastin, various hormones, body fats and lipids, and, of course, DNA. That free radicals do appear in the body is based partly on chemical logic—the ingredients are there— and partly on the detection of free radicals in body tissue by electron spin resonance (ESR) spectroscopy. ESR measures the spin of unpaired electrons found in free radicals, identifying them by the energy needed to change the direction of their spinning in a magnetic field.

Recent experiments by Dr. Barry Commoner of Washington University indicate that radiation does induce free radicals in living tissue. Furthermore, there are noticeable differences in the nature of the free radicals produced in dividing versus nondividing cells—testes versus kidney, muscle, and liver cells. And evidence that free radicals can alter both collagen and elastin has been produced by United States and Canadian laboratories.

Harman is noted for the indirect support he has accumulated, based on feeding the ubiquitous rats and mice various chemical agents that should "soak" up free radicals or block their formation. Presumably, the animals should live longer. Some early experiments along this line that did extend the life span of mice were harpooned by critics for several reasons: (1) life was extended in some strains but not others, and (2) Harman used leukemia-prone mice, whose deaths—even if put off a bit —were probably not caused by natural aging. However, restructured experiments with mice less susceptible to tumors provided parallel and cleaner results; that is, mice fed free-radical "scavengers" had a longer average life span than un-treated mice. The scavengers included butyl hydroxytoluene (BHT) and 2-mercaptoethylamine (MEA) and several other chemicals. Only BHT and MEA significantly extended the life of the mice. The MEA results are typical: mice lived three to seven months longer than the untreated animals, depending on the amount fed; normally, these mice die in about two years. While promising, the results are still questioned. Some free-radical scavengers work, others do not. And the treated mice lost weight, a currently accepted way to extend life span (sta-tistically, lean people live longer). Perhaps, his critics argue, Harman was measuring effects on diet rather than on any basic aging process. Nevertheless, his data are there, and are intriguing.

As mentioned, Harman and Curtis collaborated in an experi-mental test of the hypothesis that free radicals may be a reason for the chromosomal aberrations Curtis sees in dividing liver cells. A test was simple: free-radical inhibitors fed to animals should slow the increase in chromosomal aberrations as the animal ages. But Curtis and Harman report that "none of the compounds used significantly influenced the incidence of gross liver abnormalities." Although they attribute their disappoint-ment to a variety of reasons, including failure of enough free-radical scavengers to reach chromosomes, the experimental data has weakened their case.

The case that DNA is damaged by free radicals is yet to be made. Also, Harman's experiments, while stretching out the average life span of some mice, have not extended their maxi-mum life span of about forty months. The mice still die within their normal life span but do live a few months longer than their untreated cousins. Harman again attributes this to a failure of his drugs to reach the genetic material in the nucleus of the cell, the probable origin of the limits of life.

An interesting twist on Harman's work is provided by Dr. Aloys Tappel of the University of California at Davis. Tappel indicts the oxygen we breathe as an aging culprit. He lays it out this way: oxygen attacks body lipids, or fatty materials, creating free radicals that, in turn, launch an attack on various parts of cells, including lysosomes, often called the suicide bags because they hold enzymes that can destroy a cell. Tissue is destroyed. The damaged portions are further digested in the lysosomes. The product is a heady mix of enzymes, broken cell parts, and age pigments. Tappel's case against oxygen rests largely on an analysis of age pigments, their distribution and nature. They appear in the heart, muscle, and brain tissue of the aged and seem to contain fragments of the lipids originally attacked by oxygen. Incidentally, age pigments are veterans in the aging story, and various people have tried to pin a causative role on them. So far, there is little firm evidence that they do the cell any harm, and an alternative possibility is that they are just another by-product of a still mysterious process.

Tappel, like Harman, has a recipe for blocking the damaging effects of oxygen. It includes vitamin E, an antioxidant that blocks oxygen attack on lipids, amino acids, and other free-radical inhibitors.

We have covered two major umbrellas for the molecular reasons for aging—if we exclude age pigments—collagen that cross-links to the body's disadvantage and the steady deterioration of genetic information in nondividing cells. There is a third, which has been fed by the swelling knowledge of how genetic information stored in DNA is translated into cell function and division. This third alternative maintains that little happens to DNA during a person's life, but that the machinery through which DNA information is transmitted becomes worn with time. Errors are made, wrong molecules are produced, with an inevitable downturn in the ability of cells to do their job. It is, says Comfort, like a record that becomes more scratched with each playing; the original music is still there, but each playing makes it harder to hear. In the same way, some scientists now believe there is a steady running down in the protein-making apparatus of cells—the enzymes, proteins that turn various pieces of DNA on and off, the units where proteins are actually assembled, etc. It is an elegant theory, hip and hot, and attractive to young scientists with fresh ideas, but, until recently, with virtually no evidence to support it.

A turning point came in an experiment that is well on its way to becoming a classic. It was performed by Dr. Leonard Hay-flick, then at the Wistar Institute in Philadelphia and now at the Stanford University School of Medicine. Hayflick's experiment had a simple rationale: if dividing cells get old because their genetic apparatus wears out, then cells divided enough times will die. Hayflick proved that they did, upsetting a deeply ingrained belief in the immortality of cells. There is a limit on cell division.

Hayflick and his colleagues at the Wistar Institute isolated fibroblast tissue from a four-month-old human embryo. Fibroblasts, cells that go on dividing throughout life, make collagen and elastin and are part of the body's "cement." With special enzymes that dissolve the protein matrix that binds fibroblasts together, Hayflick was able to isolate individual cells. He gave them warmth, food, and a glass home, and let them divide away.

The cells duplicated themselves about fifty times and then died. Cells, frozen into "suspended animation" at any particular point —say, the thirtieth doubling—and then unfrozen, remembered where they were (even after six months) and continued doubling about twenty more times before dying. Other fascinations emerged. The older the fibroblast donor, the lower the number of doublings. While cells from an embryo doubled fifty times, those of a twenty-year-old doubled only about twenty times. Interestingly, as the number of cells approached their final and lethal division, the number of chromosomal aberrations—that is, the wrong number of chromosomes—rose sharply. In two rare diseases—Werner's syndrome and progeria, where the victims, although very young, display all the signs of aging, including senility—it has been found that the Hayflick experiment applies very dramatically. Cells taken from victims of these diseases doubled two or three times before dying, or ten times less than normal cells will do.

Hayflick, in keeping with the *leitmotif* of aging research, has his critics, some of whom note that Hayflick's cells divided in glass tubes, not in the body where conditions may be totally different. But there is some circumstantial evidence that Hayflick is not beating up the wrong path. The results with the progeria and Werner's syndrome victims are one piece. Another was supplied by Drs. Court Brown and Patricia Jacobs of the University of Edinburgh. They found that white blood cells taken from the elderly showed a considerably larger number of chromosomal anomalies.

In any case, Hayflick's results with human cells have been repeated and confirmed in cells taken from chickens, mice, rats, and rabbits.

But what to make of this? Curtis sees confirmation for his idea from an unexpected source—the rapidly dividing cell. Hayflick doubts that environmental injury to chromosomes or DNA may be responsible for his results and prefers another explanation. "I suggest," he wrote in *Scientific American*, "that animal aging may result from deterioration of the genetic program that orchestrates the development of cells. . . . In the idiom of the computer engineers, we might say that man, like other animals, has a 'mean time to failure' because his normal cells eventually run out of accurate programs and capacity for repair."

But what happens? What happens to the "orchestration" of a cell's genetic apparatus that explains its clocklike death at the fiftieth division? The prime instruments and their tunes are certainly known: DNA (deoxyribonucleic acid), in whose chemical architecture are the directions for making the mix of proteins a particular cell needs; messenger RNA (ribonucleic acid), an intermediate molecule that carries this information from the nucleus of a cell to the cytoplasm where proteins are actually assembled; ribosomes, protein factories, dotlike units that translate DNA information into workable proteins.

From that base, the researcher in aging tuned into molecular biology faces bewildering options. Perhaps aging is due to some subtle change in the protein complex in which DNA is bound and stabilized. Perhaps there is a subtle change in the various factors that control the start and stop of protein making. Perhaps errors pile up in the copying mechanism in which DNA information is transcribed into a messenger RNA molecule. Perhaps something happens to RNA as it moves from the nucleus to the cytoplasm where the ribosomes are. Or, perhaps something goes wrong with the ribosomes, inducing the manufacture of faulty proteins.

This DNA-to-RNA-to-ribosome route for making proteins has, of course, made headlines and won Nobel Prizes in the fifties and sixties. Yet, the fine details of this process are still being gathered. A Florentine mixture of proteins called factors have something to say about what portions of DNA are switched on and off—at least in bacteria and perhaps in man. Every cell in the body has identical DNA, implying that every cell is capable of making every protein in the body. But it doesn't happen. Each cell makes only the particular proteins it needs—be it a heart cell, skin cell, or a nerve cell. Various factors, all proteins, assure that the proper proteins are made by each cell. There are factors that control the start and finish of information transcription from DNA to messenger RNA; so-called sigma factors unwind the two strands of a DNA double helix, while rho factors release the newly made messenger RNA so it can move on to the ribosomes. Comparable fine tuning is used by ribosomes when they make proteins with information transmitted by RNA. Initiation factors start ribosomes at the appropriate point on the long messenger RNA molecule, while "nonsense words" tell them when to stop, and releasing factors snap off the freshly made protein. Other subtleties operate. Magnesium is a crucial element in protein making. Its absence may block the process, and an over- or underabundance may produce the wrong proteins.

This very brief gallop through a portion of contemporary molecular biology has a two-fold purpose: one is to indicate the very complex patterns of controls that rule a cell's division and function, and the other is to emphasize that any researcher probing for changes in these controls and relating them to aging has set himself a very hard task. Nevertheless, several groups are hard at it. To date, the results are sparse, sometimes contradictory, and often little more than suggestive hints. Still, some scientists are confident enough to begin testing drugs that can "lubricate" the fine tuning of a cell's genetic machinery.

The theoretical underpinning for much of this probing into the molecular biology of an aging cell was spelled out several years ago by Dr. Leslie E. Orgel of the Salk Institute in La Jolla, California. Orgel, now at work on the chemical origin of life, laid out his ideas in a paper called "The Maintenance of the Accuracy of Protein Synthesis and Its Relevance to Aging" that he published in 1963 in *The Proceedings of the National Academy of Sciences.*

"The basic idea is a simple one," he wrote, "namely that the ability of a cell to produce its complement of functional proteins depends not only on the correct genetic specifications of various polypeptide sequences [that is, amino acids joined in the proper order], but also on the competence of the protein synthetic apparatus." An error in a machine could be disastrous, exceeding any fault in its products. Orgel pointed out that an error in the structure of the enzyme that paces the transcription of information from DNA to RNA can be as damaging for the cell as a change, or mutation, in the DNA itself. Mistakes in the enzymes that control protein synthesis will go uncorrected. The central role of these enzymes in supplying the cell with a multiplicity of the molecules it needs to survive and function eventually leads to "error castastrophe," the point at which the cell is so error-ridden that it cannot function. Orgel, who was at Cambridge University when he wrote his famous paper, pointed out that there were no obvious selection pressures by which a cell could dispose of faults in its transcription machinery; unsaid, but implied, was that the inevitable deterioration of a cell—what some might call aging—was the strongest possible selection pressure.

Orgel suggested that one test of his idea might be to introduce deliberate errors into the proteins made by the cells of an animal and note effects on its lifetime. This can be done by feeding test animals "unnatural" amino acids—amino acids not used by nature. The experiments have been done with fruit-fly larvae and a fungus but with unclear results: no effect on life span in one case, and an increase in the other. Dr. F. Marott Sinex of the Boston University School of Medicine is testing the idea by using altered levels of magnesium to induce errors in protein synthesis. As noted earlier, magnesium is a crucial ingredient in the protein-making recipe, and differences can induce errors. The follow-up will be to isolate proteins and look for a pattern of errors—what are they, which proteins are affected, are they mounting with time, etc.?

Further along are attempts to trace the changing nature in the aging of chromatin—a complex of protein and DNA.

The protein apparently helps stabilize DNA, regulates its activity, and performs other somewhat uncertain functions. The evidence of chromatin changes with age is slim. Work with various tissues—mouse brain, beef brain and thymus, rat liver—indicates that the DNA becomes more impervious to heat with age; it toughens up. Proteins are probably responsible because "aged" DNA stripped of its proteins is no different from young DNA in its heat resistance. Perhaps inevitable "chemical accidents" forge new bonds. In any case, the DNA-protein bonds seem to strengthen with age, compacting the two, and distorting the precise transcriptions of information. However, there is an information loss even though the information molecule, DNA, is not changed. Partial confirmation comes from the experiments of Dr. Robert L. Herrmann and his colleagues at the Boston University School of Medicine illustrating a difference in the ability of young and old DNA to "prime" the synthesis of RNA.

Of interest also is the changing nature of certain histones that are part of the chromatin complex. Histones are fairly small proteins that may be "switches" activating various parts of the DNA molecule in response to cues—hormones, levels of certain enzymes, or whatever. Histones are generally classified by the amount of two amino acids, arginine and lysine, they contain; there are high and low arginine histones; high and low lysine histones. Scientists at the Gerontology Research Center found a "marked decrease in the proportion of the 'high-arginine' histones to the 'low-arginine' histones in the livers of old rats but no apparent change in the total amount of histone proteins." Perhaps they reflect a "change in the controls on transcription of information from DNA to RNA." Work by others, especially at Boston University, suggests a decrease in other proteins, aside from histones, that are also part of the chromatin complex.

Aside from these poorly understood changes, several groups are trying to measure changes in DNA and RNA with age, if indeed there are any. This is done by measuring the efficiency by which unwound strands of DNA—taken from old and young specimens—unite to form an active DNA molecule. These are hybridization experiments. RNA changes are being measured in similar fashion. Experiments so far are inconclusive, researchers having found no interesting or actual differences in young and old DNA. But the experiments are crucial, Dr. Sinex points out. If DNA differences are found, it means that age changes are occurring in the primary genetic materials, and a possible leg up for Curtis. If only RNA changes are seen, it puts the Orgel hypothesis front and center since that would indicate that errors in protein-making can be blamed on the transmittal of information rather than on the information itself.

What does this rising mountain of data—much of it tenuous and much omitted—really mean? Little, except for some preliminary evidence that changes in the regulation of protein synthesis do seem to occur with age, perhaps due to changes in the protein-DNA-RNA complex, where many of the controls are. These studies are probably the most difficult, potentially the most rewarding, and certainly the least understood in aging research. "It's easy to talk about cross-links and free radicals, but who wants to hear about histones, chromatin, transcription, etc.?" asks Sinex.

Even though the issue is only beginning to be defined, several drugs are being considered that, theoretically, should lubricate protein synthesis, extending the "mean time to failure."

Drugs to "rejuvenate" protein-making bodies within cells called ribosomes have been proposed but with questionable results so far. Various compounds have been used by Robert Kohn and others in an attempt to slow the cross-linkage of collagen. So far, nothing has worked. If too much is used, the animal dies. Too little, and the animal simply makes more collagen. "It's difficult to know," Kohn says, "whether you're interfering with maturation or aging of collagen."

Various intriguing materials are at hand, although their actual effects on human aging are uncertain at best. Denham Harman, of course, has reported increased life expectancy with some free-radical scavengers, but no human tests are yet contemplated. He does advocate diets—saturated fats such as lard, various proteins, etc.—that limit the opportunities for free-radical formation. Procaine, long an aging weapon in the European "youth clinics" so appealing to rich geriatrics, has been tested for effects on various possible aging mechanisms, such as collagen cross-linkage. None has been found. The tests on procaine, reports Sinex, "have not been encouraging, either in human subjects or rats." He does add that procaine seems to displace calcium from cell membranes, an effect that may help cells unite at the proper time. Various agents—among them vitamin E, a European "cure" called centrophenoxine, and others—have been reported to hold back the accumulation of age pigments but with no certified effects on aging itself. In fact, Harman reports that centrophenoxine can shorten the lives of mice.

Researchers are anxious to give all of these a careful hearing, feeling that it is time for aging research to cut the cards. Of course, the problem of testing a drug designed to slow a thirty-to-forty-year slide into obsolescence sobers a few. "Assuming that [a drug] was not capable of reversing established senile change," writes Alex Comfort in *Geriatric Focus*, "clinical trials in man would take thirty to forty years to show statistical results, and most of us have reservations about the risks of such prolonged administration."

Sinex gave the Center for the Study of Democratic Institutions a bill of particulars for an aging drug that included the following requirements: no adverse effects on the nervous system, although it should perk up long- and short-term memory and learning; no tumors, malignant or not; produce a pleasant feeling and be pleasant to take; stabilize normal protein synthesis; be cheap; and have been already used for other purposes, so any possible chronic, long-term effects are already known.

Of course, Sinex points out, "no drug fulfills all these criteria."

There is much more to aging research than outlined in this chapter, which is centered on molecular approaches. There is the immense and careful work on the physiology of aging which describes *what* happens, if not *why*. "At least it tells us where to look," comments one scientist. One theory, among many, which is only now beginning to pick up some steam, is the so-called immunologic theory of aging, essentially a progressive inability by the body's defenses to tell its own cells from bacteria, viruses, and other foreign matter. This accumulation of "nonself" induces a steady, documented, rise in autoimmune reaction in which antibodies attack their maker's cells. The increase with age of autoimmune diseases such as rheumatoid arthritis is one sort of evidence. More has been gathered principally by two research groups, one at the Oak Ridge National Laboratory in Oak Ridge, Tennessee, and the other at the University of California School of Medicine in Los Angeles.

All ideas about aging, diverse as they are, ultimately face the same wall: why do animals age so differently? Why does a mouse die in about two years and a man at eighty? If cross-linking of collagen and other molecules is responsible for aging man and mouse, why the gross difference in allotted time?

The cross-linking faction can only speculate at this point. Perhaps the difference is due to the wide gap in metabolic rate between the two, the much faster chemistry of the mouse accentuating—like a high-speed movie—the effects of collagen cross-linkage.

And how could age differences be explained if the riddle of aging is either in genetic material or in the machinery it uses? Dr. Horton A. Johnson of the University of Utah College of Medicine attributes the gaps—on a mathematical basis—to differences in the redundancy, or repeats, or vital molecules such as DNA. A man lives longer than a mouse because he has more spares to replace any damaged molecules.

Finally, two scientists at the University of California at Riverside attribute the difference, figuratively, to "the fickle finger of fate." They argue that aging is caused by a host of harmful genes that become active only late in life. Normally, the pressures of natural selection would eliminate these genes. But a species with few accidents, predators, and wear and tear can survive, accumulating and passing on its "death genes" that turn on late in life. Elephants live longer simply because they have fewer problems than mice have. All this implies that fewer accidents and less worry will increase life span. Of course, since the root cause is a steady accumulation of late-aging genes, any experimental test would become apparent only after several generations. The time does not seem propitious for an experimental test on humans.

An inevitable question difficult to answer is the reason for studying root causes of aging. Certainly, a public demand is missing. Most people in the field talk of the social value of enabling people to make the best physical and mental use of their alloted life span. "We're not going to increase life span but we can minimize disabilities so people can take better care of themselves," explains Nathan Shock. (Of course, heart transplants and other extraordinary procedures are helping a very few to live out their allotted span.)

Some see the aging riddle as an intellectual challenge. It is there. "Biological processes which constitute a barrier to human immortality should be of more than casual interest," writes Robert Kohn.

F. Marott Sinex has put it this way: "Application of current research in heart disease and cancer may be expected to extend life expectancy another seven or eight years. At this time, concern about failure of mental faculties, broken hips, and sensory loss will be great. Investment in basic research on the biology of aging is one of the cheapest, more foresighted, sensible investments that can be made."

Whatever the reasons for doing it, aging research has reached a sophisticated level, although the questions still weigh more heavily than the answers. The field still lacks the money and allure of other areas of contemporary biology. "It's hard to make a quick reputation in this field," says Kohn. When will all usable answers begin to pour out? Not very soon, think most researchers including Kohn, who believes that "the truth will out, but we'll be dead by then."

3

SEEKING
THE ORIGINS
OF STARS AND LIFE

It is a sad sort of story. Life is an incidental by-product, a minor happenstance in the death and renaissance of stars. In its final moments, a star swells to great size, becoming a red giant. Elements—carbon, nitrogen, oxygen, and others—swirl in its cooler outer envelope. They merge, forming momentary molecules, and separate again—an irrational chemical dance. Star matter is ejected into space, joining the remnants of other stars, drifting into the vast clouds of dust and gas that fill the spaces between stars. The ashes of exploded stars—supernovae—also drift in. Within time a cloud grows denser. The elements within, now protected by the dust, form more molecules—water, ammonia, formaldehyde, methyl alcohol, and others. These molecules absorb energy and cool the cloud, quickening its contraction just as cooling will shrink a balloon. The cloud begins to throw off infrared energy. It is growing hotter, becoming a proto-nebula, a galaxy of stars in formation. Within and without, molecules are formed and destroyed.

The proto-nebula separates into eddies of matter. Each will be a star. The eddies swirl through the galactic regions, throwing off wisps of matter that will become planets and moons. The stars burn hydrogen. On the planets, the molecules formed within the dust clouds continue to merge, growing more complex. Proteins are formed. Nucleic acids. Carbohydrates. Life is on its way.

We and our neighbors—wherever they are in our Milky Way galaxy—are negligible dross in the creation of stars.

Fantasy? Partly. Within the past decade and more intensively within the past three years, radio telescopes tuned to selected noises from space have heard the broadcasts of molecules formed deep within the clouds between the stars—the interstellar medium. A new sort of chemistry has arisen—astrochemistry, molecular astronomy, interstellar chemistry, chemistry *ad astra*—bizarre on Earth but common on a galactic scale.

A startling assortment of molecules is being created in these clouds of dust and gas out of which clusters of stars—100 to 100,000 at a time—are born. Only fairly recently have chemists, as well as the great majority of astronomers, pictured the interstellar clouds as vast chemical factories.

Mosaic of our Milky Way galaxy, from Sagittarius to Cassiopeia. Interstellar molecules are being found in the dark regions, clouds of dust and hydrogen that block starlight. *Courtesy: Hale Observatories*

Orion nebula, typical of galactic regions where molecules are being found. *Courtesy: Hale Observatories*

"It's fascinating that you are finding more complex molecules in interstellar space than you are in some of the planets," remarks Dr. Philip Solomon, an astronomer at Columbia University.

The molecules represent more than puzzling chemistry. They may become the "microscope" that astronomers will use to follow the gestation of stars within clouds. We may learn how our sun was created five to ten billion years ago. Closer to home, the molecules of space may revise the timetable for the origin of life on the Earth and other planets.

"The whole chemistry of the interstellar medium may turn out to be some sort of complicated biochemistry," Solomon says.

World War II accelerated the discovery of the molecules in space. The intense effort to develop radar familiarized a great many young scientists with microwaves—radio waves—heard rather than seen, varying in length from about 1 millimeter (about $\frac{1}{25}$ of an inch) to about 30 centimeters (about 12 inches). Microwaves are an arbitrarily sectioned part of a long electromagnetic spectrum that reaches from the wavelength of gamma rays (smaller than the diameter of atoms) through visible light to the very long radio waves (some miles long) on which we do our broadcasting.

Some of these young scientists came home still interested and started delving into microwave spectroscopy—the analysis of the energy emitted or absorbed by atoms and molecules in the microwave region. The search for molecules in space is simply microwave spectroscopy on a cosmic scale. There are many spectroscopies. When Isaac Newton held up a prism and split white light into a rainbow of colors, he was doing visible-light spectroscopy. There is ultraviolet spectroscopy, gamma-ray spectroscopy, infrared spectroscopy, all depending on which region is being studied.

Microwave spectroscopy might have stayed behind laboratory doors except for the radio telescope, first conceived in the thirties and refined after the war. The instrument overhears the sounds of stars and the matter between them; the "noises" mentioned earlier, created as atoms and molecules respond to their environment by a constant shuffle of energy, part of which is translated into radio wavelengths that can be heard by the radio telescopes; part of this energy is in the visible spectrum studied by optical astronomers. Radio stars undetected by optical telescope have been found, as have pulsars, the puzzling metronomes of space that emit energy with superclocklike regularity. The hearing of a radio telescope is formidable. One astronomer compared the total energy caught by all of them in twenty years of work to that of a single snowflake hitting the ground.

Radio astronomy has performed especially well in the interstellar medium; the dust particles in the clouds scatter the short wavelengths of starlight but pass through the much longer wavelengths of microwaves. Two decades ago United States, Australian, and Dutch radio astronomers located atomic hydrogen (H) in the interstellar medium by tuning their instruments to what has become the famous "21-centimeter line" in the spectrum. Such a feat and the power of radio astronomy can be understood by the following: Hydrogen atoms are composed of a proton and an electron, with the electron and proton either spinning in the same or opposing directions. There is an energy difference between the two spins, and when an electron transits from one to another—no one knows why but about once every 11 million years—it signals the event with the emission of a microwave 21 centimeters long.

Hydrogen is easily the most abundant element in our galaxy, dominating it as nitrogen dominates our atmosphere, but much more so. Its discovery meant that it could be mapped and that, at last, astronomers had a reliable way to determine the shape of our galaxy. Our galaxy is flat, pancakelike, composed of spiraling arms. Our sun and its satellites are dragged along on one of the outer spiral arms, and most of the stars we see in the sky belong to that region of the galaxy. Because of intervening clouds, we cannot see into the center of our galaxy—intuitively the most interesting part and probably a region of intense star making.

But radio telescopes could look in. In 1957, Dr. Charles Townes, then at Columbia University and now at the University of California at Berkeley, predicted that not only atoms but combinations of atoms (molecules) would be found in the interstellar spaces. Two-atom combinations of carbon atoms with hydrogen and nitrogen (CH, CN) had already been seen by optical telescopes because these molecules radiated visible light, but Townes said that even more complex molecules would be found with radio telescopes.

The first proof that he was right came in 1963 when a group at the Massachusetts Institute of Technology, after several tries by others, found the OH, or hydroxyl radical, in space; that is, a molecular fragment composed of an oxygen and hydrogen atom, or two thirds of a water molecule. In chemistry, a radical generally is an incomplete molecule composed of two or more atoms. A five-year hiatus followed, until molecular astronomy was deluged by new subject matter. A host of molecules were found, including ammonia, water, and a biological preservative, formaldehyde. In 1970, carbon monoxide, formic acid, methyl alcohol, hydrogen cyanide, and cyanoacetylene were added. In 1971, formamide, the first space molecule with four elements—carbon, oxygen, hydrogen, nitrogen—was added.

Why the time lapse? Officially, because the receivers needed to pick out the faint noises of a molecule against a constant background noise (even the electrons in the instrumentation emitting energy contribute to the static) had to be built. Perhaps a more basic reason was that astronomers—which included the people in charge of assigning time on the radio telescopes—simply would not believe that molecules could exist in the galactic clouds between stars.

Their argument that molecules could not exist in space was a sound one and still is, except that the molecules are there. Space is not a place to do chemistry, at least conventional chemistry. Conditions are harsh. Ultraviolet and cosmic rays permeate space and snap chemical bonds; even if molecules could form, their lives should be very short. Moreover, the likelihood of atoms meeting to form molecules is small. The density of atoms such as hydrogen in space is about one in a one-inch box; statistically, it could take years for two atoms to meet. And even if atoms—or molecular fragments—did meet, the thinking went, there is an excess energy to be gotten rid of. Unless a third body is there to collect this excess energy, two atoms meeting would usually bounce apart, just as a ball bounces off the floor because its energy is not completely absorbed. Granted, hydroxyl radicals were found. But these were simple molecular fragments, and in simplicity there is stability.

All these arguments of course came down with a bang as radio telescopes—almost exclusively in the United States—these last years reported the sighting of interstellar molecules. Chemistry was being done in space on a massive scale. Within the clouds composed largely of hydrogen gas and a bit of dust, molecules were being made. The chemistry was seemingly more intense within the dense dust clouds that measured about a light-year in diameter than in the thinner clouds, some of which measured ten light-years across. A light-year is six million million miles. A more meaningful comparison, perhaps, is that our sun is eight light-minutes away.

But how are the molecules made? The immediate response—in lieu of anything else—was the dust grains, tiny particles of uncertain constitution that are too small to be seen and make up about 1 percent of the average interstellar cloud.

"A dust grain is a fine chemistry laboratory," says Dr. David Cudaback, a radio astronomer at the University of California. "The dust clouds make dandy molecular batteries." Although not all molecular astronomers may agree with that statement, dust grains are plausible as the catalysts in forging molecules. Chemistry and, indeed, a good part of the chemical industry depend on a host of finely divided materials to speed chemical reactions. Moreover, the complex molecules—those with more than two atoms—have all been sighted within clouds.

Perhaps the most persuasive evidence that the dust grains are where the action is is the very recent discovery of hydrogen gas, or molecular hydrogen (H_2), in the interstellar region by Dr. George Carruthers of the Naval Research Laboratory in Washington, D.C. Molecular hydrogen is formed by uniting two hydrogen atoms and can be made only with the help of a third body, a dust grain. "I can't think of any other way to make molecular hydrogen except on grains," says Philip Solomon. Dr. William Klemperer, a chemist at Harvard University, points out that hydrogen molecules (and, indeed, all molecules) are broken apart very quickly by ultraviolet light. Therefore, since large amounts have been found, a very efficient hydrogen-making apparatus must be operating. Again, the dust grains suggest themselves.

But exactly what does happen on a dust grain is murky.

"Part of the problem," says Dr. Bertram Donn of NASA, "is that we have to know what the dust grains are." Donn, an astronomer turned part chemist, is head of the astrochemistry section at NASA's Goddard Space Flight Center outside Washington. The identity of the grains is a fascinating puzzle. "Right now, you pays your money and takes your choice," Donn says. Several candidates have been offered—silicates, a form of common sand; carbon in the form of graphite or diamond, and iron particles. Whatever they are, the dust grains may be coated with frozen hydrogen, although some astronomers discount that possibility. Identification may come when detectors are built sensitive enough to catch and analyze infrared radiation from these dust grains. As an interstellar cloud becomes denser, it heats up because of gravitational contraction and emits infrared energy, just as most hot materials such as a toaster will do.

Two of the leading participants in the "dust bowl" are Drs. Fred Hoyle and N. C. Wickramasinghe of the Institute of Theoretical Astronomy at the University of Cambridge. Hoyle, best known for his stout advocacy of a "steady state" origin of the universe, favors graphite, although he concedes that the answer may be a mixture of graphite and silicates. In any case, the important factor about dust grains may not be what they are but how they are shaped, whether they provide "cozy" spots for chemical reactions, and so on.

Hoyle, a prolific writer of science fact and fiction, is responsible for the first (and only) novel about interstellar clouds. It comes complete with sex, war, bumbling politicians, and triumphant scientists. The book, *The Black Cloud*, tells of the havoc wreaked when an interstellar cloud takes dead aim and moves through our solar system, blocking the sun, and alternately freezing and sweating the planets. The Cloud has an intelligence, and communication is established by a group of scientists led by Dr. Chris Kingsley, an astronomer who has a remarkable if sometimes unflattering resemblance to Hoyle. After a series of misadventures—which include the politicians firing off hydrogen bombs (the Cloud sent them back)—the intruder finally departs, leaving a relieved if shattered Earth.

But barring conscious clouds, reasonable physical processes can still account for the formation of molecules on dust grains. Klemperer at Harvard points out that carbon monoxide (CO) and hydrogen gas can in theory combine on a dust grain to form formaldehyde (H_2CO), duplicating a common chemical reaction on Earth. "The carbon monoxide molecule," Klemperer speculates, "is stuck on the grain, and then the hydrogen molecule comes along and 'skates' all over the surface until they meet." It's a slow process, but there's plenty of time in space.

Dust grains are not the only way to do chemistry in space. Klemperer and Solomon now believe—on theoretical grounds—

that diatomic, or two-atom, molecules such as cyanogen (CN), carbon monoxide (CO), and others can form without the help of dust grains.

This simpler route to diatomic molecules may provide a leg up to the formation of more complicated molecules such as formaldehyde. Diatomic molecules formed more or less by two atoms bumping together may be the raw materials for chemical manufacturing on dust grains. "That makes the whole process a lot simpler," Solomon says. Klemperer is inclined to be cautious on this point.

Molecules may also be made in stars and injected into the clouds—stellar injection. Diatomic molecules have been observed about stars, and it is probably a matter of time before more complex molecules are found. Densities are high enough in stars that dust grains are not needed. But the crucial point is whether molecules made in stars can survive the trip through open space before they reach the protection of the dust clouds. Donn estimates that most interstellar molecules, such as ammonia and water, might survive a hundred to a thousand years before being zapped by ultraviolet or cosmic rays. And that is not even enough time to leave the neighborhood of a star, much less reach the interstellar medium.

"You can't form them in a star and get them to a distant cloud," Donn explains. "If you observe molecules in a cloud, they must have been formed in that cloud."

There may be one escape route for the molecules made in stars. Hoyle and Wickramasinghe at Cambridge University point out that the stars are probably throwing off dust and that the dust grains could protect star-made molecules just as they protect molecules within the clouds.

There is little doubt that stars, including our own sun, are ejecting matter into space. The material from millions of stars moves through the galactic regions, casually and very slowly drifting together, like a Saturday night crowd at the candy store. Within the dust clouds, chemistry accelerates as the clouds slowly contract, growing denser, more protective, and gradually hotter. The chemistry that goes on within—however practiced—is exotic by the standards outlined in other chapters of this book.

But Dr. Harold C. Urey of the University of California at San Diego and others point out that it's the chemistry practiced on Earth that's really exotic.

The chemistry practiced in the clouds—on volume alone—dominates the universe. "We have a very limited point of view," said the late Dr. Richard Wolfgang, professor of chemistry at Yale University. "It's a small earth and has very peculiar conditions of temperature and what happens to be available," he says. "We have to look at the kind of chemistry that occurs in space. . . . It involves much more exotic reactants, much more exotic chemicals."

What experts in the field wonder about are the nonequilibrium conditions in which space molecules probably form. A molecule is usually doing many things: vibrating, rotating, colliding with other atoms and molecules, and so on. Each activity is rated in terms of a temperature—rotational temperature, collisional temperature, and so on. Radio astronomers usually measure rotational temperatures.

On Earth we assign one temperature to a batch of reacting chemicals, although that number really represents an average measure of several activities. We get away with it because the temperatures of molecules reacting in the laboratory are usually all the same, or, put more accurately, they have reached equilibrium conditions. In space, molecules rarely, if ever, react under equilibrium conditions. Their various temperatures, which measure what they are doing, may be quite different. Rotational and vibrational temperatures may be very low, while collisional temperatures—that is, molecules bumping into each other—can be very high.

The point of this sidestep into some chemical niceties is that these two conditions—equilibrium on Earth versus nonequilibrium in space—make a crucial difference in the way atoms and molecules react in the two places, how a molecule such as formaldehyde is formed, or, indeed, what the next step in its chemical odyssey is. Nonequilibrium chemistry is being explored by Solomon, Donn, Klemperer, and others. A sample of one approach is chemical accelerators that create beams of atoms and molecules which intersect and react. There's no time to equilibrate—nonequilibrium conditions operate—and by refined measurements the various temperatures of the reacting molecules and the products can be measured. The field is new, and results that can be applied to the puzzles of molecular astronomy are scarce. But in time these and other methods may decipher what is actually happening on a dust grain somewhere in the interior of a cloud where stars are made.

But what does it all mean? What implications lie in the discovery that molecules are being made in the vast spaces between stars? Klemperer at Harvard notes that chemists can now study the reactions of gases at temperatures and densities that simply cannot be gotten to on the Earth. "A unique laboratory if one knows how to use it," he says.

It also means, as noted before, that we now have a way to watch how stars are formed within dust clouds. In 1955, Fred Hoyle wrote in his book *Frontiers of Astronomy* that "it is only after star formation has occurred . . . that we have a chance of observing what has happened. . . . It is indeed just because we do not see these processes actually going on but only after they are completed that it has proved so difficult to understand how star formation takes place."

All that may soon change. By understanding what stories the chemistry within the clouds is telling, astronomers may be able to trace the history of a star from its conception until it brightly signals its birth.

Codiscoverer of formaldehyde Dr. David Buhl of the National Radio Astronomy Observatory in Green Bank, West Virginia, points out that "one of the very interesting questions we hope to answer as more and more of these molecules are found is what the evolutionary process is and what sort of chemistry is really involved in this proto-nebula [a galaxy in formation]. This relates very directly to what presumably took place on the earth five billion years ago when the solar nebula evolved and the sun presumably condensed out of a gas cloud very similar to those we're observing now. So this chemistry is of very immediate significance in terms of the origin of the earth."

That stars are born within the interstellar clouds is evidenced

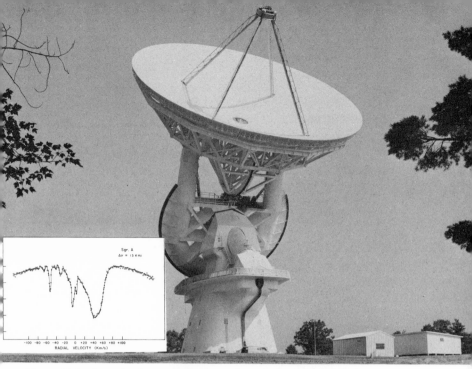

Formaldehyde and other interstellar molecules have been found with this 140-foot radio telescope of the National Radio Astronomy Observatory, Green Bank, West Virginia. Inset shows signal from interstellar formaldehyde. *Courtesy: National Radio Astronomy Observatory*

by very bright, very intense blue stars that burn themselves out in a million years or so, a mere flicker by astronomical time scales—too short for these stars to have come from elsewhere. These blue stars, which shine forty to fifty times more brightly than our sun, are usually found in the clouds. And a leading United States astronomer, Dr. Jesse Greenstein of the California Institute of Technology, once pointed out in *The Scientific Endeavor* that "for the bright stars to exist, there must be a reservoir of matter (and nuclear fuel) out of which they continue to be born—the interstellar gas. Exhaustion of nuclear fuel (largely hydrogen), and the slow, small change in the composition of the gas is the only real history of stars."

But as implied at the beginning of this chapter, the molecules may play a dramatic role in this history of stars. As the molecules form within the protective cover of a cloud, they take in, or absorb, energy which cools the cloud and accelerates its contraction to the point where "critical masses" become high enough to form stars and planets.

"What we have essentially," explains David Buhl, "is interdependence where the clouds are necessary to form the molecules. And then the molecules, in turn, are necessary in order to cool these clouds to form stars and planets. So the chemistry of the interstellar medium may be very vital in terms of the formation of stars and other astronomical processes going on."

(It might be noted that we have a cosmic chicken-or-egg paradox. Did the clouds or stars come first?)

But if some molecules are cooling the clouds, others are quite "hot," emitting an unusually intense amount of radiation, much higher than could be accounted for just by their abundances. A rough analogy would have a single match boiling a pot of water. Scientists now suspect that this intense radiation by certain chemicals in space—water and hydroxyl radicals are two —may be one result of the energy thrown off by germinating stars. If true, these hot molecules may have a fascinating story to tell.

This seems a fairly implausible story. But we have devices on earth that do just what is done in the cosmos—momentarily raising certain molecules to high energy levels and then emitting and guiding the energy returned when these molecules descend to normal, stable levels. These earthly counterparts to what nature seems to do in the cosmos are masers and lasers. The maser emits its energy in microwaves and the laser in light or optical waves. Both instruments are used in industry as well as in laboratories.

Ironically, part of the group that first observed the oddly intense signals from space was Charles Townes, a physicist who shared the 1964 Nobel Prize in physics for devising the principles that enabled masers and lasers to be built. These devices are very complex, and even after Townes had written down the equations, experimentalists had a hard job building them. Yet the clouds in space seem to have no trouble operating them. How they do it remains a major mystery.

It may be an interesting aside—in an age when astronomy is also puzzling over quasars and pulsars, possibly remnants of exploded galaxies and stars respectively—that the extraordinary energy emitted by some interstellar molecules would have mystified researchers, except that the maser had already been invented. "They probably would have had to think up something like a maser," observes Bertram Donn.

The most fascinating molecule found in space—at least from our parochial point of view—is formaldehyde. One radio astronomer called it "the experiment that blew the lid off the interstellar molecule business." Formaldehyde to an organic chemist is a simple molecule composed of just four atoms—CH_2O, one each of carbon and oxygen and two of hydrogen. But its discovery snapped heads because its presence in space suggested that even more complex molecules could be found. That suspicion, of course, has been confirmed by the subsequent discovery of the first five-atom molecule in space—cyanoacetylene (CH_3N), then formic acid ($HCOOH$) and methyl alcohol (CH_3OH)—all one or two atoms more complicated than formaldehyde. The discovery of formaldehyde at the National Radio Astronomy Obervatory (NRAO) also suggested that the chemistry in space could be versatile enough to form molecules usually associated with life. Buhl, an electrical engineer with a dramatic flair, reportedly remarked after seeing formaldehyde signals from nine galactic clouds that the group was "witnessing nine civilizations in the process of formation."

In addition to Buhl, the formaldehyde group included Dr. Lewis Snyder, then at NRAO and now at the University of Virginia, Dr. Patrick Palmer of the University of Chicago, and Dr. Benjamin Zuckerman of the University of Maryland. They used the 140-foot NRAO telescope in Green Bank. This was in 1969 when the possible existence of fairly complex molecules in space was still not taken seriously.

It might be noted that radio astronomers must have a fairly good idea where in the radio spectrum they want to tune the receivers for the radio telescopes. The radio spectrum is much larger than the optical spectrum used by optical astronomers. The latter can cover their regions by exposing one or two plates. But the radio astronomer making a blind search has a problem somewhat akin to finding a particular shortwave station without knowing its call letters. There simply isn't enough time for a blind search. Moreover, any signals received could be missed unless they are expected. The "call letters" of probable interstellar molecules can sometimes be measured with laboratory instruments and sometimes they can be roughly calculated with mathematical equations. Formaldehyde was no problem; its call letters were already available in the scientific literature.

Formaldehyde was picked for a go for several interlocking reasons. Its elements—carbon, oxygen, and hydrogen—are fairly abundant in the galaxy, and its molecular structure is the simplest possible combination of the three. Moreover the NRAO telescope at Green Bank had detectors with the capacity to pick up the very weak microwaves six centimeters long that formaldehyde molecules broadcast.

"The hundred and forty foot telescope is ideally suited to six centimeters," Lewis Snyder points out. "And it turned out that at the time we wanted to do this, telescope time was available."

The first formaldehyde signals were heard about an hour after the search began. The signals were quite weak and hardly positive proof that a new era in molecular astronomy had begun. The group kept up their search. Stronger signals appeared, verifying the presence of formaldehyde. These signals were absorption signals, meaning that formaldehyde molecules passing between a star and the NRAO telescope were absorbing some of the star's energy. Laboratory experiments on earth, in which microwaves were sent through formaldehyde vapor, had provided the wavelengths at which formaldehyde molecules absorb energy, whether in space or elsewhere. And the absorption spectrum seen at Green Bank—"like shadows on a bright field," Buhl explains—closely matched the laboratory predictions. (The actual signals were displaced slightly from their expected positions because the formaldehyde clouds were moving.) "Next to ammonia," says Snyder, "it's the most well-confirmed spectroscopic identification in the radio spectrum."

In fact, just as the ubiquity of atomic hydrogen in our galaxy has been used to map its shape, the distribution of formaldehyde is being used to trace the outlines of the center of our galaxy, a region of active star-making. It appears to be distributed in a series of rotating, concentric rings, the inner ones growing smaller and the outer ones larger. How to interpret this is still uncertain, but this early work backs up the recent comment in *Nature* that "the study or the interstellar molecules is rapidly forging a useful tool for the investigation of our galaxy."

Buhl and Snyder have also found hydrogen cyanide, a molecule that chemists—particularly Dr. Leslie Orgel of the Salk Institute—have linked to the chemical origin of life. Hydrogen cyanide appears to be an ideal material for the formation of purines and pyrimidines, relatively complicated molecules that suitably linked with other atoms become the building blocks for the genetic materials DNA and RNA.

Hydrogen cyanide, formaldehyde, and other molecules found in space are *prima facie* evidence for a case that some sort of prebiology is being practiced in the galactic regions. Several decades of theory and about two decades of experiments have established the probability that life arose on earth from a steady accumulation of simple molecules into more complex ones, such as the cited example of hydrogen cyanide.

The supposition has always been that the process began about four-and-a-half billion years ago when the earth formed and that it took about a billion years before life appeared. But some people wonder if a billion years is enough time to create life. Now, with the discovery that extensive chemistry is being done in space, there is the possibility that the process of assembling complex chemicals of life began in the galactic clouds and that when we look at formaldehyde, hydrogen cyanide, and the others, we are indeed, as David Buhl says, witnessing the beginning of civilizations that will make their mark in several billion years.

This view is not entirely a flattering one. Life becomes subordinate to star making. "Life," Lewis Snyder explains, "might be connected with stellar evolution. Perhaps the evolution of a star is a basic process going on in the galaxy, and all other processes which we are familiar with, such as life, are simply side processes that stem from this basic process."

If that star theory of life is correct, then even more complicated molecules might be found in space. Snyder and Buhl (and others) are now thinking seriously about very big game

—amino acids. These, of course, are building blocks of proteins. That amino acids may be in space is not outlandish, and, in fact, discoveries reported in late 1970 give their existence a high probability. First, chemists at the University of Miami found that simply heating ammonia and formaldehyde—both molecules in space—will produce amino acids. Hard on that came the report by a combined group of experimenters (NASA, University of California at Los Angeles, Arizona State University) that they had found sixteen different varieties of amino acids in the Murchison meteorite that fell in Murchison, Victoria, Australia, on September 28, 1969.

Amino acids have been found in meteorites before, but strong possibilities of contamination have always marred the results. For instance, past measurements have turned up the amino acid serine, which is also dominant in fingerprint marks. However, the group found no serine, and that fact as well as other evidence enabled them to present a strong case that they had found the first amino acids not made on earth.

Of course, meteorites come from within our solar system, probably from the asteroid belt between Mars and Jupiter and not from the galactic regions beyond that molecular astronomers are probing. However, this work has intensified the search for amino acids in the clouds between stars. The portion of the radio spectrum in which amino acids might be found is unknown. Measurements of these wavelengths in the laboratory is difficult because the molecules must first be vaporized, which breaks their chemical bonds. Probable wavelengths can be calculated, but they may not be precise enough to justify a search. Klemperer at Harvard thinks that wavelengths will be determined in the laboratory, that ways will be found to vaporize amino acids and keep them intact long enough to measure their microwave spectra, although "one might have to be clever about it." Snyder now estimates that it will be the late seventies before enough information is available to justify a search.

The field of molecular astronomy, like a lusty infant, is changing rapidly. One example is a new and grand technique with a ponderous name: very long base-line interferometry (VLBI). It simply means that two radio telescopes separated by hundreds or even thousands of miles are coupled by open telephone lines or other means so that they can exactly coordinate their search of a particular section of the galaxy. The reason for pairing widely scattered radio telescopes this way is to get an accurate idea of both the size and location of the clouds of water, formaldehyde, etc., that drift in the interstellar medium. The resolution achieved is extraordinary and is of the kind that enables a press release from the Massachusetts Institute of Technology to point out that the resolution of two 'scopes separated a few hundred miles "is equivalent to an observer in New York being able to tell the difference between a fifty-cent piece and a dime suspended over Fargo, North Dakota."

Looking at radio sources in the galaxy is like looking at a finger in front of your face with one eye closed; the finger's position will shift depending on which eye is open, but neither position is the true one. Only when both eyes are open do you really know where the finger is. And with objects light years away, the farther apart the "eyes," the better fix astronomers have on their true position. Radio telescopes in Sweden and California have been coupled to establish a base line of several thousand miles, and astronomers now dream of putting a radio telescope on the moon.

It may strike some readers that molecular astronomy has been largely an American science. The reasons are several, the most obvious being that radio astronomers in Europe and Australia were busy with other matters. That may change. The United States, which built most of the 'scopes with which the molecules were found in the late fifties and early sixties, now has few significant plans to expand its instrumentation. However, major new telescopes are in operation, under construction, or planned in Germany, Holland, Italy, and Australia.

In common, the scientists working in the new field of molecular astronomy agree that only a beginning has been made. They are looking at pieces of a puzzle with little idea what the puzzle will tell them or, indeed, how many pieces are in the puzzle. But eventually understanding will come and researchers will be able to write the scenario for the formation of stars and planets from clouds of dust and gas. Jesse Greenstein once said that the universe is "enormous, strange, and untouchable."

It is becoming less strange and less untouchable.

4

THE SEARCH FOR
SUPERHEAVY ELEMENTS

Just past magic ridge and over magic mountain looms the sea. Beyond, in the mist, past unseen submarine alps, is the goal— the island of stability. If that sounds like a not-too-clever fairy tale, consider this: People in the United States, Sweden, Germany, the Soviet Union, and elsewhere are busily filling blackboards with schemes for reaching this mythical island. Balloons are breaking records to find it, one man has gone underground to look for it, and four countries are building machines to reach it.

This time, effort, money, and analogy swirl about a new stage in the creation of matter, undreamed of a decade ago and still a cause for wonder. Chemists and physicists have in sight a new group of fairly stable elements. Certain confirmation that they exist would confirm that men are closing in on the true matter of matter.

Dmitri Mendeleev would be delighted. In the nineteenth century he grouped elements by their chemical properties and created the periodic table of elements. Mendeleev put sixty-three elements in his table and predicted the discovery of three more. Now his table is crammed with ninety-two natural elements, and nuclear scientists have added thirteen synthetic ones, with several more in sight.

But as the element makers continued their climb beyond uranium—number 92 in the periodic table—their creations became more and more mischievous: they disappeared in minutes, seconds, or fractions of a second after they were made. Added to their instability was their scarcity; only about a hundred or so atoms of the most recent synthetic element, 105, were actually made.

Now the audacious proposal has been made by element makers that beyond this rising sea of instability in which they are treading are islands of stability—further groups of stable elements, which, because of their atomic masses, are called the superheavies.

Predicted superheavies range up to an atomic number of 164, with current searches focusing on two islands of stable superheavies: those with atomic numbers 110 to 114 and 120 to 126.

The race for the superheavy elements—few participants deny they're in a race—is taken very seriously. The first one to find or make them will pioneer a territory of matter whose exploration may consume significant portions of the talents and monies of the world's most advanced technologies.

The theory that superheavies exist was put together by an international group within only the past several years. Already, in 1971, British and Indian groups have reported possible sighting of superheavy elements 112 and 114. Accelerators that can make them are being built. One is "on beam," ready for a go. This is the ALICE machine at Orsay, about twenty miles

KNOWN AND PREDICTED REGIONS OF NUCLEAR STABILITY, SURROUNDED BY A SEA OF INSTABILITY

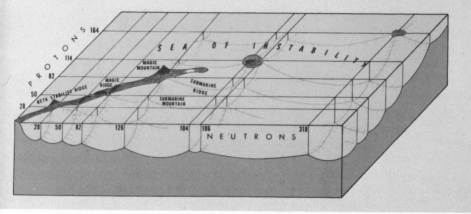

southwest of Paris, where the science campus of the University of Paris is located. Four other machines are being built or planned—at the Lawrence Radiation Laboratory of the University of California in Berkeley, at Dubna, located just outside Moscow, and at two places in Germany: Heidelberg and Darmstadt. These machines, capable of accelerating heavy atoms at energies and intensities needed to reach the superheavy island, will go on beam one by one between now and 1975.

The heavy-ion accelerators will have the common goal of hurling a heavy ion—an atom stripped (e.g., by passing through mercury vapor) of many of its electrons—against target atoms. What will happen when they meet is still moot. Dr. W. J. Swiatecki of the Lawrence Radiation Laboratory (LRL) summed it up this way at a meeting in Heidelberg:

$$A_1 + A_2 + \text{Hope} = \text{Superheavy Nucleus}$$

$A_1 + A_2$ are heavy nuclei—one a target, the other a bullet—whose forced marriage should produce a lusty offspring. That technique has already been applied to the creation of several synthetic elements, including element 105.

An element's atomic number denotes the number of protons

within the nuclei of that element's atoms; protons are matched by an equal number of electrons orbiting about the nucleus. Except for hydrogen, the atomic nuclei of all elements contain neutrons, uncharged particles with about the same mass as protons, an atom's mass being the total number of protons and neutrons. While the number of protons gives an element its identity, its number of neutrons can vary, which is why there are several isotopes of most elements. Isotopes of an element have the same atomic number but differ in atomic weights because of the differing number of neutrons. Thus, there are various isotopes of uranium differing in mass— $^{235}_{92}U$, $^{237}_{92}U$, and $^{238}_{92}U$ —all sharing the same atomic number 92. If you subtract 92 from the mass numbers (the atomic weights), you will obtain the number of neutrons for each uranium isotope.

How do heavy-ion accelerators work? The concept is simple, although execution is difficult and costly. As many as possible of accompanying electrons are removed, or stripped, from atoms. For instance. a uranium atom, which normally has 92 electrons, may be stripped of 22 electrons. Stripping turns the atoms into ions and also gives them a charge that electrical and magnetic fields of the accelerator can use as a "handle" to hurl them against target atoms. These fields must be exactly coordinated to achieve the speed (about 1/5 of the speed of light) or energies needed for nuclear reaction. The ion beam must not be allowed to diverge, as any stream of like charges ordinarily will. To keep "down time" to a minimum, the machine must be accessible to quick changes of ion source and target.

The design of an accelerator can be agony as scientists and engineers trade off dream and reality. What does the nuclear scientist want and at what energies? Will the machine be adequate in ten years? (The Berkeley machine was inadequate thirteen years after it went on beam.) These are serious issues for machines where magnets are measured in tons, electrical power in millions of watts, and cooling water in thousands of gallons per minute.

To date, virtually all the effort in creating synthetic elements with heavy-ion accelerators has been done at two places: the Laboratory of Nuclear Reactions at Dubna and the Lawrence

Albert Ghiorso of the Lawrence Radiation Laboratory beside apparatus used to detect isotopes of synthetic element 104. *Courtesy: Lawrence Radiation Laboratory, University of California*

Radiation Laboratory. LRL, which gets first credit on most of the synthetic creations, is perched on a hill overlooking Berkeley and San Francisco Bay, where—except for occasional smog, a newcomer to the scene—one can look out to the Golden Gate and the Pacific. Many factors account for LRL's supremacy so far. Basic was the drive of E. O. Lawrence, who built the first cyclotrons, or circular accelerators, and attracted the kind of people capable of launching a massive attempt to make elements. There are too many to mention, but a few are better known: Dr. Edwin McMillan, codiscoverer of element 93 and now LRL's director; Dr. Glenn T. Seaborg, who took part in the creation of over a half-dozen elements and former chairman of the United States Atomic Energy Commission; and Albert Ghiorso, in charge of the element-making machine at LRL since the fifties and now preparing to make superheavies. Ghiorso is a paradox in the usually tightly knit scientific establishment. He has no Ph.D.. lacks formal training as a nuclear scientist, and first came in contact with LRL as a sort of high-grade repairman who fixed its Geiger counters. Now, after having participated in the discovery of almost every synthetic element, he is regarded as the master of the supreme art of making elements and in the detection of a few atoms with fleeting lifetimes.

The creation of element 105, claimed by LRL, is illustrative. Two millionths of an ounce of a californium isotope, an amount just barely visible, was bombarded with nitrogen ions, which have the requisite amounts of electrons and protons, accelerated in the Heavy Ion Linear Accelerator (HILAC), the laboratory's "cranky old lady." They were accelerated at concentrations intense enough and energies high enough to form a compound nucleus, the momentary mingling of nucleons (protons and neutrons) in the nuclei of target and projectile atoms before they rearrange themselves to form the nucleus of the new element.

A stream of helium gas swept the atoms of the newly formed 105 out of the target area onto a metal wheel that rotated at intervals carefully clocked to place these new isotopes of 105 in front of a sequence of detectors. By measuring the energies of alpha particles (2 neutrons plus 2 protons and equivalent to the nucleus of a helium atom), these detectors could identify particles produced as the new element decayed to a known synthetic element, lawrencium. Detection of the appropriate

Interior of Super HILAC. *Courtesy: Lawrence Radiation Laboratory, University of California*

amount of lawrencium atoms provided the case that a new element, 105, had been made.

But the HILAC is not versatile or powerful enough to accelerate the very heavy ions that will be needed as bullets in the creation of superheavy elements, and was shut down early in 1971 for conversion into, of course, a Super HILAC. While LRL's timetable calls for the Super HILAC to be back "on the air" within months, some nonresident observers have some doubts about that timetable. "We aren't dubious," Ghiorso insists. "We think we can actually go faster than that." He may be right. Many of the components for the new Super HILAC have already been built, and Ghiorso has a reputation as a forceful ramrod, quite willing to work alongside his workmen to make sure they're properly motivated. The spur is not only pride but the other machines being built. ALICE at Orsay is on, but its beam of heavy ions apparently is not intense enough to have a high probability of forming a compound nucleus, the way station to a superheavy. "ALICE is just on the edge as far as forming a compound nucleus," Ghiorso explains. But most new accelerators begin life with low intensities, and ALICE may become a more formidable competitor as she grows up.

More serious is the challenge of the Russian and two German machines. The Dubna machine is a cyclotron whose diameter has been widened to permit it to accelerate ions as heavy as the isotope xenon-136. The Russians, led by one of their great nuclear scientists, Georgii N. Flerov, are not giving out timetables, but the guessing is that they will be ready for a go sometime in 1972. The Germans are working on an unnamed machine in Heidelberg and on their UNILAC in a forest outside Darmstadt. The Heidelberg machine will be ready about July 1972, and UNILAC in 1974 or 1975. UNILAC will be "the Cadillac of the new accelerators," according to a United States observer, Dr. H. Marshall Blann of the University of Rochester. UNILAC's advantage, of course, is that it is a new machine, while those at Berkeley and Dubna are conversions of older accelerators. UNILAC will certainly underline the renaissance of German science. Some 22 million dollars will be spent on the project, with 12 million going to the machine alone. About 3 to 4 million is being spent to reconvert the HILAC.

Four hundred and forty people, including 190 scientists, will man the UNILAC complex. The machine will be able to accelerate ions as heavy as uranium at continuously variable energies; while the maximum energy of the Super HILAC is fixed, it can be degraded to lower energies. The UNILAC beam of ions may also be more intense—that is, its current higher—than any of the other heavy-ion accelerators now being built, according to Blann.

The emergence of the foreign machines probably means that Europe will become dominant in fields where heavy-ion accelerators are needed, such as in element making, studies of nuclear fission, and the production of isotopes. "The ability to read German, French, and Russian should be invaluable in this regard," Blann told a probably glum audience of United States physicists.

Their frustration was probably heightened by a report early in 1971 that British scientists—in a kind of backstairs approach—may have already made a superheavy element, 112. This group—a mix from the Rutherford High Energy Laboratory, the University of Manchester, and the Universities Research Reactor—bombarded two targets of very pure tungsten metal with protons. Occasionally, a tungsten atom, like a horse stung by a bee, would recoil when hit by a proton and fly off with enough energy to collide with another tungsten atom. The hope was that the collision was energetic enough to produce a momentary compound nucleus that would decay down to the nearest island of stability in the superheavy region, most likely to element 112. Since the chances of two tungsten atoms meeting with enough energy are small, the group bombarded their targets for up to a year in a proton accelerator at the European Organization for Nuclear Research (CERN) in Geneva, Switzerland. The irradiated targets were taken to Manchester, dissolved, and the various radioactive elements formed during the proton bombardment separated. Mercury was deliberately added to a dissolved solution and then precipitated, a technique that would remove 112, which by its position in the periodic table of elements should behave chemically like mercury. When the samples were placed in radiation detectors, the Britishers observed two things that gave them a case for the first sighting of a superheavy: the appearance of alpha particles with an energy that could not be explained by what is known of the decay of lighter radioactive atoms; and the detection of fission fragments, indicating that atoms were breaking apart spontaneously, something that mercury does not do. While that makes a case for the detection of a superheavy element, the case is by no means airtight, with contamination by other radioactive elements such as thorium a clear possibility. The British were properly cautious, titling their report in *Nature*, "Evidence for the Possible Existence of a Superheavy Element with Atomic Number 112."

However, the technique while imaginative is also limited, not designed as heavy-ion linear accelerators are, to create both a variety and sizable quantities of superheavy elements.

There is another route to superheavy territory which is also beginning to produce glimmerings of success. This is to look for superheavy elements in nature. American and Russian scientists looked for evidence of elements 110 and 114 in platinum and lead ores, respectively, and failed to find them. These two superheavy elements, because of the way their 110 and 114 electrons are arranged, may be somewhat akin in their chemistry to platinum and lead. They are usually called eka platinum and eka lead, eka being Sanskrit for "one," which was Dmitri Mendeleev's label for the next unknown element in a family of known elements.

Russian scientists in Dubna think they may have seen eka atoms fissioning in some of their samples. These came from colorfully dramatic sources—old church windows made with leaded glass, ancient ceramics, and the like. The issue is clouded since the events the Russians reported may have come from radioactive impurities such as uranium or thorium, or fission events induced by an energetic cosmic-ray particle. Time will tell.

An exhaustive and disappointing search for evidence of natural superheavies was also made by Dr. Gunter Herrmann and his colleagues at Johannes Gutenberg University in Mainz, West Germany. Superheavy elements, when they do fission—or break apart because the nucleus is unstable—should spit out an unusually high number of neutrons: ten per event as opposed to two or three when an element such as uranium fissions. Since neutrons have no charge, they can pass through a large amount of matter relatively undisturbed. Putting these facts together, the scientists at Mainz passed hopefully fissioning ten- to one-hundred-pound lots of metal ores such as gold, platinum, lead, and iridium under neutron-counting devices. They found no evidence of superheavies, merely detecting neutrons from known sources.

Nevertheless, neutron-counting techniques in which the neutrons produce detectable flashes of light in liquid scintillators have been adopted by both Dubna and Berkeley searchers. While Georgii Flerov is leading the search at Dubna, Dr. Stanley Thompson, codiscoverer of five synthetic elements, heads the Berkeley search for natural superheavies. He now has metal ores some eight hundred feet underground, in a tunnel of the Bay Area Rapid Transit (BART) System now being built. So far no superheavies have been discovered, although by going underground, Thompson has increased the sensitivity of his neutron counting a hundred- to a thousandfold. Thompson now knows that if relatively stable superheavies exist in nature, their numbers are very scarce indeed—perhaps fewer than one in ten million.

The joker in this search for superheavies on Earth is that they may not be stable enough to have lasted the passage of several billion years, when the Earth was created, until the seventies. The search for natural superheavies is based on the logical assumption that they were made when most heavy elements—heavier than iron, anyway—were created, probably in the cataclysmic explosion of a star, a supernova.

What happens when stars explode is that elements already formed by the carbon-nitrogen cycle and other routes (as in the chapter on neutrinos) are exposed to a very intense shower of neutrons that are energetic enough to barge into atomic nuclei. Many elements respond by fissioning or decaying to lighter elements. In some cases the nuclei hold together, while neutrons are added successively and very rapidly, raising an atom's mass. Occasionally, a neutron transmutes to a proton (beta decay), which raises the atom's atomic number, thereby creating a higher-numbered element. The net effect of this process—called the r-process or rapid multiple neutron capture—is the creation of new elements. This is what goes on in exploding stars and, on a considerably lesser scale, in nuclear explosions. For instance, isotopes of the synthetic element fermium, atomic number 100, were found in the debris of an underground explosion. Apparently, they had been made by neutron additions to plutonium nuclei with subsequent beta decay. As of now, the confidence that superheavy nuclei with their extraordinary masses can be formed in a nuclear explosion is low. And, even if formed, recovery and detection may be improbable. Bets are still on the accelerators.

Theorists estimate that some superheavies should be stable enough so that a portion is still with us today. But their calculations depend on some assumptions that may not hold up, including the predicted masses of superheavy nuclei and the binding energies (a measure of cohesive forces) of the protons and neutrons within these nuclei. When physicists gather to discuss these things, they evaluate them in terms of millions of electron volts, or mevs.

"If you jiggle things around by an mev or two, that makes a pretty big difference," Thompson points out. Indeed. An error of one mev in the calculations could mean a million-year difference in the half-life of a superheavy element. Half-life—nominally the time it takes one half of the atoms of an element to fall apart, by definition giving the rate of decay—gives a direct reading of an element's age, or stability.

Any superheavy element with a half-life shorter than about a hundred million years would be gone by now. Since that is uncomfortably close to the half-lives calculated by theorists, it's probable that Thompson, Flerov, and the others may simply be too late to find superheavies.

Partly to escape this time trap, British and American scientists have sent balloons to the edges of outer space in the hope of detecting superheavy elements in cosmic rays—streams of protons, electrons, and very small amounts of heavy elements. Cosmic-ray particles move at energies far higher than achieved by any earthbound accelerator, which is why some scientists call

Balloon used for carrying emulsion and plastic detectors of cosmic rays and superheavy elements. *Courtesy: General Electric Research and Development Center*

them the "poor man's accelerator," although working on them is far from cheap. Since cosmic rays probably come from outside our solar system—most likely produced in supernovae—they might be younger than the elements of the solar system, which must be at least four to five billion years old, that is, as old as our earth. If cosmic rays are considerably younger than our solar system, any superheavy elements they are carrying should still exist and be detectable.

The first report of heavy elements in cosmic rays came from Professor Peter H. Fowler and his colleagues at the University of

Bristol in England. Fowler sent up detectors in 1967 from Palestine, Texas. Palestine has both a scientific ballooning facility and overhead magnetic conditions that screen out the nuclei of lighter elements that might obscure detection of very heavy elements. Fowler and his people soon joined forces with an American group that included Dr. Robert M. Walker of Washington University and Drs. Robert L. Fleischer, George E. Nichols, and P. Buford Price at the General Electric Research and Development Center.

Each group used different detectors. Fowler used special photographic emulsions that are standard tools in nuclear science. They are generally thicker than ordinary film and considerably richer in grains of silver halide. They are easy to transport and can be stacked on one another. A charged particle —such as a heavy ion—will alter the silver compounds so that, as in a common photograph, more-or-less standard development will reveal the tracks and, by comparison with known tracks, their maker's identity.

Walker and company used a "fission track" technique that he, Fleischer, and Price created when they were all at General Electric. Charged atoms moving at high energies, as they do in cosmic rays, will carve a track of shattered molecules in materials that have an orderly molecular structure, such as crystals and certain plastics. The tracks are chemically etched and, again by comparison with known samples, the track-maker identified. The American group used plastic detectors for their cosmic-ray work.

In past balloon flights, the emulsion and plastic detectors, stacked together, agreed on the sighting of cosmic-ray elements as heavy as uranium but in 1969 diverged dramatically when Fowler reported that he may have seen element 104. But there were many doubts, and Fowler himself could only be 65 percent certain that he had caught an element heavier than uranium. The plastic detectors, flown by the American group on the same flight where Fowler detected 104, indicated element 92, uranium, as their heaviest element seen. Both groups have now compromised on element 96, curium, as the particle sighted in both emulsion and plastic detectors.

Why the discrepancy between the two techniques? P. Buford Price, now professor of physics at the University of California at Berkeley, points out that Fowler's detectors were not covered during the forty-hour flight when 104 was seen. "During that time the relative humidity changed considerably," he explains. "The emulsions took in and let out water so that it's possible that the sensitivity of the emulsions could have changed during the flight."

In cosmic-ray work, it's hard to predict where trouble will come from next. A balloon sent up late in 1970 from Minneapolis and supposed to stay up for two days, instead—because of a mechanical failure—stayed up for two weeks and took off for a flighty journey to the West Coast, out over the Pacific, finally returning to Canada and crashing near Fork River, Canada, about a hundred miles northwest of Winnipeg. The scientific package, containing plastic and emulsion detectors, separated earlier and came down more-or-less intact in a field of flax near Regina, Saskatchewan.

Price has been looking elsewhere for superheavies. "The other approach we're taking at Berkeley," he explains, "is to look at moon samples with very large crystals that came right from the surface."

The moon, as Glenn Seaborg once said, is "a massive virgin target of cosmic rays." And the particular lure of a moon sample is that, unlike meteorites or the surface of the earth, it has not been eroded. Superheavy elements barging into moon matter will stop at the skin and remain there.

Price thinks that he has found the track of a superheavy element in one of his lunar samples. "I've got one now that has got to be particularly heavier than uranium, but I can't prove it," he says. It is possible that comparison with the tracks made by intermediate weight elements such as krypton may help him prove his case. More likely, he'll have to wait until his nascent neighbor, the Super HILAC, is in business.

A more assertive case for the sighting of superheavy elements in the cosmos was made in 1971 in a report to *Nature* by Indian researchers from the Tata Institute of Fundamental Research in Bombay. Rather than cosmic-ray detectors, the group, led by

Lunar crystal with possible track of superheavy element. About one millimeter long. *Courtesy: P. Buford Price, University of California*

Dr. N. Bhandari, used meteorites, voyagers through space that should have been bombarded by superheavy elements during their travels. Their search was based on the fact that the length of track carved in a crystalline material, such as a mineral grain, is dependent directly on its charge and energy. With that in mind, a search was begun for tracks made by the fragments of a superheavy element that has fissioned spontaneously. The Indian group painstakingly extracted and then, with acid, chemically etched mineral grains from meteorites, as well as moon dust returned by the Apollo missions. A careful examination under the microscope revealed, in the case of one meteorite, some 1,500 tracks, 9 of which were of the length expected of the fission fragment from a superheavy element. The group now believes the superheavy element they have detected is 114. Similar evidence has been found in the moon samples.

An alternative to the moon as a superheavy probe is the manned orbiting workshop planned by NASA for the late 1970s. This will give scientists an opportunity to expose very large detectors for a very long time, factors that will improve the chances of finding superheavies.

While this terrestrial and heavenly scrambling has already gained tentative evidence for the existence of superheavy elements, it has also underscored what many scientists already suspected: if superheavies are found in nature, their numbers will be very scarce indeed and, therefore, to do any meaningful work on them, they will have to be made. The new generation of heavy-ion linear accelerators that are and will be ready this decade are inescapable tools for exploring the new matter dreamed up by theorists.

"Dreamed" is an unjust word for the very hard, often brilliant work of many scientists from several countries—Germany, Poland, the Soviet Union, Sweden, and the United States—that has gone into building the theoretical case that there are islands of stable elements, perhaps beginning at atomic number 110.

The case rests on a complex intertwining of pictures, or models, of the nucleus of the atom—the liquid-drop model and the shell model. Neither one completely explains the nucleus, both may be wrong, but each helps rationalize some nuclear peculiarities. The liquid-drop model of the atomic nucleus was resuscitated in 1939 to explain the astounding report out of Germany that a uranium atom had been fissioned by the simple insertion of a neutron. Physicists were puzzled that so little energy was needed to split an atom. It was as if, one later wrote, a rock had been split by a pencil tap. The liquid-drop model compared the fissioning of atoms to the splitting of liquid drops as their spherical shape is increasingly distorted. The analogy is so useful to a comprehension of nuclear fission that scientists, including Stanley Thompson at LRL, have taken slow-motion pictures of dividing drops. A liquid-drop nucleus became a balancing act between the natural repulsion (because they have identical charges) of protons within it and surface tension, or nuclear force, that held the nucleus together, much the same way that the surface tension of a water droplet holds it together.

Difficulties for this theory came with the heavier elements such as uranium which have a sizable number of protons and neutrons whose interactions, ignored in the liquid-drop model, could no longer be ignored. Out came the shell model of the nucleus. Here protons and neutrons are independently sorted into shells and subshells, quite analogous to the way that electrons are arranged in shells and subshells about the nucleus. Electronic arrangements determine an atom's chemical propensities, differing from the arrangement of protons and neutrons which may determine an atom's existence and certainly its stability.

Each picture of the nucleus gained its own jargon. A very stable liquid-drop nucleus is a "spherical" nucleus, while in the shell model a stable nucleus has "closed shells" of protons and neutrons. The shell view of the nucleus also contributed "magic" numbers, an apparently fortuitous number of protons and neutrons that for still uncertain reasons gives a nucleus special stability. An element whose atoms had 2, 8, 20, 50, 82, or 126 protons or neutrons had a magic nucleus. And if it had both a magic number of protons *and* neutrons, it was, of course, doubly magic. Thus an isotope of lead, say lead-208, is doubly magic: its atomic number is 82, that is, its nucleus has 82 protons, and its mass is 208, giving it 126 neutrons (208 minus 82). Isotopes of an element, it might be remembered, differ in the number of neutrons but are alike in the number of protons, which determines their atomic number.

A chain of dramatic calculations in the late sixties brought the realization that islands of stable elements might exist, with the nearest island centered about element 114. What essentially happened was that theorists surmounted some handicaps of their nuclear models, both shell and liquid drop. The weakness of the liquid-drop view in predicting stable regions of elements was overcome. At the same time, the shell model was refined so that it could be applied to calculations outside the region of magical numbers of protons and neutrons—that is, to distorted, non-spherical nuclei. This confirmed that a superheavy nucleus might be a stable one.

Essentially, the heavier the atoms, the less certain are the magical combinations of protons and neutrons that will give them stability. The extremely complex and difficult calculations discussed here reduced that uncertainty. Researchers realized that superheavy nuclei need not break up through spontaneous fission. With that barrier up, two other independent routes of nuclear breakdown were also sealed. These were alpha decay and beta decay. In alpha decay, as explained earlier, the nucleus of a helium atom—two protons and two neutrons—pops out of the nucleus. In beta decay, an improbable electron emerges, improbable because electrons have no business in the nucleus; they are formed when a neutron transmutes to a proton (beta decay).

All three ways of losing a superheavy element—spontaneous fission, alpha decay, and beta decay—operate independently of each other and had to be accounted for before stable, detectable superheavy elements became something more than coffee-time chatter.

But which are the superheavy elements? The uncertainties in the theoretical attack are testified to by the numbers game that's been played in identifying the probable islands of stability. Attention was initially focused on element 110 and 114, with 110 more likely on the basis of "survival of the fittest." Now the favored elements are those with a nucleus of 120 to 126 protons in combination with 184 neutrons to achieve stable superheavy status.

"I kind of like these ideas," says Ghiorso. "I think they're great." As one of the people leading the United States try for superheavy territory, Ghiorso would rather shoot at elements in the 124 range than 110. The reasons are arithmetic and realism. To reach element 110, which has a predicted mass of 298, Ghiorso must come up with a combination of elemental target and projectile that will give him a compound nucleus of 110 protons and as close to 184 neutrons as he can get. The island of stability has steep shores, and any element with a marked scarcity of neutrons will fall back into the sea; in an indicative experiment in 1971, Ghiorso found that the addition of 2 neutrons to the artificial isotope fermium-256 reduced its stability 25 million times!

But there is no plausible arrangement of target and bullet that will put him in 110 range. When Ghiorso bombarded a californium target with argon ions, he had the right number of protons but came up 14 short on neutrons. If a superheavy was formed, it fell apart in something like a billion-billionth of a second, beyond the reach of even Ghiorso's ingenuity. He can, however, measure the half-lives of atoms in nanoseconds, a billionth of a second. And, Ghiorso says, a technique now being developed may detect atoms with half-lives as short as a thousandth-billionth of a second.

The feeling on the "Hill"—LRL at Berkeley—is that the only way to gain the island of stability around 114 (if it's there) is to deliberately overshoot the target by creating a nucleus that is unstable and will either decay or fission down to the nearest island of stability. One way—actually called the "overshoot reaction"—is to bombard uranium with krypton, giving a product that will decay by alpha and beta emissions to a stable superheavy element. In nuclear shorthand, it's written:

$$^{238}_{92}U + {}^{86}_{36}Kr \longrightarrow \left[{}^{324}_{128}X \right] \xrightarrow[\text{decay}]{\text{alpha}} {}^{292}_{114}X \xrightarrow[\text{decay}]{\text{beta}} {}^{292}_{110}X$$

The ultimate reaction (until the day superheavy nuclei are accelerated against a target of superheavy elements) will be the bombardment of uranium with uranium, which, hopefully, will produce a compound nucleus that will fission down to a stable superheavy element.

Ghiorso, however, is content for now to plan the production of stable superheavy elements in the 120 to 126 regions with less dramatic nuclear reactions. "If I were going to try a reaction tomorrow," he muses, "I would bombard a target of curium-248 or californium-252, or possibly plutonium-244 with iron-56 or zinc-60."

To understand that, remember that Ghiorso's problem, if he is going for element 124, is to create a nucleus with 124 protons and 184 neutrons. Take one example: the reaction between californium-252 and iron-56. Californium and iron have 98 and 26 protons, respectively, in their nuclei. A forced Super HILAC reaction between them might work out this way:

$$^{252}_{98}\text{Cf} + {}^{56}_{26}\text{Fe} \rightarrow {}^{308}_{124}\text{X}$$

The product is an element with 124 protons and 184 (308, the combined masses, minus 124, the combined protons) neutrons. Calculating the possibilities for the other bullet-target combinations is equally straightforward. (Appropriate atomic numbers are 96, 94, and 30 for curium, plutonium, and zinc.)

"My guess is that we'll be the first to try any of these things with any hope of success," Ghiorso says, "and we'll quickly know whether the thing is easy or not. If we don't find anything in the 120 to 126 range, we'll have to fall back to uranium on uranium to try to get to 114."

A thin target will be used so that the element will be able to escape. Its flight will be guided by magnetic fields onto detectors that will measure its traveling time and, indirectly, its mass. A search for possible decay products will be made just in case the superheavy element is less stable than thought. But if the synthesis is difficult and a thick target has to be used, "then things get a little sophisticated."

Whether this attempt at Berkeley or the other nascent superheavy capitals will work is still moot. No one is quite sure what will happen when heavy ions meet at high energies.

Part of the problem is that a superheavy nucleus, although stable, is also very brittle. Swiatecki of LRL, who led the theoretical attack from the liquid-drop side, compares it to a piece of very fine crystal. "It is very stable and permanent if left to itself, but beware of distorting it much from its symmetric shape," he explained at a Heidelberg meeting. "If you do, it will shatter at once. This brittleness may be the biggest factor in cutting down cross sections [probabilities] for the formation of superheavy nuclei in heavy-ion reactions, because heavy-ion reactions are violent affairs." It'll be like cutting diamonds in a car factory. It seems possible, but the distractions are considerable. We should know in a year.

Even the formation of a compound nucleus, the intermediate on the road to superheavy territory, is an uncertain art. "The compound nucleus is heavily excited," Stanley Thompson points out. "Imagine two balls flying at each other, spinning, and sticking. Their spinning [or angular momentum] may be enough to pull them apart again."

What will these superheavy elements be like if and when they become reality? That depends largely on whether 110, 114, or 124 electrons are spinning about a superheavy nucleus. Although electrons because they orbit only the nucleus are largely irrelevant to element makers constructing a nucleus, their arrangement in shells and subshells spells out the chemistry of the new element. Several people—notably at the Los Alamos Scientific Laboratory—have made careful computer-assisted calculations of the probable electronic structures of the superheavy elements. Glenn Seaborg, as he did for the earlier synthetic elements, has used this and other information to place the elements-to-be in particular slots in the periodic table.

The highest element is calculated at 164, which should bear some resemblance to element 114 (eka lead), which, as the name implies, is placed in the lead family. Seaborg calls 164 eka-eka lead. Whether this element or any of the other superheavies will actually resemble the known elements they're grouped with is debatable.

"The predictions of properties are certainly estimates only," Seaborg told an audience of chemists, "and may well depart substantially from experimental values if they are ever measured."

However, Dr. O. Lewin Keller, Jr., and his colleagues at the Oak Ridge National Laboratory have gone out on a limb to the extent of listing properties for some superheavy elements, such as 114. Based on extrapolation from data on existing elements, it will be a solid melting at about 160°F. and boiling at about 300°, extraordinarily dense, and reacting like a metal, generally giving up two electrons in combining with other elements.

To what purposes might superheavies be applied? That's an unanswerable question, just as it was when Seaborg, Thompson, Ghiorso, Flerov, and others were fashioning the transuranium elements, the synthetic elements 93 to 105. But one man-made element, curium, was used for the first chemical analysis of the moon's surface. Another, californium, such an intense emitter of neutrons that a speck amounts to a "hip-pocket reactor," may be the base of a new technology, especially now that its price is dropping precipitously. A third synthetic element, americium, is being used in a variety of industrial sensing devices such as fuel gauges.

But such "cost-benefit" considerations are not really on the minds of the men at Orsay, Darmstadt, Heidelberg, Dubna, and Berkeley. They know that if superheavy elements are found or created as predicted, it will be a very dramatic sign that centuries of speculation on the nature of matter are getting somewhere.

Dr. Stanley Thompson, nuclear chemist at the Lawrence Radiation Laboratory, showing model representing calculations that suggest the existence of a superheavy element, eka-platinum 294, which he has looked for in nature. *Courtesy: Lawrence Radiation Laboratory, University of California*

5

NEUTRINOS: HOW
THE SUN SHINES

Ramon Guthrie was emphatic about it: ". . . if you ever find
yourself holding sweet converse with a neutrino, better watch
it!" The poetic warning streaked through my mind as an elevator
took me into the depths of a gold mine in Lead, South Dakota.

I had arrived in Lead* late at night, driving forty-five miles
from the nearest airport at Rapid City over an empty superhigh-
way onto a twisting road that took me through Deadwood
(where Calamity Jane and Wild Bill Hickok are buried), and
finally into Lead. It was a pretty moon-filled night, and I could

* Lead is pronounced "leed." A Homestake brochure says the name
means a ledge or outcropping of ore.

see outlines of the Black Hills that bring summer tourists to this western edge of the Dakotas. It would have been more appropriate, I thought, to have come on a bright day when I could see the reason for my journey to Lead: our nearest star, Phoebus Apollo, Sol Invictus, the giver of life, Father Sun.

The next morning, the sun was again hidden, this time by snow-packed clouds. I drove up to the Homestake gold mine, started in 1876, two years after a military expedition led by General George A. Custer explored the area. Today, about 5,600 tons of low-grade ore—each ton containing about a third of an ounce of gold—is milled every day. Homestake and the Carlin Mine in north-central Nevada are now the only major sources of native United States gold.

I parked my car by the administration building near the mine entrance and went inside to meet my guide, Harold Munger, a division foreman, who, I later learned, started with Homestake as a miner some thirty years ago. After outfitting me with boots, helmet, and a miner's lamp, Munger took me for my jolting ride in the elevator, or man hoist, to the 4,850-foot level of the mine. The current working depth is 6,800 feet, and some South African mines go to 13,000 feet.

I followed Munger through the mine tunnel, which was brighter than I expected. Passing a bend, we came to a steel door that Munger unlocked and swung open. Inside was a very large chamber—30 by 60 by 32 feet, according to Homestake—that contained what I had come to see: a spectacularly large tank, painted white, big enough to hold 100,000 gallons, or 610 tons, of liquid—what it takes ten railroad cars to carry.

We looked down on the tank, having come in through the higher of two entrances, and could see the maze of piping and wiring leading from it. Nearby was a glass-enclosed control room that bristled with dials, gauges, and knobs to turn. Fixed to the roof of the chamber by eight-foot bolts, Munger told me, was wire screening to keep debris from falling on the tank.

The tank and its accessory parts seemed almost ludicrously out of place in the space economy of a gold mine. Yet, this tank, almost a mile below the Black Hills of South Dakota, was a probe into the very heart of the sun, some 93 million miles away.

Tank containing 100,000 gallons of dry-cleaning fluid for the detection of neutrinos from the sun. *Courtesy: Raymond Davis, Jr., Brookhaven National Laboratory*

For the first time, it enabled men to "see" into the center of the sun and study the sources of the heat and light that bathe our earth and sustain its life.

The Homestake tank, an observatory for the interior of the sun, represents a practical product of decades of work on the question: How does the sun shine? In operation since 1967, this solar observatory has produced enough data about the center of the sun that physicists have begun to "fine tune" their ideas of how the sun creates energy. The tank is a detector of neutrinos, the products of reactions occurring at the heart of the sun that supply the sun's energy and sustain its structure. The neutrino is a creation of physicists which many still regard as more art than nature. It is a particle—for want of a better word—that is ejected from the sun's center, travels some 400,000 miles to the sun's surface, streams through the solar system and the galaxy beyond, passing through the earth without even the wink of a ghostly eyelash. It is a particle with virtually no mass and no charge, and has been aptly described as simply a packet of pure energy. Named by an Italian and meaning "little neutral one," the neutrino was created by physicists in the 1930s to explain otherwise unexplainable losses of energy in the decay of certain radioactive materials. Neutrinos, they decided, were the thieves. Neutrinos existed only in equations until 1956, when they were caught by experimenters working with a large nuclear reactor at Hanford, Washington.

The neutrinos become something of an article of faith for the layman. Either he believes in them or he doesn't. Physicists consider them an established member of the fraternity, while most of us boggle at believing in particles that travel at the speed of light and, because of no mass or charge, are almost oblivious to matter. Ramon Guthrie said it for the common man in his poem, "THE NEUTRINO AND MR. BRINSLEY."

> *no, x does not mark the spot, because*
> *it isn't there anymore and wasn't*
> *there in the first place—*
> *not in any accepted sense of the word there . . .*
> *since, by any weekday sort of reasoning,*
> *that which is is, and that which isn't,*
> *concomitantly, is not. And that which, being,*
> *in the phenomenal sense, discrete*
> *yet has not mass, is (in this same*
> *phenomenal sense) not.*
> > *Which,*
> *since they are traveling nonstop at some*
> *186,000 miles a second and can penetrate*
> *a wall of anything up to ten billion*
> > *earth-diameters thick,*
> *is just as well.*

If ideas about how the sun burns its energy (we'll get to specifics in a moment) are right, then billions upon billions of neutrinos are passing through this page and through you every second, most of them having come from the center of the sun. A good estimate is that 3 percent of the sun's energy is packaged as neutrinos. If neutrinos could be detected and their energy and amounts measured, then theoretical physicists would have some direct experimental data to hone their ideas on what is going on inside the sun.

But, like the proverbial recipe for rabbit stew that first advises the cook to catch a rabbit, solar neutrinos first had to be caught. The fact that they were the *only* particles that could leave the center of the sun, travel through space, and flit right through the earth meant that neutrinos would be extremely difficult to catch.

That the attempt has now been made—as represented by the giant tank in the Homestake gold mine—is due in no small measure to the faith of the man who declared that "it should not be too difficult to understand such a simple thing as a star." This was Sir Arthur Stanley Eddington—bachelor, Quaker, conscientious objector, Plumian Professor of Astronomy at Cambridge University, and the leader of the assault in the 20s and 30s on the sun's mysteries. Sitting in his easy chair in the home that went along with the observatory he directed, Eddington thought about what went on inside the sun. He was a great and perceptive scientist, among the first to understand the implications of the new theories being proposed by Albert Einstein, and also somewhat of a mystic, not afraid to venture beyond the plausible.

"Because we are unable to render exact account of our environment," he once said, "it does not follow that it would be better to pretend that we live in a vacuum." It was Eddington's unique tolerance for the mystical that enabled him to successfully apply his scientific knowledge to the problems of astronomy. "Science saved his mysticism from running to extravagance; mysticism saved his science from claiming the last word," an admirer said.

About the middle of the nineteenth century, several people realized that the composition of the sun's surface could be discerned by comparing colors in the spectrum of sunlight (from a prism) with the color produced in a flame by any of several elements. This came only about fifty years after the French philosopher Auguste Comte cited, with Gallic logic, the chemical composition of the stars as an example of knowledge that could never be gained.

It quickly became apparent that the sun was almost exclusively hydrogen and helium, with almost all the other chemical elements now known making up less than 1 percent of the sun's mass. But the mystery of how the sun burned remained a mystery. A succession of measurements, from analysis of sedimentary layers laid down by geological ages to measuring the age of meteorites, has upped the sun's age now to about 4.5 to 5 billion years.

But even in the 20s, when he started thinking about the sun, Eddington knew it had to be very old, that it was mostly hydrogen and helium, and how much light and heat it produced. He knew that this energy, aside from peripherally making our planet habitable, also helped prop up the sun.

"The outward flowing radiation may . . . be compared to a wind blowing through the star and helping to distend it against gravity," Eddington explained. Some sort of interior furnace was countering the pressure of the overlying weight of the sun. Also, since the sun is neither cooling or heating up noticeably, the furnace was supplying just enough energy to make up its losses by radiation. Knowing these things, Eddington, with the assurance of a mystic, made his declaration: "No source of energy is of any avail unless it liberates energy deep in the interior of the star."

It meant that some 400,000 miles into the center of the sun was its secret: a central furnace that sent out the heat needed to prop it up and warm its satellite planets. What fueled the furnace? Hydrogen atoms fusing together to create helium and a bit of energy, said Eddington. The equation which every school child now quotes but which was new to Eddington and his colleagues, $E=mc^2$, said that matter and energy are convertible. When hydrogen atoms merge to form a helium atom, there is about a 1 percent loss of matter that, according to Einstein, becomes energy. Hydrogen is the fuel, helium the ash, and the difference is the sun.

Properly, hydrogen nuclei fuse to form a helium *nucleus,* since the intense heat inside the sun strips away all or almost all of the electrons that are an ingredient of atoms. A hydrogen atom is a positive proton with a much lighter, negative electron spinning about it. A helium atom is two neutrons (neutral protons) and two protons, with the latter's positive charge counterbalanced by two electrons.

Eddington's proposal that the sun was merely a particularly flamboyant way of making helium left several details unsettled, partly because the niceties of atomic structure—mathematical and physical—needed to fill out his idea were still unsettled.

"We have taken the present-day theories of physics and pressed them to their remotest conclusions," he acknowledged.

Perhaps the most mystical part of Eddington's sun was the exact route from hydrogen to helium. Eddington and others realized that direct conversion was out since that would use up even the sun's massive supply of hydrogen (now known to be going at five hundred tons a *second*) at too fast a rate, cutting its lifetime drastically. A slow way to make helium was needed.

The problem was taken up and solved by one of the many "gifts" of Nazi Germany to American science: Hans Bethe. He left Germany in 1933, the year Hitler came to power, and taught in England for two years before coming to Cornell University, where he is now professor of physics. Bethe has become a public figure in recent years in part for the technical arguments he has mounted against the antiballistic missile (ABM) system. In 1967, he received the Nobel Prize in physics, in part for proposing two ways that the sun makes helium from hydrogen.

The first (also discovered independently by the German astronomer Carl von Weizsäcker) is the proton-proton cycle. As the name implies, the cycle begins with protons, the equivalent of hydrogen nuclei—hydrogen atoms without their accompanying electrons. Two protons merge to form a heavier variety, an isotope, of hydrogen called deuterium. It is, in its chemical behavior, almost identical to hydrogen but just a bit heavier (heavy water is made with deuterium, instead of hydrogen).

Laboratory measurements show that it takes about fourteen

million years on the average for any two protons to merge into a deuterium nuclei. But that patience is rewarded by a lifetime of only about six seconds before deuterium merges with still another proton to form a light isotope of helium called helium-3. Two of these light helium isotopes then merge to form one nuclei of common helium, or helium-4. Other products of the reaction are two protons from the helium isotopes that can re-join the cycle and a modicum of energy.

Other reactions in this proton-proton cycle, in addition to the main one just outlined, momentarily form beryllium, lithium, and boron. But all these creations, like the roads to Rome, eventually lead back to helium. These processes, the main one and the side ones, produce energy to keep the sun going, do it slowly enough to justify the sun's calculated age, give it an internal temperature of about 20 billion degrees Fahrenheit, and satisfy Eddington's germinal idea that the sun shines by "burning" hydrogen to make helium.

Our sun—"a middle-aged citizen in the community of stars" —apparently runs mainly on the proton-proton cycle. But older stars depend largely on the second scheme proposed by Bethe, the carbon cycle. Three protons or hydrogen nuclei add to a carbon nuclei to form nitrogen. When this nitrogen nucleus merges with a fourth proton, helium is produced, and carbon reappears. Overall, hydrogen is consumed and helium and energy created, while carbon rises like the phoenix from the ashes to catalyze another cycle. Some three hundred years are needed to complete a cycle, making it a very slow rise from the ashes indeed. Helium remains in the sun, while the energy created warms our solar system.

All this is imaginative but circumstantial. While Bethe and others transported their knowledge of nuclear physics to the inside of a star and while the rates and probabilities for many of the reactions described in the Bethe cycles were measured in laboratories, there was still no direct proof. "Our telescopes may probe farther and farther in the depths of space," Eddington said, "but how can we ever obtain certain knowledge of that which is hidden behind substantial barriers?"

The huge, white, almost incongruous tank in the Homestake

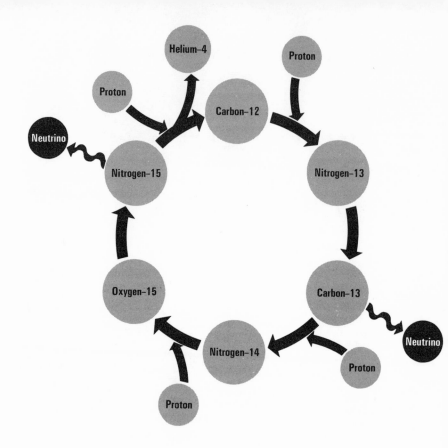

Carbon–nitrogen–oxygen (CNO) cycle which creates a helium nucleus from four protons, or hydrogen nuclei. The catalyst, carbon-12, is regenerated, and energy and neutrinos are released.

mine is one answer to Eddington's plaint. It is designed to catch neutrinos and learn what "is hidden behind substantial barriers." In the forties, two physicists—Dr. Luis Alvarez of the University of California at Berkeley and Dr. Bruno Pontecorvo, then in Canada and now in the Soviet Union—pointed out that when an isotope of chlorine called chlorine-37 is hit by a neutrino, it is transmuted to argon-37, a rare radioactive gas that decays back to its parent chlorine. (Isotopes of an element, it should be remembered, are varieties of an element differing in weight but not significantly in chemical properties.)

Professor John N. Bahcall of the California Institute of Technology calculated in the sixties that reactions in the proton-proton cycle could produce neutrinos energetic enough to transmute chlorine to argon. One is the "pep" reaction, in which a proton, electron, and another proton combine to form a deuterium atom plus a neutrino. The second is a very minor reaction—representing about a tenth of 1 percent of the reaction routes in the proton-proton cycle—in which a boron atom transmutes to beryllium and spits out the most energetic neutrino of all. Beryllium then splits in two to form two helium atoms—the sun's ashes.

None of these profundities was really running through my mind as I scrambled around the big tank in the Homestake mine snapping pictures and trying to keep my helmet on. Baffled by the maze of circuitry and plumbing that went with the tank, I regretted that the man who built this apparatus—a solar neutrino "observatory"—wasn't there. This is Dr. Raymond Davis, Jr., of the Brookhaven National Laboratory, a huge installation of the United States Atomic Energy Commission located near the eastern end of New York's Long Island. Davis, a physical chemist, has spent most of his professional life at Brookhaven studying nuclear reactions, cosmic chemistry, and, more lately, neutrino chemistry. When Bahcall at Cal Tech calculated that it was possible—"disappointingly low, but possible"—to detect solar neutrinos using the chlorine-to-argon-capture scheme, Davis, with his colleagues Kenneth C. Hoffmann of Brookhaven and Don S. Harmer of the Georgia Institute of Technology, proposed in 1964 that an actual attempt be made.

The AEC provided funds, and the effort to back up Eddington and his successors with data from inside the sun began. For his source of chlorine-37, Davis turned to ordinary dry-cleaning fluid. It's cheap, easy to get, and rich in chlorine, as implied by its chemical name, tetrachloroethylene, and chemical formula, C_2Cl_4, or two parts carbon and four parts chlorine. Davis initially tried his scheme for catching neutrinos with two five-hundred-gallon tanks placed in a limestone mine in Barberton, Ohio.

While the Barberton test confirmed that the experiment was

feasible, it also made clear that a deeper mine and one hundred times as much dry-cleaning fluid would be needed. (The deeper mine is needed to ward off cosmic rays that could also create argon-37 in the tank).

Davis, with the help of the United States Bureau of Mines, found several mine sites that fit his requirements. After some initial negotiations with the happily named Sunshine Silver Mine in Idaho, Davis finally went to the Homestake Mining Company. Their mine in Lead was deep enough, the rock harder and more stable than the granite carved into presidential images at nearby Mount Rushmore, and the costs reasonable—about $360,000 for chamber, tank, and liquid.

A contract was signed in December 1964, and the tank was in place the following summer. Some 7,000 tons of rock were carved out to make the main chamber for the tank. "Not particularly difficult to do: the kind of thing we do everyday," according to my guide, Harold Munger. Two entrances, upper and lower, were built and vapor-proof doors were put in so that the whole chamber could be flooded if additional protection from extraneous radiation was necessary—even more than 4,850 feet of Dakotan earth and rock.

The tank was built and installed by the Chicago Bridge and Iron Company, a firm that specializes in unusual construction, including space chambers for the National Aeronautics and Space Administration. The tank was put together in pieces, some weighing several tons but small enough to fit into the man hoist for the ride down to the 4,850-foot level. The sections were welded together almost like a patchwork quilt, and an X-ray machine used to check the welds. Also, after the work was finished, the gas-tight chamber was flooded with helium to make a test for leaks. Much of the circuitry was installed by Brookhaven personnel with Davis doing some of the intricate work himself, winning the admiration of the practical-minded miners.

In June 1966 the tank was filled with 100,000 gallons of tetrachloroethylene shipped to the mine in 10,000-gallon-railroad-tank cars. After the tank cars were carefully checked for contaminating radioactivity, the liquid was transferred to much smaller tank cars that could fit into the man hoist. It took 144 trips down the shaft to fill the neutrino tank.

"With a little practice, we found that we could empty in one day one large tank car," Davis remembers. "Starting about six o'clock in the morning, we could empty a tank and have it ready to roll again by ten o'clock in the evening."

After the full tank was flushed for several weeks with helium, which carried out any trapped gases, including argon, the Homestake neutrino observatory was open for business. An estimated 4,000 billion billion neutrinos were expected to pass daily through the tank. If the ideas on the sources of sunshine were right, then, according to prediction, on the average of five times a day neutrinos made in the two steps of the proton-proton cycle deep inside the sun should strike at least one of trillions of chlorine-37 atoms in the tank and transform it to argon-37. Over a three- to four-month run, several hundred argon atoms should appear in the tank.

Successive experiments were run in 1968, 1969, and 1970. Each time, the tank, cleansed of air argon by helium gas, was "exposed" to the neutrino shower. After about four months during the first experiment, helium was again bubbled through the tank, hopefully carrying out with it atoms of neutrino-created argon-37. The helium passed through a charcoal trap cooled by liquid nitrogen to −320°F. The charcoal traps argon atoms much as the charcoal filters of cigarettes trap smoke particles. Procedures for subsequent experiments were much the same.

To a chemist, this experiment is audacious, although Davis tells people it's "only plumbing." He hopes to isolate and identify a few hundred atoms in 100,000 gallons of liquid composed of some 10^{31} (10 followed by thirty zeros) atoms. Davis proved that he could get the argon out by deliberately adding some "dead" or nonradioactive argon to the big tank and then successfully recovering 95 percent. Not until he did this experiment could he be sure that the Homestake setup would work.

"In outline, it is simple," he says, "mainly because the chemistry of argon is simple. It doesn't form any compounds and is just there as a gas. You can remove it by bubbling helium

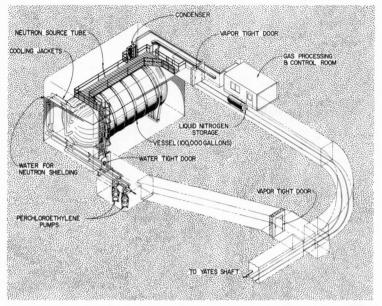

Arrangement of neutrino tank and accessory equipment at the 4,850-foot level of the Homestake gold mine in Lead, South Dakota. *Courtesy: Raymond Davis, Jr., Brookhaven National Laboratory*

through, and it's just physical adsorption on the charcoal that enables you to isolate it from the helium."

The argon was removed from the trap by simply warming it. After purification, this hard-won (and historic) sample was flown to Brookhaven—this was 1968—where specially made radiation detectors, or counters, were waiting to catch the signal of neutrino-created argon atoms reverting back to their parent, chlorine. The signal in this case would be the appearance of an electron of known energy.

Incidentally, a piece of exotica in the counting apparatus at Brookhaven is a twelve-inch naval gun barrel which helps shield it from extraneous, or background, radiation. The signal of the electron is so weak that the slightest contamination by radiation would smear it. Davis's problem was something like trying to find a snowman in a snowstorm.

But, after all this effort and years of planning, nary a neutrino

was to be found. Davis did not see the average number of neutrino "hits" predicted by the theorists.

Actually, neutrino hits are measured in solar neutrino units
(SNU), with a "snew" being the chances of one chlorine atom
capturing a neutrino. This in a number is 10^{-36}, or 10 with thirty-
six zeros *before* it. Turning that inconceivable number around,
it means, as Bahcall wrote in *Scientific American,* "that an atom
of chlorine-37 would have to wait 10^{36} seconds, or roughly 10
billion billion times the age of the observable universe, before
capturing a neutrino." But since the Homestake tank of dry-
cleaning fluid contains some 10^{31} chlorine atoms, the chances
of a hit are considerably greater—by as much as 10^{31}. When the
capture rate is one SNU, Bahcall writes, "the average waiting
time . . . is about six days per capture."

But, however measured, Davis did not see enough neutrinos.
There was at least a twofold gap between what he saw and
what Bahcall and others had calculated should be the number
of neutrinos produced by the sun. Davis's report that the sun
was apparently not cooperating had several immediate effects.
Other solar-neutrino searchers operating in mines in South
Africa and the United States, realizing that their experimental
approaches to measuring neutrinos simply could not match
Davis's, gave up the hunt. More to the point, theorists became
"rather excited." There was apparently little quarreling with
Davis's experiment, already probed at by some of the best
physicists in the world. "Ray is universally regarded as a very
careful experimenter," says Dr. Icko Iben of MIT, one of the
theorists involved in the solar-neutrino search. A rechecking was
begun of the assumptions and numbers used in constructing
"standard solar models." The nuclear cross sections—probabilities of interactions among nuclei and particles—were remeasured
in the laboratory. New data on the sun's composition were
calculated. For instance, the sun was found to contain more iron
in its interior than had been assumed in the calculations made
earlier of expected neutrino flux. More iron increases the density
of the sun, making it more opaque. But to provide the heat and
light that we *know* the sun is producing, because we can measure that on earth, the increased opacity must be compensated

for by a higher temperature, which increases the rate of solar reactions, raising that neutrino count. So, more iron means more neutrinos coming from the sun and an even greater gap between what Davis was reporting and what the theorists hoped he would find.

Very intensive efforts have been made by Bahcall, Iben, and others to reduce that gap. "An attempt has been made," Iben points out, "to reduce as far as possible all uncertainties in the input parameters that are necessary to make a solar model. The result is that if you change them as far as you can, within experimentally determined limits, you end up with something that is still five times as big as what Davis finds."

Some elegant ways out have been proposed. For instance, there is actually a dichotomy in the neutrino—an electron neutrino and a muon neutrino. Bruno Pontecorvo in Russia argues that, while electron neutrinos leave the sun, by the time they reach the Earth some 93 million miles away, about half have become muon neutrinos. A muon is somewhat like an electron but heavier. The point is that muon neutrinos do not react with chlorine and are essentially invisible to Davis's detector in South Dakota. "Thus," Iben says, "you'd have a neutrino flux of the type that would turn chlorine into argon at only half of the rate had there been no mixing." But even with this dichotomy, the needed neutrino count is still too big.

Iben also points out that if there was a way to get rid of the solar reaction in which the most energetic neutrinos are produced—the transformation of boron-8 to beryllium-8—"the number you get is remarkably close to Davis's number." The problem is how to get rid of boron-8, whose parent in the sun is another isotope of beryllium, beryllium-7. "The only possibility," Iben says, "is to cook up some reaction that will get rid of beryllium-7 in a much more rapid rate." While a good deal of chalk and blackboard work is going on, the boron-8 hypothesis and other ideas why the sun is too free with its neutrinos are still more hopeful than real.

The basic problem is that the numbers on the composition of the sun's interior are still partly guesswork, based largely on what we see on the sun's surface. However, various mixings of interior with exterior data could alter those numbers and produce both satisfied physicists and a happy Davis. Few are yet ready to give up on the sun. "There's just too darn much observational evidence that couldn't be fitted any other way," Iben says. John Bahcall of Cal Tech, who made the calculations that justified Davis's experiment, says that "if his [Davis's] sensitivity is increased by a factor of two and he doesn't find anything, then I think the theory of stellar evolution is in very serious trouble. If he increases it by a factor of six and doesn't find anything, then the whole theory of nuclear fusion in stars is in trouble. I personally don't think we're going to have that trouble. I believe in that theory."

While physicists have been scratching their heads, Davis has been refining his instruments to lessen that margin of error inherent in every experiment where a phenomenon of nature must be translated into numbers. For instance, he's tried moving his counters out to Homestake in the hope of improving their sensitivity. Also, he is working hard to get a better "fingerprint" of the electron emitted by argon-37 when it reverts back to chlorine-37—the event that signals that a solar neutrino has been detected. Even though the counter is small and very well shielded, the intrusions of other electrons cannot be discounted. However, the electron produced by argon-37 decay has a specific energy and produces a specific pulse on the charts. Its pulse has "a fast rise time," Davis says.

"With this improved counting arrangement we can reduce the background of our counters because we now require an argon-37 event to have the right energy and the right rise time."

Davis now thinks he has seen some solar neutrinos, at least pulses that had the right fingerprint. However, the counts are still seven to ten times lower than what theorists calculate he should find. Davis's confidence in his experiment is firm. "The chemical arguments say that if a solar neutrino does make an argon-37 atom that I would indeed get it out, and that it would finally end up in my counter. I know my counting efficiency, and if it's there, I ought to see it."

But while theorists wait for further word from South Dakota and while Davis cranks up his big tank, both groups are already thinking of other ways to catch solar neutrinos, particularly less energetic ones made in different parts of the proton-proton cycle.

"I tell people we're doing the easy one now," Davis says. He's right. For instance, Davis is now doing start-up work on the use of lithium salts to look for certain neutrinos. If a lithium ion meets a neutrino, it becomes beryllium, whose presence can then be looked for. However, separation of beryllium, measurement of its radioactivity, and the need to handle enormous amounts of lithium are requirements that blanch bench chemists.

In the meantime, the white, improbable tank sits several thousand feet down in the gold mine, slowly gathering the evidence that may or may not vindicate man's solution to the sources of the sun's fire.

Perhaps a final word about Davis is in order. He is a patient man, unassuming, ready to be helpful. There is none of the intense, frenetic air about him common to many of his peers. Davis has devoted some fifteen years of his professional career to the solar neutrinos, and that—in what is still a publish-or-perish profession—took quite a bit of courage.

"But," as he says, "there's a carrot out there at the end of the string that just might be within reach.'

6

UNRAVELING THE MYSTERY OF ANCIENT GLASS

While researchers throughout the world seek to create new elements and others explore the sun, still others are applying science to understanding some very tangible matter. By wedding modern analytical science to the perspective of the archaeologist, scientists are piecing together a history of the technologies that thrived thousands of years before the "chymistry" of Robert Boyle.

"The more you examine the works and technology of the ancient artisans and craftsmen—glassmakers, potters, metallurgists—the more you realize that they not only had great skill with their hands, but they also had an appreciation for the technological aspects of their work," says Dr. Robert H. Brill of the Corning Museum of Glass in upstate New York. A physical chemist, Brill has spent over a decade unraveling the methods of ancient artisans, particularly in the way they fashioned glass. His work and that of others—notably Dr. Edward V. Sayre of the Brookhaven National Laboratory—have uncovered a stunning sophistication in ancient glasswork, whether from Mesopotamia, the ancient kingdoms of Egypt, or the budding cultures bordering the eastern Mediterranean. Glassworkers, with trial and error and a few words to their gods, learned how to make glass, to control its texture with various ingredients, and to create colors, often by careful control of fires, and to fashion the material into salable shapes.

They did all that without a clear idea of what glass is, which remains a puzzle today. There seems to be no simple definition of glass. One textbook devotes seven pages groping for a definition; Brill wrote an eleven-page article defining it and its chemistry for archaeologists. Most simply put, glass is a material intermediate between a liquid and a crystal, its atoms not mobile as in a liquid but not fixed in orderly arrangements as in a crystal. With apologies to Gertrude Stein, glass is glass is glass.

It's simpler to talk about what goes into glass than what it is. Most glasses, ancient or modern, have three basic ingredients: silica from quartz sand, an alkali such as soda to act as a flux, and lime as a stabilizer. Silica is the basic stuff of glass; lime protects the glass from water, chemicals, or any foreign matter; and the flux lowers the melting temperatures of the quartz to workable levels and also helps "wet" the lime and silica.

Egyptian, Roman, and Mesopotamian glassmakers all used this basic tripartite recipe. Occasionally, instead of soda, particularly in the Islamic period, lead oxide (PbO) was used as a flux. About medieval times, after the tenth century, potash, or potassium oxide (K_2O), was substituted for the soda alkali (Na_2O). Aside from being a convenient boundary for glass historians, this switchover to a different alkali has trapped forgers trying to pass off potash glass as premedieval creations.

Where did glass come from? Many experts suspect that its

immediate ancestor was faïence, a glazed material used by the Egyptians as early as 3000 B.C. Faïence is made by mixing crushed quartz pebbles with a small amount of alkali. When the alkali is melted, it forms a matrix which cements the quartz grains together. Once the Egyptians had faïence, says Brill, glass wasn't very far behind.

"If someone added a little too much alkali or if they used too high a temperature or if, perhaps, they ground up some of the wastes from earlier experiments and threw them back into the mixture, the chemical reaction could have been pushed far enough so that they might have dissolved all of the quartz grains and formed a glassy network. The discovery of glass probably came about through an accidental firing or, perhaps, an intentional tinkering with faïence ingredients."

When and where glass was first made—accidentally or not— is difficult to pin down, although glass beads were probably first made somewhere between 2000 and 1500 B.C., possibly in Egypt. Glass vessels have been traced to Egypt's Eighteenth Dynasty, early in the fourteenth century B.C. These are cored vessels, made by lining the outside of a clay form of a desired shape with strips of hot glass, then scraping the clay form out through an opening after the glass cooled. Glassblowing was invented shortly after 100 B.C., probably in Syria, although, typically, the Romans were the first to apply the technique to mass manufacture. The Romans put a tax on glass, and there was even a special quarter near the Tiber for the glassworkers.

Much of this is archaeology, information gleaned from patient and ingenious picking through rubble and historical writings. What scientists have done is to analyze hundreds of ancient glass pieces, often without damaging them. That work is described below. With that information a map has been assembled —a technological map, if you will—which researchers confronted with an unknown piece of glass can use to find their way.

Dr. Edward Sayre of the Brookhaven National Laboratory has done a good deal of this foundation work. Others include Brill; two Englishmen, W. E. S. Turner and H. P. Rooksby; M. A. Besborodov of the Soviet Union; and W. Geilmann of Germany.

Sayre has analyzed well over four hundred pieces of glass,

Dr. Robert H. Brill excavating in 1965 beneath a nine-ton slab of glass found at Beth Shean in Galilee. The slab was created about 1,500 years ago. *Courtesy: Robert H. Brill, Corning Museum of Glass*

many of them collected and their authenticity established for him by Ray W. Smith, a millionaire who, among other things, is fascinated by ancient glass. A pattern, albeit with exceptions, has emerged: The earliest glasses, those dating back to the second millennium from Egypt and Mesopotamia, all have fairly high concentrations of magnesium—about 4 to 5 percent. Not until about the seventh century B.C. does glass with a low magnesium content, around 1 percent, begin to show up.

This change from a high to a low magnesium content reflects a new source or sources of alkali. Glass artisans in ancient times derived magnesium from ashes of plants rich also in alkali;

the magnesium-laden chinan plant that still grows in the marshes and deserts of Mesopotamia probably was the alkali source for the glass factories. For some reason—a war, cheaper prices, or aggressive trading—artisans turned to other alkali sources, including the Wadi el Natrun, a valley of eleven lakes that still exist in the desert between Cairo and Alexandria. The lakes are fed by the Nile through an underground route and they flood the valley as the Nile rises in late summer. When the waters recede and evaporate, clumps of crystalline sodium carbonate, or natron, are deposited. Natron, which takes up water, was used by the Egyptians to dry out bodies for mummification as well as an alkali for glassmaking. Natron, *low* in magnesium, can be traced from samples—in its use as a staple of the glass industry—to no earlier than about the seventh century B.C. However, high magnesium glasses reappeared, in Europe, about the tenth century A.D. when glassworkers came full circle back to wood ashes—probably beechwood—rich in magnesium.

The silica portion of the glass recipe came from different sources, judging from historical writings. Like the Egyptians of 3000 B.C. the land-locked Mesopotamians used crushed pebbles, which are still used today by faïence makers in Iran. The Romans at times used fine beach sand from the mouth of the Belus River, in what is now Israel. This beach sand as well as desert sand contained enough lime to complete the basic recipe for making glass.

Sayre, largely with neutron activation analysis (NAA), has extended his study of ancient glass to cover extremely small amounts of various trace elements such as lead that provide a "fingerprint" of a particular sample. In NAA, neutron "bullets" from a nuclear reactor, by striking stable elements, transform these elements into unstable isotopes, which in turn emit various decay products that can be measured. Because these decay products and their rate of production is known, the amount and identity of particular elements in the glass sample are determined. Increased sensitivity of the detectors of these decay products—particularly for gamma rays—has made NAA a popular tool for analyzing small quantities of elements.

Neutron activation analysis of ancient glass objects has uncovered a great deal of information, some of it quite puzzling. For instance, glass pieces supposedly made from natron contain relatively high amounts of the rare element europium. But neither ancient (from mummies) nor modern natron (from the Wadi el Natrun) have much europium. The conclusion: either the alkali source was not natron or the natron was mixed, accidentally or not, with other materials that contained europium.

Significant clues to the many puzzles of ancient glasses have come from a study of their colors. Anyone who has wandered through a reasonably good collection of ancient glass is struck by the richness and diversity of the colors. There are opaque yellows, whites, and reds, and beautifully rich and transparent blues and greens, and amethysts and ambers.

Glass from the second millennium, whether it comes from the Bull Kingdom of Minos, the Mesopotamian Ziggurat at Tschoga Zambil, or from the palace of Amenhotep II at Thebes, is colored in remarkably similar fashion. Counterpoising these similarities, noted Edward Sayre, are such things as Chinese glasses—given their distinctive colors in totally different fashion.

Whatever the culture or civilization, various pigments were used throughout. Copper- and cobalt-containing materials were used to create blue glasses; calcium antimonate ($Ca_2Sb_2O_7$), and tin oxide (SnO_2) were used successively for white opaques; Naples yellow, or lead antimonate ($Pb_2Sb_2O_7$), and, later, lead tinate ($PbSnO_3$) gave yellow opaque glasses. However, each colorant had its own suite of impurities—"accompanying elements" is the proper label—which also provide a fingerprint for sorting out the various glasses.

For example, the cobalt-blue glasses found in Egypt and Mycenae in southern Greece contain similar trace amounts of nickel, zinc, and manganese, whereas Mesopotamian blues, with the same impurities, contain different quantities. Sayre's conclusion is that the cobalt ore for the Mycenaean and Egyptian glasses came from the same source, while the Mesopotamian was unique. A similar pattern was found with copper blues.

Sayre found that different glass objects contained the same levels of trace elements. This indicated, he thinks, that the glass for these objects came from the same glass ingots, or blocks. Apparently, unfashioned glass was sold and traded like any other commodity.

The chemistry of metals such as copper, cobalt, tin, antimony, nickel, indeed any element, is generally governed by the number of electrons in those orbits farthest from the nucleus of the element's atoms—what chemists call the valence electrons, electrons of an atom that can be transferred to or shared with another atom. Elements vary in their number of valence electrons, depending on the chemical environment the elements operate in. In a chemical reaction involving an exchange of electrons, the atom or molecule that gives up electrons is said to be oxidized, while the reactant gaining them is said to be reduced. In an oxidizing situation, electrons are taken away, and an element, such as copper, will have fewer valence electrons than in reducing conditions, where it often gains electrons. The important point is that for these different valence states—where the number of outermost electrons differ—the chemical properties of the elements will also differ. It was this chemical fact that glass artisans were inadvertently applying when they produced different colors with the same colorants. Copper in its oxidized, or cupric, form will give a glass a beautiful blue color; in its reduced, or cuprous, form, the glass will be red. In the cupric form two electrons are lost; in the cuprous, one electron is lost. Red or blue in part depended on the fire. An oxidizing fire—where the flame is clear and smokeless and oxygen is not shut out—gave a blue glass; a reducing fire—smoky, wet, and without oxygen—gave a red glass.

A similar miracle was performed with antimony. An antimony pigment—calcium antimonate—normally gave an opaque white glass, that is, when in its oxidized form, five short of its normal complement of electrons. If antimony gains two electrons, it is reduced and responds chemically in glass by producing no color at all—a transparent glass. This gain of electrons may come from another ingredient in glass—iron atoms, which give poor-grade glasses their "bottle-green" color. When iron loses electrons (which means it is oxidized), the bottle green virtually disappears, leaving a beautifully clear glass. This is obvious to a chemist, but it must have sent the artisan who wanted an opaque white glass and got a beautifully clear one instead to the nearest temple for meditation.

This achievement in glass chemistry was remarkable, considering nothing usable was known of elements, atoms, or electrons. Moreover, the working temperatures and atmospheres of the fires—reducing or oxidizing—had to be precisely controlled to achieve the high-quality glasses that now populate museums, such as the excellent one in Corning, where Brill does his work.

"Of course," Brill says, "they didn't understand what they were doing in the same terms that we understand it today, but they did have an appreciation for controlling conditions of manufacture so as to get certain desired effects."

Brill's lab is a rather small, necessarily crowded room, adorned by little of the glassy bric-a-brac that distinguishes most chemical laboratories. The only scientific instrument in sight is a microscope, still the best single tool in scientific archaeology. Brill generally works in concert with people expert at certain analytic techniques—when he has work calling for more than a routine look at a glass piece.

"This way I can keep ten or twelve experiments going on at one time," he points out. "If I had a laboratory, I'd only be doing one or two.'

In the late sixties, he examined some glass fragments from Kenchreai, an abandoned port city for ancient Corinth, a Grecian city-state that straddled the Isthmus of Corinth, which used this position to become a trading power. Kenchreai, on the Saronic Gulf, was Corinth's window to the East, a port for the ships that sailed the Black Sea, the eastern Mediterranean, and Homer's "wine-dark" Aegean. It was "the most famous town of all the Corinthians," as wicked as any port city could be, and a melting pot for religions. There were temples for Grecian gods and goddesses as well as a sanctuary for Isis, the Egyptian goddess of fertility. An earthquake shattered the city in A.D. 365 and thirty years later Visigoths sacked Corinth. Another earthquake struck in A.D. 527 and Kenchreai was then abandoned.

When in 1963 Kenchreai was explored by a joint archaelogical team from the University of Chicago and Indiana University,

View of chamber where *opus-sectile* panels were found. *Courtesy: Robert Scranton, University of Chicago, and* Archaeology

led by Dr. Robert L. Scranton, professor of classical art and archaeology at the University of Chicago, their explorations took in a building submerged a few feet offshore. It was church-like, with an apsidal, or semicircular, wall at one end. The team examined the building, Scranton wrote in *Archaeology*, "in response to an almost casual curiosity. Our curiosity had been aroused by a thickening of the wall at the shoreward end of the building, but as this was explored it proved to represent the top of a flight of steps leading down beneath the surface of the sea."

They followed the steps down to a submerged, rectangular room with a mosaic floor. Leaning against its walls were wooden crates containing door-sized panels covered with glass inlays. Images of the Nile could be seen—egrets and ibis among lotuses and papyruses, a man on a crocodile. The glass pieces forming these images were embedded in a thin, resinous matrix, the latter held together by beds of broken pottery, or shards.

Summer ended and the team sealed their extraordinary find. Next year they came back. The little room was pumped dry, reasonably dry anyway. The floor buckled under their feet. Water seeped through everywhere—walls, floors, even over the top on stormy days.

Using steel supports to lift the panels, they managed to get two of them out of the water and onto dry land for a closer look. The panels had been crated two at a time, face to face, and time and the sea had fused the glass faces together. So, Scranton and his colleagues got their first good look backward —by scraping off a portion of the pottery and resinous backing. It was obvious that the panels were the best example yet found of a type of inlay work called *opus sectile*.

Scranton suspects that these glass pictures, as he calls them, may have been bought by the Roman aristocracy. "In ancient literature you read that Pompeii built a theatre in Rome with the second and third stories lined with glass. It could be just this kind of thing. Also, little bits of colored glass found in ruined Roman palaces may have come from this kind of panel."

The colors in the resurrected Kenchreai panels were striking: bright reds and yellows, greens and blues, and even a unique flesh color. But the greatest delight was a figure in one of the panels, about four feet high and standing on a pedestal with an inscription identifying it as Homer. Two other figures are on two different panels: one is probably Plato, the other Theophrastus, successor to Aristotle. Finding Greek philosophers among Nile scenes doesn't surprise Scranton: "By this time Plato and Homer belonged to everybody."

"This time" is about the fourth century A.D., a date picked by Scranton largely from the pottery and coins also found at the site. Perhaps the panels were stored in the apsidal building when the earlier earthquake hit, submerging the building, and making retrieval of the panels difficult, if not impossible.

Other questions remained. Where had the panels been made? Locally? Or somewhere else—Alexandria, the Rome region, or Naples? Who made them? And what were the panels doing

Opus-sectile panel from Kenchreai showing Homer. *Courtesy: Robert Scranton, University of Chicago*

there? Were they intended for the apsidal building, possibly the sanctuary for Isis mentioned by a Roman travel writer, Pausanias?

These are archaeological questions. But Scranton was anxious to know more about the nature of the glass itself, as well as the resinous plaster and pottery base that held everything together. Where did the materials used for the *opus sectile* inlay stand in the history of glass? Technologically, did they represent some ancient technique or a new, medieval one?

He turned to Bob Brill for possible answers. Brill visited the site, primarily to help preserve the badly corroded panels from further deterioration. Many were taken to a little museum in Nauplia, a two-hour drive south of Kenchreai, to be restored by Mr. Charalampos "Babis" Deilakes, a skilled restorer for whom Brill has the highest praise. The remaining panels are in storehouses near the Corinth Canal.

Several small pieces of glass were carefully removed from some panels, and, with others that had dropped off, were examined at the Corning Museum of Glass. "Our objective," Brill says, "was to use every scientific means we could think of to study each material contained in the panels in order to learn everything we could about them—how they were made, and, perhaps, when and where they were made."

With two common analytical techniques, X-ray fluorescence and X-ray diffraction, useful for identifying the type and structure of chemicals in glass and other materials, Brill found what seemed to be two yellow pigments in his samples. One pigment was the ancient Naples yellow, containing lead and antimony; and the other was the later pigment made with lead and tin, placed at about A.D. 400, also the tentative date given the Kenchreai panels. But why two yellow pigments? A reply came from the electron microprobe, an instrument that seems almost too good to be true.

The probe can scan a very tiny surface area—as small as a twentieth of the width of a strand of human hair—and directly read its elemental composition. The instrument is large enough to squeeze Brill right out of his laboratory. He used a probe at the Corning Glass Works operated for him by Dr. William T. Kane and Mr. Norbert J. Binowski. Its principle is essentially simple, although execution calls for special talents. A sample is

Mr. Charalampos Deilakes cleaning the upper panel of a stack of *opus-sectile* glasswork found at Kenchreai. The panels were found as shown, except for the sand and mud that has been cleaned away. *Courtesy: Robert H. Brill, Corning Museum of Glass*

placed under the probe and a microscope with crossed hair pieces is used to aim the instrument. A beam of electrons guided by magnetic lenses is directed at the target. As the beam hits, electrons in the atoms of the sample, in response to this sudden charge of energy, emit, or fluoresce, X rays. As the X rays scatter from the target, they are caught by detectors that split them into various wavelenghs, just as a prism will split a beam of natural light into a rainbow pattern. Since each element emits a characteristic spectrum of X-ray wavelengths, the element can be identified, while the intensity of the particular X-ray spectrum will give the concentrations of the element. While both the probe and neutron activation analysis give comparable information on elemental makeup, the probe reveals how elements are distributed within a selected area, while NAA provides an overall count.

Brill pioneered the application of the probe to intricate glasswork, notably *millefiori* (lit.: thousand flowers) glass and miniature mosaic plaques, both made by Roman artisans by fusing tiny canes or rods of colored glass to form various patterns. In fact, the first glasses of any sort to which the talents of the electron microprobe were applied were these ancient glasses. Now, the instrument is used routinely for analyzing ancient *and* modern glasses.

"If you remove even a small sample that you could use for analysis, the damage is very evident," Brill explains. "You remove a significant part of the object itself. Secondly, you can't get a decent sample because they are such tiny pieces of glass. If you tried to sample the yellow glass, you'd bring out some blue or red with it. By using the probe you can study these little pieces in detail without doing any damage at all."

Recently, a variation of the microprobe idea has been tried, using a laser beam instead of electrons. A tiny hole is burned into the sample, but it is too small to be worrisome. Identification is based not on X rays but on a small plume of the elements vaporized by the laser beam. The laser-microprobe technique, exploited by Dr. William J. Young of the Boston Museum of Fine Arts, has been applied to clays, glazes, Chinese bronzes, and ancient glass.

To learn why there were two yellow pigments in the Kenchreai glass, Dr. Kane, who was working with Brill, set up the electron microprobe to obtain a direct display of the nature and intensity of the X-ray pattern coming from the atoms in the yellow pigment as they were disturbed by the electron beam. The beam moved slowly over the sample area, and the distributions of lead, tin, antimony, and calcium were read individually. A picture was taken of each elemental distribution of different chemical elements near the surface of the sample being analyzed. Overlapping them produced a "television picture" that told the story. Tin and lead formed almost identical patterns. Wherever tin appeared, lead could also be found. However, the same fraternal company was not kept by lead and antimony. Rather, wherever antimony appeared, lead was noticeable by its absence, and there was instead a richness of calcium. The conclusion: lead and tin are combined into the same molecules which were present as flakes of the "new" lead-tin yellow pigment that glassworkers began using about A.D. 200–300. Antimony and calcium were combined as calcium antimonate, a colorant for the white opaque glasses as early as the seventeenth century B.C.

The Kenchreai glassmaker had mixed old with new by melting together two pieces of glass—each containing a different pigment—and used the dominant yellow result in this part of his *opus-sectile* work. "The craftsmen who made them," says Brill, "probably salvaged glasses from earlier sources, remelted them, and then fashioned these little bits of glass."

The fact that the Kenchreai glass did contain lead pigments —whatever the reason—gave Brill another entry to locating sources from which the Kenchreai glass could have come. Lead, which is easy to mine, was one of the first metals to be widely used, perhaps as early as 3500 B.C. Simple heating of its common ore galena, or lead sulfide, recovers the metal. The Romans called the metal "plumbus," which explains both "plumbing" and the chemical symbol for lead, Pb. Aside from its attraction to early metalworkers, lead has some other properties which are particularly useful to a contemporary scientist, whether he wants to know how old the moon is or where some piece of rotted glass came from. Lead has four stable isotopes, which contain an equal number of protons and electrons (eighty-two) but differ in the number of neutrons in their nuclei. But while their atomic masses (protons plus neutrons) are unequal, they will all react in just about the same way in a chemist's test tube or a glassmaker's furnace.

The actual proportions, or ratios, of these stable lead isotopes in lead minerals will differ from place to place depending on geological happenstance. These lead isotopes are formed from the decay of radioactive uranium and thorium isotopes, and since these decay rates are well known and cover millions of years, they make a very nice "clock" to date ancient materials, including moon rocks returned by the Apollo voyagers. However, Brill wasn't especially interested in the geological age of the lead in his Kenchreai glass; that would only tell him the minimum age of the Earth. But the fact that lead-isotope ratios in ores differ from location to location suggested that the source of lead in a particular relic might be traceable.

"There is one large advantage of this technique over chemical analysis," Brill points out. "In the past, literally thousands of analyses have been done on bronzes and copper and so forth. But the frustrating part is that every step you take a metal through affects its chemical composition, making the results very difficult to interpret. But in the case of the lead-isotope studies, nothing that you do to lead will change its isotope ratio unless you mix it with lead from another source. So, the technique is useful for lead from different materials—metals, corroded or not, pigments, glazes, glasses, alloys, etc."

Even before the Kenchreai glasses came to Corning, Brill, with Dr. J. M. Wampler, then at the Brookhaven National Laboratory, had already determined lead-isotope ratios in about seventy ancient materials including samples from England, Pompeii, Greece, Egypt, and from as far away as the Mesopotamian city of Ur, south of the Euphrates. A meaningful pattern emerged. The ratios fell into several groups that Brill and Wampler labeled L, E, S, and X, each representing leads that looked like the leads from known mining areas—Greece (Laurion), England, Spain, and an uncertain group from sites near the eastern Mediterranean.

Laurion was the famous lead-mining region southeast of

Athens, best known for its silver that paid for the ships that stopped the Persians at Salamis. Remains of the Laurion mines can be seen today, including a portion of the underground galleries that totaled about one hundred miles. Lead mines were operated by the Romans throughout England south of Hadrian's Wall. The locations of the Mesopotamian mines are still uncertain.

The labels Brill gives his leads don't necessarily specify where a particular lead comes from. A "Laurion" lead—a lead with isotope ratios similar to leads from Laurion—could possibly have come from places in Turkey or Iran, where similar leads are mined.

William Shields of the National Bureau of Standards determined isotope ratios for lead extracted from two pieces of the Kenchreai glasses—the yellow and red opaque glasses. In the yellow glass the lead is in the form of the lead-tin pigment. The colorant of the red glass is cuprous oxide with a dash of lead added by the artisan for two reasons: to help dissolve copper oxide in the glass melt and to assure complete and uniform precipitation after the glass cooled.

The lead isotopes from the two glasses were studied with the mass spectrometer, an instrument that can separate atoms or molecular fragments through differences in weight and charge, making it ideal for isotope analysis. Lead is extracted and tiny samples are placed on a filament, which is then heated. As they sputter off, the lead atoms are guided by magnetic fields down the mass spectrometer's "racetrack," the individual isotopes separating because of mass differences as they fly down the track. At the finish, detectors note the trajectories and intensities of the different lead isotopes, information that is then used to identify the mass and amount of each lead isotope.

Shields found that the lead in the two Kenchreai glasses had somewhat different isotopic fingerprints; in other words, the leads originally came from different sources. Perhaps each glass was made at a different place. Or, as Brill suspects, the glasses may have been made in a place where no local lead was available, so the glassmakers used whatever imported lead they could get.

One thing, however, is certain. Neither lead comes from the Laurion mines, which means a low probability that the glasses were made in Greece. Although it can't yet be said where either of these leads were mined, Brill points out that the lead in the red glass from Kenchreai is similar to that found in some early glasses from Egypt and in glass mosaics at Shavei Zion and Beth-Shean, both located in present-day Israel. The lead also matches metallic specimens from Jelemie, another archaeological site in Israel, as well as lead extracted from some glasses, bronze coins, and a bronze statue, all from Istanbul.

The lead from the yellow Kenchreai glass resembles the lead in two glasses found on Rhodes and one from Egypt as well as that in several bronze coins minted in Asia Minor (Turkey).

Even though the exact origins of these leads cannot be specified (they resemble some ores occurring in Turkey), Brill points out that they do provide some very useful information. The two most likely places where the glasses could have been manufactured are Alexandria, in Egypt, or somewhere in the neighborhood of Rome or Naples, in Italy, judging from what's known of the history of glass manufacture. But among all of the ancient leads that they have analyzed so far, no leads resembling those from either of the Kenchreai glasses have been found that can be associated with Italian sources. Thus the evidence seems to point toward the conclusion that the Kenchreai glasses themselves were made in Alexandria or somewhere else in the eastern Mediterranean region rather than in Italy.

Working with Professor Robert Clayton of the University of Chicago, Brill is now evaluating the use of an isotope of oxygen —oxygen 18—as another tracer of source materials. Oxygen, of course, is more ubiquitous than lead, and the oxygen-18 content of various naturally occurring forms tends to be highly variable. Their work has shown that the oxygen-18 contents of ancient glasses reflect the oxygen-18 contents of ingredients from which they were prepared. Moreover, they have evidence that melting conditions do not affect the glasses' content of oxygen-18. For these reasons, oxygen-18 analysis may become a powerful tool in archaeology.

Brill also hopes to analyze the Kenchreai panels in the little

museum in Nauplia with X-ray fluorescence spectrometry. It
has been used in similar situations.

In X-ray fluorescence spectrometry, a radioactive source is
placed against the sample, which responds by emitting X rays.
What happens is that electrons are knocked out of their normal
orbits by the radiation, and the empty orbits are immediately
replaced by electrons from other orbits. This exchange leaves a
bit of excess energy that is emitted as X rays. The energy and
wavelengths of the X rays emitted identifies the material.

Dr. Isadore Perlman and Harry Bowman (Lawrence Radiation Laboratory of the University of California) have developed
a portable X-ray fluorescence instrument which can analyze archaeological objects and works of art in the field and in museums.

The importance of on-the-spot analysis of the Kenchreai
glasses is amplified by Brill's discovery that, by identifying the
weathering products on the surfaces of these glasses, their original colors can be traced.

The wood used to crate the panels has been identified, using
carbon-14 dating, as a pine dating back to about A.D. 300, give
or take some seventy years. It's a common wood in the Mediterranean area. The resinous matrix in which the glass pieces were
embedded has been identified by Dr. Curt Beck at Vassar College as a combination of crushed limestone and pine resin, the
stuff from which turpentine is made. "The mixture makes a very
good adhesive," Brill points out, "because when it is hot, it is
soft and pliable. But when it cools and hardens, you can literally drive a nail through it." Brill extracted the pine resin
chemically and, by the carbon-14 technique, dated it to about
A.D. 305, implying that the panels were about thirty to ninety
years old when the earthquake struck.

As a final note, it should be pointed out that all this technical
probing has only suggested some sketchy answers to basic
archaeological questions—where did the panels come from, who
made them, and what was their purpose. Indeed, little of the
work that chemists have done on antiquities has as yet answered
the first-line questions of archaeologists and curators. But the
steady accumulation of background material is beginning to pay
off.

7

ON THE TRAIL
OF RIBONUCLEASE

What would you do if you had a million dollars? Most of us, abandoning the Puritan ethic, would list various joyful enterprises. David Harker said, "I'd take ten years or so off and get the structure of a protein." Seventeen years and $2 million later, he did just that. Harker is now director of the Center for Crystallographic Research, affiliated with the Roswell Park Memorial Institute in Buffalo, New York.

The protein that led Harker through a molecular version of *Pilgrim's Progress* is called ribonuclease. It is one of perhaps 100,000 enzymes—all proteins—each charged with seeing that a particular cell reaction proceeds at the proper rhythm and pace compatible with life. Enzymes function as molecular metronomes, guiding the rhythm of biochemical reactions—two to three thousand per cell—that together constitute life. In the watery, cool, and chemically bizarre environment of a living cell, each enzyme must find the material it's designed to work on and break it apart or condense it with another molecule, and do it all much faster than can a chemist using a test tube. What happens when an enzyme is missing or mismade is illustrated by the Lesch-Nyhan syndrome and other genetic diseases discussed in the first chapter.

The particular role of ribonuclease is to smooth the dissolution of ribonucleic acid (RNA), a necklacelike molecule that is part of the cell's machinery for making new proteins, including ribonuclease. RNA codes the information, or blueprints, needed by a cell to make a particular protein. This information is derived from the genetic molecule, DNA. When the protein is made, RNA becomes excess baggage and is broken apart by ribonuclease so that its building blocks can, presumably, be used again to make another RNA molecule. While ribonuclease is found within cells, plentiful amounts of the enzyme also pour out of the pancreas, where it is made, into the intestines, where it helps to digest RNA in foods.

Ribonuclease, like any protein, is made up of a variety of amino acids linked together in a definite order. Within the past decade, chemists have learned that order, deciphered the shape into which the amino-acid chain is twisted, synthesized the molecule, and learned a good deal of what gives ribonuclease its almost magical (to a chemist) enzyme powers. These and parallel achievements have stripped away the almost mystical aura that surrounded enzymes. A treasure chest of possibilities has been revealed: application to genetic diseases, custom-made enzymes for specific uses, and, inevitably, a revolution in the laboratory creation of new molecules.

Harker got a picture of the ribonuclease molecule, from which he learned its three-dimensional shape. When he first dreamed of getting the structure of a protein, ribonuclease was yet to be named and little was known about other enzymes or, indeed, any protein. This was about the mid-thirties after he had taken a turn at industry for a couple of years, and earned a Ph.D. under Linus Pauling at the California Institute of Technology, where he learned how to use X rays to decipher molecular shapes. In 1936, he signed on as an instructor in the chemistry department at Johns Hopkins University. At that time, proteins were still somewhat murky objects, believed by many to be conglomerations of amino-acid chains of various lengths held together by some sort of unspecified bonds. The idea that a protein could be one molecule made of a specific, repeatable chain of amino acids was still a minority view. The idea that the shape of a particular protein molecule was fixed was outrageous.

But then the prospects for learning more about proteins brightened. Twenty-four years earlier, Max von Laue, a German physicist, musing in a Munich beer garden, realized that X rays should be bent, or diffracted, as they pass through a crystal. A crystal—to a chemist—is an orderly, regular array of atoms or molecules; someone called it frozen music. Once the crystal pattern is known, the position of each atom or molecule is also known. An X-ray beam going through a crystal will be deflected by each crystal unit in exactly the same way, because each unit is in exactly the same position as its neighbors. Just as a beam of light focused on a wire mesh will "etch" a pattern characteristic of the mesh, X rays can etch a pattern characteristic of the atoms' arrangement in a crystal on a photographic plate. X-ray beams are used because of their shorter wavelength; the wavelength of ordinary light is too long to distinguish individual atoms in the atomic lattice of a crystal. This is the basis of X-ray diffraction.

One of the most famous father-and-son teams in science, Sir William and Sir Lawrence Bragg, immediately realized that von Laue's discovery could be applied to solving the atomic structures of crystals, and shortly thereafter, Sir Lawrence worked out the structure of table salt—sodium chloride. This was in 1912.

Serious work on proteins began decades later in 1934 at the University of Cambridge when J. D. Bernal and Dorothy Crowfoot (now Hodgkin) took an X-ray diffraction picture of pepsin, an enzyme used in digestion to break up other proteins. Two years later, Max Perutz, a Viennese-born chemist, came to Cambridge and soon took X-ray pictures of chymotrypsin, like pepsin a digestive enzyme, and hemoglobin, the oxygen carrier in blood. What they each got was a symmetrical array of dots that might amuse a devotee of contemporary art. But to the Cambridge groups, the dots revealed that protein structure made sense; every protein molecule in a crystal looked exactly like the other, down to the most minute atomic details. Proteins had lost their amorphous nature, and emerged as reasonable creatures that, *in principle*, could be deciphered; it took Perutz twenty-two years to learn what hemoglobin really looked like.

While Perutz and company were beginning to realize the import of their dots, Harker was amusing his Johns Hopkins colleagues with the idea of "doing" a protein. At the time, he was continuing the work he had started at Cal Tech and was deciphering the structures of various "simple" molecules—simple in comparison to proteins, anyway. Harker recalls that his turn to proteins was inspired in the 1930s by a visiting lady mathematician from Cambridge University, Dr. Dorothy Wrinch.

"She had a theory of how protein structure was arranged, based on very rigid rules. That got me interested in the notion of trying to find out what the structure of protein really is, instead of just hypothesizing about it. I was discouraged by the older people who knew how to do X-ray crystallography. And I did not get any support at that time." There was little faith that the X-ray diffraction techniques he and others had learned in the thirties could be applied to molecules as large and complex as proteins.

Indirect help arrived from industry in the form of a job offer at the General Electric Research Laboratories in Schenectady, New York. The offer came from Dr. Irving Langmuir, a prestigious scientist in his own right and one of the few industrial researchers to receive a Nobel Prize (for work on surface chemistry).

By the spring of 1941, Harker was established in GE's metallurgy department, doing anything but protein structure—various metal alloys, boron compounds, etc. "General Electric, of course, couldn't justify to its stockholders going into a program of research on protein structure," Harker points out.

Harker spent almost ten years at General Electric, generally happy, turning out productive research and papers but still dreaming of proteins. He got out, as he got in, with the help of Langmuir. At a party to honor the retirement of Langmuir and other eminent GE researchers (who were immediately rehired as consultants), Langmuir asked Harker what he'd do if he had a million dollars. Harker, supported by two martinis, declared his ambition to do a protein.

"And I thought no more about it," he remembers. "But two weeks later he came into my office and said, 'Harker, did you mean what you said the other night? Because I think we can swing it.' "

Some of the money, $25,000 a year, came from a foundation set up by Langmuir's brother, Dean Langmuir, a lawyer. The Rockefeller Foundation supplied additional funds, a guarantee of $35,000 a year for five years. It wasn't a million but enough to enable Harker to quite GE and join the faculty of the Brooklyn Polytechnic Institute in 1950. He went to Brooklyn Poly in part because New York City was the only place where he could get a large computer not completely tied up by Korean War work. This was the IBM 650 computer at the Watson Laboratory of Columbia University. In addition, Brooklyn Poly had a protein chemistry laboratory and X-ray diffraction equipment.

"So I established myself there and that turned out very well. They gave me two thousand square feet in a building they rented, and I set up there. I bought apparatus, hired young people, built equipment, did theoretical work, and tried to crystallize the protein we decided to work on—ribonuclease."

Ribonuclease had been crystallized earlier, in 1940, by Dr. Moses Kunitz of the Rockefeller University (then Rockefeller Institute) in New York City. It had been isolated and named two years earlier by Dr. René Dubos, also of Rockefeller. Harker had some difficulty crystallizing the enzyme. He and Dr. Murray Vernon King visited Kunitz's lab to learn how the master did it, apparently brought back some seed crystals on his coat, and thereafter had no difficulty crystallizing the enzyme. Eventually,

Dr. King got fourteen different crystalline varieties of the enzyme, one of which was chosen for a go at the three-dimensional structure. A more common example of crystallization occurs when dissolved sugar becomes rock sugar. However, proteins, because of their large, complex structure, are notoriously difficult to crystallize.

Harker got crude ribonuclease from meat packing companies, which had no use for this enzyme which was a by-product of the packer's process for making trypsin, another enzyme medically useful and salable because it dissolves blood clots. At first the enzyme was free, but it now costs about two or three hundred dollars a gram; the meat packers learned there was a market for their throwaways.

While X-ray diffraction technique is simplicity itself, interpretation is another matter. A speck of ribonuclease crystal is sealed in a capillary tube and placed in front of an X-ray source. As the capillary tube is slowly turned, X rays pass through and are scattered onto a photographic plate. The X rays are bent, or diffracted, by the electrons of the atoms in the crystal. The X-ray patterns recorded on the photographic plates—arrays of dots—actually contain enough information to work out the pattern of the electron distribution in a crystal. The task of Harker doing ribonuclease, Perutz doing hemoglobin, and others was to find the structure that could produce the particular patterns of dots they recorded—like trying to shape a man from his shadow. Tens of thousands of dots were recorded, each dot recorded several times. Various correction factors such as angles and intensities had to be applied. An almost infinite number of comparisons had to be made. The calculations involved millions of numbers to be manipulated. All this would have been impossible without the high-speed computers that came into being about the time the crystallographers were turning X-ray beams on large organic molecules such as proteins.

Both Harker and Perutz ran up against a common stone wall. While they could measure the intensity of the dots on their film, which told them the spacings between atoms, they found that in large molecules there was so much overlap—so many chemical bonds of the same lengths and in the same direction—that it was impossible to sort them out. They were lost in a forest of identical trees. To put it somewhat more technically, they could measure the intensity of the X rays coming through their crystals but not their phases—how individual waves were retarded or advanced with respect to each other. Their picture became undecipherable maps, a strange language without a dictionary. In effect, the pictures were of several molecules mixed together. The phase problem was solved first by Perutz, and subsequently by Harker, whose inspiration came from his colleague, Dr. King, who had accidentally dyed his pants made of wool—a protein. The two reasoned that if wool could be dyed, then a protein could be "dyed" in similar fashion by attaching heavy atoms to the ribonuclease molecule. After several false starts, they did get pictures of dyed and undyed crystals differing slightly in intensity, enough to help them find their way through the molecule. The protein molecule was big enough and spacious enough that the insertion of the heavy atoms—usually uranium and platinum—made little difference in their three-dimensional structure.

"The difference between those intensities and the ones you got from an undyed crystal gave us a chance to get the vital information needed to get not just the direction of the interatomic distances but the atomic positions themselves," Harker explains.

Perutz labeled the technique isomorphous replacement, meaning same shape, and used it to push on with hemoglobin, whose structure he finally solved six years later in 1959. It took Harker's group another eight years to solve the structure of ribonuclease.

While Harker and others—notably Dr. C. H. Carlisle of Birkbeck College, University of London—were pursuing a picture of ribonuclease, the *overall* shape, others were tracking it quite differently. Chemists at the National Institutes of Health in Bethesda, Maryland, and Rockefeller University went after the enzyme's molecular, or chemical, structure; that is, the order in which the amino-acid building blocks were arranged. The chemical arrangement of the atoms in ribonuclease was essential both to understanding how the molecule worked and to getting the three-dimensional structure. While X rays can detect the position of atoms, they can rarely identify them.

That people were working at all on the chemical structure

of ribonuclease was due in good part to a shy British chemist, Frederick Sanger at the University of Cambridge, who in 1955 cracked the structure of insulin, a protein made of two amino-acid chains held together by chemical bonds. In 1958, Sanger

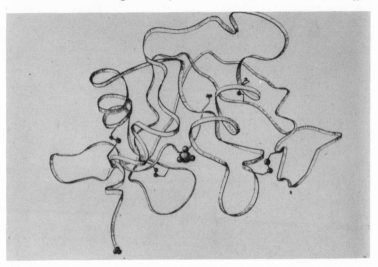

Outline of ribonuclease molecule. *Courtesy: David Harker, Roswell Park Memorial Institute*

Model of complete ribonuclease molecule as determined by X-ray crystallography. *Courtesy: David Harker, Roswell Park Memorial Institute*

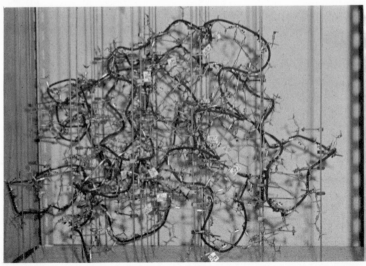

received the Nobel Prize in chemistry. Sanger's achievement, after ten years of very hard work, was the protein chemist's equivalent of Roger Bannister's four-minute mile. If Sanger could do insulin, then even considerably larger molecules such as ribonuclease were realizable.

The problem that faced protein chemists at the time (and still does) was to identify one by one and in the proper order the amino-acid beads in the protein necklace. Not only do these amino acids look remarkably alike, but their chemistry is distressingly similar.

Each amino acid contains an amino group (H-N-) and a
$$H$$
(with H above N)
carboxyl group (-C-OH), which represents the "acid" portion.
$$O$$
(with O above C)
The two are joined together by a carbon atom to which is attached a hydrogen atom and a group of atoms (given the arbitrary general label of R). Therefore, the general structure for an amino acid is H-N-C-C-OH. If R is a hydrogen atom, then the amino acid is glycine; if R is a methyl group (carbon and hydrogen, H-C-H), it is alanine.

When two amino acids—glycine and alanine, for example—are joined, a molecule of water (HOH) is lost, with OH coming from the carboxyl group and the second H from the amino group. The product formed is a dipeptide, glycylalanine. Chemically, it's written this way:

glycine   +   alanine   ⟶   glycylalanine   + water

Since amino acids, as they join together, lose some of their atoms, chemists talk of the amino-acid *residues* in a protein rather than just amino acids.

That proteins and peptides (smaller, less complicated amino-acid chains) were made of amino acids was already known in the nineteenth century. By 1904, Emil Fischer, one of the great German chemists, found that proteins are long chains of amino acids.

Fischer, incidentally, was probably the first scientist to bridge the gap between biology and chemistry. In addition to proteins, he did pioneering work on sugars, fats, and purines. The latter are building blocks for the genetic material, deoxyribonucleic acid, or DNA. He speculated about enzymes, making the memorable remark that "a ferment [enzyme] fits its substrate as a complicated key its lock."

Insulin is composed of two amino-acid chains. Frederick Sanger in his work on insulin in the 1950s found that these two chains are held together by cystine bridges; these are formed when the sulfur atoms from the amino acid cysteine pair up and form a chemical bond.

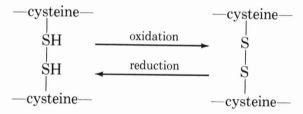

Sanger broke the sulfur bridges apart, separated the chains, and deciphered the structure of each chain—one made of thirty amino acids, the other of twenty-one amino acids. Two tools were crucial: paper chromatography, invented several years earlier by two British chemists, and DNP analysis, invented by Sanger and his colleagues. Paper chromatography is based on the fact that a liquid traveling along a piece of filter paper will carry different substances along at different speeds. If the proper liquid is picked, even minute amounts of very similar materials can be separated and identified. DNP stands for a dinitrophenyl group, a chemical that forms a bright yellow compound when attached to amino acids. Sanger broke the individual insulin chains apart by splitting the bonds between amino acids with acid. He separated the shattered fragments with paper chromatography, attached DNP to the amino-acid group at one end of each fragment, lopped this terminal amino acid off, and identified it. That process repeated over and over produced the structures of the fragments. Therefore, he knew the identities of the amino acids in each chain, and with one-by-one DNP analysis he knew the order. From there, Sanger was able to write down the structure of two chains of beef insulin. In just as difficult work, he found the points on the chains where the sulfur bridges formed.

Beef insulin has 777 atoms in it; ribonuclease taken from the pancreas of a cow has 1,876 atoms. Aside from its larger size, there were other problems that precluded the step-by-step approach used by Sanger unless chemists were willing to face decades of work, which they were not.

Automatic methods for measuring the amounts of amino acids were developed in the fifties by the ribonuclease group at Rockefeller University, which included Drs. William H. Stein, Stanford Moore, C. H. W. Hirs, and D. H. Spackman. Column instead of paper chromatography was used. A mixture of amino acids is passed through the top of a glass column packed with a special resin that has varying affinities for the individual amino acids. As a result, when the packed column is washed with a solution that removes the amino acids, they flow out one-by-one with the solution at the bottom, where they react with a chemical, ninhydrin, a normally colorless substance that forms a blue color with amino acids, the "blueness" measuring the amount of the amino acid. This scheme was automated by the Rockefeller group.

Dr. Christian B. Anfinsen of the National Heart and Lung Institute, one of the units of the National Institutes of Health, in the 1950s proved that ribonuclease, unlike insulin, was one single chain of amino acids. He did it by cleaving the sulfur bridges that folded up the ribonuclease chain into its specific shape (which Harker was trying to learn) and then using DNP to prove that there was only one terminal amino group, hence only one chain. (A protein by convention begins with an amino group and ends with a carboxyl group.)

The Rockefeller group attacked the chain's structure using the same divide-and-identify technique pioneered by Frederick Sanger. However, instead of using acids, which produce a discouraging mixture of amino-acid fragments, they turned to proteolytic enzymes (also used by Sanger). These attack other proteins, breaking them apart at *specific* points. It's the difference between a rapier and a broadax; the proteolytic enzymes make surgical incisions along specific points in a protein chain, while acids simply smash away, breaking all chemical bonds between amino acids. For instance, the proteolytic enzyme trypsin breaks only the bonds following the two amino acids arginine or lysine.

Each of the ribonuclease fragments was then deciphered, using, principally, a technique (Edman degradation) devised by a Swedish chemist in which amino acids are chemically snipped off one by one, like a child unbeading a necklace. Concurrently, the sulfur-to-sulfur bridges, which had a tendency to shift positions unless properly handled, were located for ribonuclease.

About 1960, a tentative chemical structure of ribonuclease was offered. Corrections were made about two years later based on the work of Dr. F. M. Richards of Yale University and others. Chemists now knew that ribonuclease consisted of 124 amino acids of 19 different varieties, and they knew the exact order in which these amino acids were arranged. They also knew that there were four points in the molecule where sections of the chain were linked together by the sulfur-to-sulfur bridges bending the molecule into a precise shape. That shape was crucial. If the sulfur bridges were broken and the molecule uncoiled, it lost all its activity. It was no longer an enzyme.

But Harker was having his problems learning that shape. A new president was installed at Brooklyn Polytechnic Institute who, he says, believed that an engineering school, such as Brooklyn Poly, should not be spending money and space on biological research. Harker was offered a professorship in electrical engineering if he would give up his pursuit of ribonuclease; the president would not sign Harker's grant applications for work on proteins. In 1959, a recruiter from the Roswell Park Memorial Institute arrived looking for someone to head a department of biophysics. Harker suggested himself, was invited to give a talk on his work, and offered a job by Roswell's director at the time, Dr. George Moore.

"I said to Dr. Moore," Harker recalls, "I want to go on working to find the structure of the ribonuclease molecule and if that's biophysics according to you, I'll accept. And he said, 'It sounds like biophysics to me.'"

Harker moved to Roswell Park in 1959, taking with him two colleagues—Dr. Gobinath Kartha, who did the X-ray work, and Dr. Jake Bello, who focused on the chemistry of ribonuclease. Even though the phase problem had been resolved, seven years remained before Dr. Kartha, normally a serious fellow, smiled and announced he had the structure of ribonuclease. What he had done was to bring the X-ray picture of ribonuclease into sharp enough focus to see the continuous ribbon of electron density that indicated the main chain of the molecule. That is, the dots, which contain three-dimensional information produced as the X-rays bounce off the electrons of the atoms in the protein crystal, were measured for their intensities and phases. The more spots measured, the sharper the resolution of the image. A special mathematical treatment—Fourier synthesis—translates the intensity and phase information into contour maps of electron density that look rather like the contour maps that mark elevations on a geological map. (Fourier synthesis essentially treats a molecule as a continuous cloud of electron density rather than a cluster of individual atoms.) Parallel slices of the electron density are obtained in section by section of the molecule and are contoured on Plexiglas sheets by their being stacked on top of each other. What emerges is the pattern of electron density for the entire molecule, from which the crystallographer, at last, can begin to learn the structure of his beast.

Harker, Kartha and their colleagues had to measure and analyze over 7,000 spots for each of the dyed and undyed forms of ribonuclease. Fourier calculations were made and contour maps drawn. In 1967, they had good-enough resolution to pick

Plexiglass stacks showing electron density distribution for ribonuclease. Portion of main chain is marked. *Courtesy: David Harker, Roswell Park Memorial Institute*

out the main chain of the ribonuclease molecule and some of the bulkier side groups. They could see their molecule. Their friendly competitor, C. H. Carlisle of Birkbeck College, had announced a different structure of ribonuclease a bit earlier, but his resolution was considerably poorer, and his structure has not held up. Carlisle, in effect, took a gamble and lost. Harker, incidentally, didn't feel he was competing with Carlisle in the style of the competition for the structure of DNA spread before the public by Dr. James D. Watson in his book, *The Double Helix*. "A horrible book," says Harker.

Harker and Kartha could not identify individual atoms in their ribonuclease model, but they were able to fit the chemical structure worked out at Rockefeller into the overall shape of the molecule. "We knew the structure in that sense," Harker says.

"The known sequence fit into the electron density at that resolution."

The molecule is roughly kidney shaped, with a deep depression or cleft in one side. Someone said it looked like Napoleon's hat. That Harker's structure was sound was confirmed in another, somewhat sophisticated way. All enzymes, including ribonuclease, have an active site where they come in contact with the material, or substrate, they act on. For ribonuclease, of course, it's RNA, a molecule the enzyme apparently stretches at specific points so that it's easily destroyed. The active site is a relatively small part—just a few amino acids—in a sizable protein. The usual analogy is a lathe, where a small cutting edge does the actual work with the rest of the machinery used to bring edge and object together. The active site of an enzyme is the cutting edge, but what the rest of the molecule does is still being debated. In the case of ribonuclease, only three or four amino acids out of 124 are known to be indispensable for activity; others can be blocked with some but not complete loss of activity; and still others can be blocked with no loss at all. The indispensable amino acids for ribonuclease include the amino acid histidine in positions 12, 48, and 119, and lysine in position 41. (The numbering begins with lysine at position 1, the first amino acid in the chain.) The intriguing part is that these particular amino acids are widely scattered in the stretched-out version of the molecule. They must somehow come together if they are to function as the active site; in Harker's folded molecule they do. Harker and his group have done intensive studies to locate the active site in the molecule, and indications are that it is indeed located at the point where the vital histidine and lysine molecules become neighbors.

There's more circumstantial support for Harker's structure. A look at the molecule indicates that it has a "tail" made up roughly of the first twenty amino acids. Apparently, part of this tail is more exposed than the rest of the molecule, making it vulnerable to chemical attack. In the late fifties, Dr. Frederic M. Richards at Yale used a bacterial enzyme, subtilisin, to snip this tail off between amino acids 20 and 21—alanine and serine. The broken but not parted enzyme was still fully active, but all

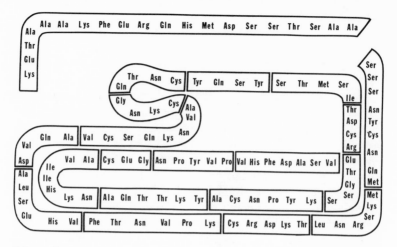

Ribonuclease-S. When the "tail" is mixed with the main portion of the enzyme, full enzyme activity is restored. Chemists at Merck Sharp & Dohme research laboratories synthesized the fragments shown of the main portion of the molecule, combined them in proper order, and, together with the tail, produced ribonuclease. *Courtesy: Merck Sharp & Dohme Research Laboratories and* American Scientist

activity was lost when the two portions—which Richards called S-protein and S-peptide (the tail)—were separated. However, simply combining the two portions, without having to repair the broken bond, restored complete activity. Richards used the S-peptide as a probe for studying how the enzyme worked by modifying it, mixing it with the S-protein, and measuring the effects on activity. As noted earlier, Dr. Richards and his colleagues in 1962 pointed out an error in the chemical structure of ribonuclease proposed by the Rockefeller University group in 1960. In 1967, when Harker reported the three-dimensional structure of natural ribonuclease, Dr. Harold M. Wyckoff of Richards's lab solved the X-ray structure of ribonuclease-S, the form of the enzyme when the bonds between amino acids 20 and 21 are broken. This structure looked very much like the native enzyme, except for expected differences of shape in the area where the enzyme was broken by subtilisin. Wyckoff did the job in about four years, but he had the advantage of some of Harker's hard-won techniques.

Ribonuclease now was the best-known enzyme in terms of its structure and shape and how it worked. The next step was obvious—synthesis of the enzyme. An attempt would be made to create ribonuclease in the laboratory, making it the first enzyme *not* made by a living cell.

Emil Fischer had followed up his classic early twentieth century studies of proteins by synthesizing a chain of eighteen amino acids. However, his choice of amino acids and possible combinations was limited. This, however, didn't save him from newspaper reports that he had solved "the riddle of life." A landmark in peptide synthesis was reached in 1953 when Dr. Vincent du Vigneaud of the Cornell University School of Mediine synthesized two small natural peptides—oxytocin and vasopressin, both nine amino-acid chains. Oxytocin contracts the muscles of the uterus and is sometimes used to aid delivery, while vasopressin stimulates the kidney into increased reabsorption of water, making it an antidiuretic. Du Vigneaud received a Nobel Prize for his achievement. Other peptides were made, notably adrenocorticotrophic hormore (ACTH), fully synthesized about 1963 by a Swiss group. And about the same time, ten years after Sanger had the structure, beef insulin had been created in the laboratory. American, German, and Red Chinese chemists all had a hand in this achievement, with the moral credit going to the Chinese who, in spite of almost no communication with their Western counterparts, competed successfully on a very sophisticated level of protein chemistry.

However, this insulin race left blood on the laboratory bench. The results of one group were challenged by another. A lack of complete insulin activity by one group brought claims of spurious results by another. The Americans were the first to synthesize one of the two insulin chains; the Germans made both; and the Chinese solved the problem of recombining the two chains that had plagued both groups and were able to make the first fully crystalline, completely synthetic insulin. Later, the American group was able to improve the yield of active insulin considerably.

The race in the late sixties to create ribonuclease, while intense, was cordial. There were two groups: one at the Merck,

Sharp and Dohme Research Laboratories in Rahway, New Jersey, and the other—in true ribonuclease tradition—at the Rockefeller University.

The two groups used completely different methods, and their approaches reflected the high sophistication that protein synthesis has reached since the 1950s when du Vigneaud received a Nobel Prize for hooking nine amino acids together in proper order.

The Merck group pursued ribonuclease by using more-or-less "classical" techniques—classical usually meaning anything that has worked at least once. Essentially, the protein is made from individually synthesized fragments that are hooked up to create the complete protein. The advantages of this fragment method are several: the chemist has greater control over each synthetic step, and he gets pieces of the protein in various sizes that he can purify and test for activity, modify, and so on. The disadvantages are also plentiful: every time one amino acid is hooked to another the product must be isolated, purified, and its structure confirmed before another amino acid is added. These necessary steps may run into the hundreds or even thousands before a protein emerges. And with each step—no matter how elegant the bench work—a little bit is lost; a 100-percent yield is always an idle dream in protein chemistry. The result is that the protein chemist is somewhat in the position of a balloonist high in the sky who is losing his gas and wondering if he can get to the ground before everything is gone. The protein chemist pursues a vanishing species.

The Merck group actually synthesized ribonuclease-S, the split version of the enzyme created by Richards of Yale several years earlier. They prepared nineteen fragments, varying in length from six to nine amino acids, and joined these together to create the S-protein, the larger portion of Richards's split enzyme. They mixed this with synthetic S-peptide, the tail of the ribonuclease molecule, already synthesized in 1966 by Dr. Klaus Hofmann of the University of Pittsburgh. The result was an active, synthetic enzyme. The effort was led by Dr. Robert G. Denkewalter, vice-president for exploratory research at Merck, and Dr. Ralph F. Hirschmann, director of peptide research.

The Merck group used several innovations in their classical synthesis that considerably simplified the built-in difficulties of joining amino acids. Amino acids have several reaction points. Just arbitrarily joining two amino acids will produce a variety of products only a part of which may be what is wanted. Therefore, all irrelevant reaction points must be blocked. And those left open—those that must join—must be activated with special chemicals that supply the energy they need to react. Once two amino acids are joined, the proper blocking group must be removed so that the next amino acid could be joined. This is not only very difficult chemistry but calls for careful planning and tactics to avoid running into a dead end. The Merck chemists simplified some of these problems by using phosgene ($COCl_2$), a World War I poison gas, that combines with amino acids. It simultaneously blocks one reactive center while activating the one that is to be joined. This ability of phosgene to react with body proteins is also the reason for its more lethal uses.

By carefully controlling conditions, the Merck chemists were able to turn out fragments at a relatively fast clip, with the actual joining taking about two minutes, and the necessary isolation and purification considerably longer. Other chemical innovations were created by the Merck chemists for their historic synthesis, especially to prevent sensitive amino acids, such as cysteine, from being changed as the ribonuclease chain was synthesized.

Across the Hudson, on the east side of Manhattan, chemists at Rockefeller University, led by Dr. R. Bruce Merrifield, were putting together ribonuclease in a totally different, almost radical fashion. Instead of making fragments and hooking them together, they were "growing" the enzyme from a single amino-acid bud, roughly imitating nature, and eliminating the problem of classical synthesis—isolation with each new step, purification, and so on.

In 1959, while his Rockefeller colleagues—Moore, Stein, etc.— were unraveling the structure of ribonuclease, Merrifield contemplated the hazards of making proteins and opted for another way. "You got a little discouraged even making small ones," he recalls, "so it seemed to me that to make large ones we needed a new approach to the problem so that one could accelerate the synthesis and simplify it, minimizing the number of operations involved in the laboratory." It would take until 1968.

Merrifield's idea was simple but elegant. He proposed to attach the first amino acid to an insoluble support of some sort, then attach the next amino acid, and so on, until he had the complete chain. The final step would be clipping the whole chain off the support. The basic advantage of this stepwise approach was that the growing amino-acid chain was never dissolved during the entire synthesis. Since it was attached to an insoluble support, it could be filtered, washed, and reacted with blocking groups, more amino acids, etc., without the need to isolate and purify the product after each new chemical manipulation.

Merrifield's idea was heretical, representing a departure from the mainstream of protein chemistry, and some generous doses of teutonic scorn were tossed at it.

His difficulties at first were enormous, and it took Merrifield three years to learn how to hook just two amino acids together with his "solid-phase peptide synthesis." The insoluble support from which the protein was grown had to be resistant to all the chemical reactions used to make a protein but still react with the initial amino-acid bud. Moreover, it had to give up the finished chain easily enough so that the finished product wasn't torn apart in the final parting. Merrifield finally settled on a special form of polystyrene—a common plastic used in commercial products—in the form of very small beads almost invisible to the naked eye. In proper solution these beads swelled to double their size, increasing their volume eight times, making it possible to grow as many as a trillion peptide chains on a single bead.

"It took a long time," he remembers. "I seemed to pick wrong conditions each time, and it was a trial-and-error process. Then, after the first successful synthesis, things went a little better and we could make improvements."

By 1964, Merrifield produced a natural peptide called bradykinin, made with nine amino acids. It does several things in the body: lowers blood pressure, increases capillary flow, and contracts smooth, involuntary muscles. The latter reaction was used to confirm that the synthetic product was indeed identical to natural bradykinin.

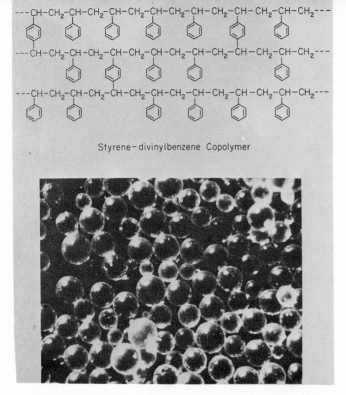

Styrene–divinylbenzene Copolymer

Polystyrene beads used as "anchors" for the solid-phase synthesis of proteins. *Courtesy: R. Bruce Merrifield, Rockefeller University*

The next year, Merrifield and a colleague, Dr. J. M. Stewart, were able to automate the whole procedure, a step he had in mind when he first conceived solid-phase synthesis. "That was the whole purpose of trying to develop this method, because if you can accelerate and simplify a method, then the way to carry that to its logical conclusion is to automate the process."

In automated peptide synthesis, amino acids, reagents, and washing solutions flow through a selector valve and out again. Twelve steps, in proper order, with proper amounts of reactants, are needed to attach a new amino acid to the growing chain. Control is through a series of switches operated in turn by pins stuck into a rotating drum. Comparison to a player piano or music box is inescapable; Merrifield calls the tune, and his protein machine plays it.

"What we have to do," he explains, "is to weigh out six different types of amino acids, dissolve them, and put them in little reservoirs. Once that's done, these six amino acids will be added one at a time to the peptide chain, all automatically."

It takes about twenty-four hours to add six amino acids. The protein machine, once "fed," starts growing peptides, without coffee breaks, dropping test tubes, or asking for a day off.

In 1967, Merrifield and a student, Dr. Arnold Marglin, using the automatic approach to protein synthesis, made the two chains of insulin, and then combined them to produce active insulin. Of course, insulin had already been made by classical methods, but now it had been made automatically, considerably faster, and—in terms of time and manpower—at considerably less cost. Some 5,000 individual steps were needed to make the two insulin chains. They were all performed in sequence automatically, under the direction of one man. Once the method was perfect, insulin could be made synthetically in a few days.

Now that Merrifield knew that his technique was mature enough to turn out respectable amino-acid chains, he prepared to crank one out four times larger than an insulin chain—ribonuclease. It took Dr. Bernd Gutte, a research associate from Germany working in Merrifield's laboratory, about a year to make synthetic ribonuclease, carrying on Rockefeller University's love affair with this particular protein. The final synthesis of ribonuclease involved 309 reactions divided into almost 12,000 operations, all done in a few weeks.

The Merck and Rockefeller groups revealed their success in the same issue of *The Journal of the American Chemical Society* and in a joint press conference early in 1969. That ribonuclease was made by two groups independently and at the same time twenty-nine years after it was first crystallized by Moses Kunitz tantalizes laymen. It's less surprising to scientists aware of the slow accumulation of necessary data and technique, information that is available to all takers. In science, as in politics, there are ideas whose time has come.

Both groups got only partially active products but enough specific ribonuclease activity to support their claims that they had indeed made an enzyme. The activity of ribonuclease is measured by its ability to split RNA specifically but not DNA,

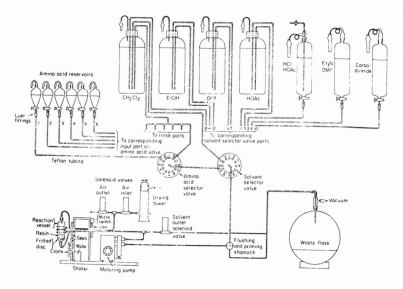

Diagram of solid-phase-synthesis apparatus. From "The Automatic Synthesis of Proteins" by R. Bruce Merrifield. Copyright © 1968 by Scientific American, Inc. All rights reserved

Professor R. Bruce Merrifield at the control panel of the solid-phase synthesizer. *Courtesy: The Rockefeller University*

closely related. Merrifield's synthesis was particularly criticized. A hazard in his technique is that if a reaction where an amino acid is added doesn't go to 100 percent completion—that is, if nearly all the trillion or so amino-acid chains on a bead don't completely react—then he is left with a mixture of products, some of which may be what he wants and others only remnants, missing one or more amino acids. Even in 1970 critics were pointing out this "failure sequence" problem with solid-phase peptide synthesis. All this nettles Merrifield a bit since he acknowledged the problem in the paper he published on his solid-phase method in 1963. "Sure we know about the problem, and we're doing all we can to avoid it."

Synthesis of an enzyme or any large protein is essentially a molecular game of blindman's bluff, with results uncertain until the final product is made and its activity synthesized. As Drs. Denkewalter and Hirschmann of Merck have noted, a chemist has no way of telling how this synthesis is going until he gets a biologically active material.

Today, both groups have their critics, people who doubt that they have in fact made the complete ribonuclease chain.

Merrifield throws his hands up at this. "There are some people who'd say that even if it were crystalline, even if you had X-ray data on it, it wouldn't prove it. We take the view that you get as close as you can."

Neither ribonuclease team is ready to be very positive on the applications of its work. Both are still busy trying to crystallize their product to get a purer specimen. Both talk in terms of altering the enzyme, perhaps training it to work on molecules other than RNA. Merck, in addition to further purifying the enzyme, is actively trying to learn more about what makes ribonuclease an enzyme, in the hope of, perhaps, making a shorter, more easily manufactured version that duplicates ribonuclease activity if not structure.

As Merrifield put it as the press conference: "We may someday be able to make an enzyme that's simpler than the naturally occurring ones. Perhaps you can retain part of the molecule—the active center, the binding site—making the other parts dispensable."

Denkewalter of Merck also pointed out that "at this moment, we don't want to play the kind of game of saying how many enzymes we can make. But we do want to understand in depth how any enzyme works, and we will probably concentrate on ribonuclease to become familiar with it."

More is known in toto about ribonuclease than any other enzyme, with chymotrypsin, a digestive enzyme, a close second. A host of other enzymes and proteins have been and are being deciphered. The effort is intense. Some forty to fifty laboratories have been involved in the pursuit of ribonuclease, and a recent review listed five hundred references to reports on ribonuclease research.

Other enzymes will surely be made, patience and government largesse willing. And the techniques for "cracking" enzymes will become more genteel, sophisticated, and considerably less brutal than they were in the past two decades. The "sense of blood, sweat, and broken research students," to quote *Nature*, "is replaced by one of sureness of aim and mastery of technique." Efforts that will expand the gallery of protein portraits considerably are underway in many places—Bethesda, Maryland; the two Cambridges; Pasadena, California; Lafayette, Indiana; and West Germany.

And, inevitably, as the workings of enzymes—their mechanisms —come out of the shadows, chemists can begin to mimic them, by-passing, in part, the laborious step-by-step linking of amino acids. It may be possible to substitute other molecules—and several groups are already trying—that imitate the shape and charge distribution of an active site. It may be possible, for example, to use the same chemicals that go into plastics to imitate enzyme action. Then, the chemist achieves his ultimate goal—synthesizing *function* rather than structure.

Of course, to put all this in perspective, no one yet fully understands what makes an enzyme, what enables it to speed reactions a billion times faster than chemists can. One clue emerged in mid-1970. Dr. Daniel E. Koshland, Jr., of the University of California at Berkeley proposed that enzymes may achieve their great catalytic powers because they can "steer" reacting molecules and atoms together, giving them an optimum chance to react. More precisely, Koshland proposed, and supported with experiments, that enzymes may be able to align the electrons orbiting about reacting atoms. Chemical reactions are essentially a give and take of electrons, and anything that simplifies that process presumably hastens a reaction. Koshland devised "holders" for two reacting molecules that enabled them to react a million times faster than they would normally. With very slight adjustments in the holding angles, the speed-up disappeared. In effect, the holders acted as enzymes. Although Koshland is careful to rule out universal application of his "holder" hypothesis, it does represent a pioneering insight. Typically, opponents of Koshland's idea appeared in print in 1971 with counterexperiments. But Koshland is too good an enzyme chemist to be radically off base, and it may be that he has hit on a part of the truth but that modifications will have to be made in his hypothesis.

The work on enzymes has reached a high plateau, one that would astound and please "old man Fischer." Yet, we should remember where we are. It took the chemists at Merck and Rockefeller over a year to make ribonuclease. A living cell does it in minutes.

8

NITROGEN FIXATION:
MORE PROTEINS
FROM AN OLD PUZZLE

Nitrogen is a paradox. It makes up most of our air, and we use a considerable amount of energy breathing it in along with very necessary oxygen. But we breathe it right out again, leaving us no better off.

Nitrogen is an inert material—a colorless and odorless gas—that dilutes oxygen sufficiently so that we don't risk everything whenever we strike a match. Yet, that same nitrogen that we have little direct use for finds its way into proteins, including all enzymes; the nucleic acids, DNA and RNA; membranes that contain living cells; protoplasm within these cells; and so on.

In short, nitrogen is a foundation for the kind of life we know.

That this is so, that a seemingly inert substance in the air is indispensable to life, is due to a scattered assortment of microbes and primitive plants that have little in common but their ability to transform the nitrogen of air into a form that can be used by plants and, in turn, by animals. These are the nitrogen fixers.

Until the sixties, if you asked the experts for the molecular details of how nitrogen fixers operate, you'd have gotten a great deal of verbal arm waving and, in time, an embarrassed confession of ignorance. Adding to the chagrin were the brute-force methods used in technological man's imitation of the nitrogen-fixing powers of nature: in the manufacture of ammonia via the industrial Haber process, which uses temperatures and pressures so exorbitant that German workers who first confronted the process walked off their jobs. When the German workers rebelled, engineers came in and reset the dials so they would register at lower readings; of course, temperatures and pressures remained as high as ever. In essence, the Haber process forces the merger of hydrogen and nitrogen to make ammonia by using iron catalysts in combination with temperatures up to 900°F. and pressures of two hundred to three hundred times normal.

In contrast to these brute-force methods, nitrogen fixers add usable nitrogen to the soil at everyday temperatures and pressures, although they require an unusually large amount of energy to do it. Now, because of a swelling interest in the science of nitrogen fixation, we know a good deal more than we did ten years ago about how the "bugs" do it, although not enough to exactly imitate them.

In typical (and healthy) fashion, the work has split off in several directions. Strenuous efforts are underway to learn the structure of the enzyme used by nature's nitrogen fixers. In part because the enzyme is a complicated beast to decipher, several chemists are creating simpler molecules that to a degree imitate the enzyme's effects. And groups in several countries, ignoring biological constraints, are simply trying to find better and milder ways than the Haber process to induce nitrogen into reacting. The Haber process, in spite of its considerable industrial clout and the cheapness of the ammonia produced, remains an affront to scientists accustomed to more elegant chemistry.

A participant in this boomlet in nitrogen-fixation research writes that "practical advances in biological nitrogen fixation have not yet been made." Nevertheless it is not premature to suggest rewards. Nitrogen fixation, as already stated, makes nitrogen of the air available to life on earth. Without that nitrogen, plants could not grow or exist, and neither could we. The fertility of grassland, forest, and farmlands directly depends on nitrogen available to it. The nutritive value of crops depends on their protein content, and that depends on their nitrogen content, which comes either from natural nitrogen fixation—meaning the bugs—or from fertilizer. The research now underway will bring understanding and through it may come methods of raising the intensity and ubiquity of natural fixation, perhaps inducing nitrogen fixing in nonfixer plants, such as corn and wheat.

The essential act of nitrogen fixation is the stunningly straightforward reaction (on paper!) in which nitrogen and hydrogen gas combine to form ammonia:

$$N_2 + 3H_2 \rightarrow 2NH_3$$
$$\text{Nitrogen} + \text{hydrogen} \rightarrow \text{ammonia}$$

In this straightforward chemical equation lies the nature of our world. As one expert writing in *Scientific American* put it, the supply of food "is limited more by the availability of fixed nitrogen than by any other plant nutrient."

Ammonia is a reactive substance, which is why it has such a pungent odor. Ammonia, or materials derived from it, such as nitrates, are soluble in water and seep into the root hairs of plants. Inside, these materials combine with various other compounds to form amino acids, which then join together to form peptides and proteins. Eventually, the cycle is closed as other microbes—denitrifying bacteria—restore nitrogen to air. Nature, unlike man, is frugal with her wastes and carefully harbors the remains of our decaying bodies and plants.

Most reactions in this nitrogen cycle, while not fully studied, are within chemical reason. It is the creation of ammonia, the initial step in the cycle, that is mystifying.

Nitrogen gas, which constitutes about 80 percent of the air we breathe, is actually composed of nitrogen molecules, or two atoms of nitrogen linked together:

$$N + N \text{ becomes } N_2$$

This combination of two nitrogen atoms is formidable and resists strenuous efforts by chemists or anyone else to pry them apart, although nitrogen fixers seem to have no trouble at all when they set out to make ammonia. The reason is that two nitrogen atoms together form a "comfortable" arrangement of electrons, and electrons form chemical bonds. Specifically, the two atoms merge to form a triple chemical bond, or three pairs of electrons, between them, an arrangement that is extremely close-knit. Each dot in the following diagram is an electron.

$$\cdot \ddot{N} \cdot + \cdot \ddot{N} \cdot \longrightarrow \; :N: \; :N: \; \text{ or } \; N \equiv N$$

The natural nitrogen fixers are a random lot, including blue-green algae, microscopic plants that maintain the fertility of rice paddies as well as of Antarctic regions. They even grow on tiled rooftops. When the explosion of Krakatoa in the summer of 1883 sterilized the island, the first signs of life to reappear were blue-green algae. More diverse are the nitrogen-fixing microbes. There are two kinds: those that fix nitrogen without any direct help, and those that must do it in combination with plants. The former are the free-living bacteria that have the enzyme systems needed to fix nitrogen and pick up nutrients they need—metals such as molybdenum, carbohydrates, etc.—from surrounding soil. The microbe and plant combinations are examples of a symbiotic relationship, and the microbes that fix nitrogen this way are called symbionts, with the major group called *rhizobia*. The relationship is beneficial to each member; the plant gets usable nitrogen, while the microbe obtains the nutrients it needs from its host plants. Symbionts usually infect root hairs,

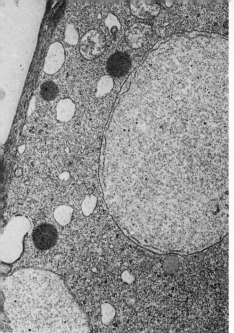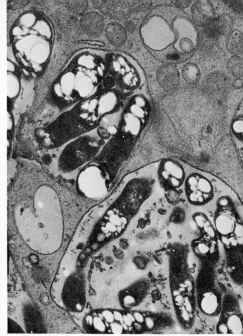

(*Left*) Uninfected root cell of soybean. (*Right*) Root cell of soybean infected by *rhizobia,* a nitrogen-fixing symbiont. Both photographs taken with an electron microscope. *Courtesy: R. W. F. Hardy, E. I. du Pont de Nemours & Company*

forming tiny nodules, or swellings, on the roots of plants such as the legumes—alfalfa, peas, beans, etc.

The common link of this microbiological zoo is an enzyme, nitrogenase, that gives nitrogen fixers their unique ability to induce chemical changes in the nitrogen of our air. Nitrogenase's existence was long assumed; it was named in 1934. Not a good deal is known about it, and efforts are now underway to learn its molecular structure in the fashion that the structure of ribonuclease was pieced out.

The essential act of nitrogen fixation is to induce a nitrogen molecule to accept electrons, or, to put it chemically, reduce nitrogen. How it's done remains a mystery. Nitrogenase, in some still uncertain way, does the persuading, or activating, of the nitrogen molecule, while electrons are transported to the appropriate site by a chain of molecules intricate in its constitution but simple in its purpose. Among the agents involved are ferrodoxin and flavodoxin, proteins that are able to take up and release electrons. In practice, the nitrogen molecule is apparently split by nitrogenase into its two constituent atoms before electrons are delivered. Once electrons are delivered, hydrogen is simply added naturally—most easily from water—and ammonia appears.

Nitrogenase was exposed to public view in 1960 through a landmark achievement by four Du Pont Company scientists—Dr. James E. Carnahan, Dr. Leonard E. Mortenson. Dr. Howard F. Mower, and Dr. John E. Castle. What they did, and what many before had tried to do, was to split open a nitrogen fixer, take out its nitrogenase, and, by feeding it appropriate nutrients, have the isolated enzyme fix nitrogen. It was like making a stew without the pot.

This ability to fix nitrogen in a cell-free system—i.e., without the need or the presence of an intact microbe—not only meant that nitrogenase could be isolated, but more importantly that its nitrogen-fixing ability could now be watched under all sorts of conditions.

Until then, scientists in the field had a "black box problem." They could grow nitrogen fixers under different conditions, observe the product, and from that make some guesses at what was happening in between. The work had gleaned some useful information. For instance, nitrogen fixers absolutely need the element molybdenum, which explains why legumes grown on Australian fields did poorly; the soil was poor in molydenum. Nevertheless, the inability to peer inside an operating nitrogen fixer blocked any substantial work. The Du Pont work opened the door, or floodgates to be more precise, as other laboratories not only confirmed the results of Carnahan and company, but also prepared cell-free systems of a wide spectrum of nitrogen fixers, both free livers and symbionts.

There were several reasons why Carnahan and his colleagues succeeded where others failed. For one, they carefully kept oxygen away from their system; nitrogenase is essentially poisoned by oxygen and must be shielded from it. In some cases, where the presence of oxygen is unavoidable, the fixer will speed up its metabolism, which means that more oxygen is "burned" and less is available to interfere with fixation.

But the most important reason that the Du Pont people succeeded is that they hit upon the same source of electrons that natural fixers use—a simple carbohydrate called pyruvate, a metabolic product of sugars, amino acids, and other materials found in living cells. As pyruvate is transformed, or oxidized, by other chemical changes, it gives up electrons that are caught up by the electron-transferring agents mentioned before, such as ferrodoxin, a brown iron-containing protein.

Pyruvate has a secondary role. It charges the "power package" that supplies the energy needed for the few but crucial events in nitrogen fixation. The power package is called adenosine triphosphate, or ATP, a material that stores and then releases the energy derived from the foods we eat and needed to drive the diverse chemical processes necessary for life. ATP is often referred to as the "energy currency" of the living cell.

Thus, pyruvate is the key: it supplies electrons to nitrogen atoms and produces ATP, which powers the nitrogen-fixing process. This helps explain the value to soil fertility of straw, compost, dung, or root stubble. These are carbohydrate materials and may be progenitors of pyruvate.

Nitrogenase itself is starting to come into coarse focus. It is a complex entity, not only larger than most enzymes but also more diverse in its talents. This nitrogen-fixing enzyme is really more of a molecular *system* since it is composed of two quite different proteins, which are probably linked when at work, although exactly how is unknown.

Both protein portions harbor metals. The smaller contains iron (Fe-protein), while the larger contains molybdenum and iron (Mo-Fe protein). The best guess at the moment is that the working nitrogenase system is composed of two Fe-proteins and one Mo-Fe protein.

The two portions are sizable, their reported molecular weights varying with the source of the nitrogenase and the researcher. The smaller protein has a molecular weight around 55,000. The larger fraction has been assigned a molecular weight of 270,000. Ribonuclease, in comparison, has a molecular weight of 14,000.

Richard D. Holsten (*left*) and Ralph W. F. Hardy of Du Pont at "klinostat," used for laboratory studies of nitrogen fixation by soybeans and other plants. *Courtesy: The Du Pont Company (Photo by Alex Henderson)*

Both proteins have been extensively purified, largely through the efforts of two groups, one at Purdue University led by Dr. Leonard E. Mortenson and the other at Du Pont led by Dr. R. W. F. Hardy. Mortenson and his people have even begun the very formidable job of trying to learn the amino-acid sequences of both proteins. X-ray crystallography, to learn the three-dimensional shapes of the proteins and eventually the entire nitrogenase assemblage, is further away, hampered to date by the lack of crystals large and stable enough for X-ray work. However, an X-ray study is underway through a cooperative effort between researchers at Du Pont and the University of California at Los Angeles.

What each protein portion does, whether they act in concert or sequentially in a one-two processing of electrons and nitrogen atoms, is uncertain. However, both parts are vital to fixation. If split in two, there is no reaction; if reunited by simple mixing, fixing begins again and ammonia is produced.

Nitrogenase intrigues chemists not only because it does something easily that they find very difficult, but also because of its remarkable versatility. Hardy calls it a "superchemical catalyst." Most enzymes are quite exacting about what materials they act on. Ribonuclease works on RNA but not on DNA, which is chemically similar; deoxyribonuclease is needed for that.

In contrast, nitrogenase can add electrons to an impressive list of materials aside from nitrogen, including azides, cyanides, acetylene, and many others. The denominator here is the identical arrangement of electrons that these substances have. Put another way, they have the same kind of triple chemical bonds that knit nitrogen atoms together to form nitrogen gas.

This fortuitous versatility of nitrogenase is at the heart of the second most important thing that's happened in the field: detection and measurement of nitrogen fixation without nitrogen.

Microbes that fix nitrogen are singularly slow about it, as well as being inefficient in how they use nutrients provided them by surrounding soil and plants. Their slowness and low rate of fixation has made it very difficult to follow the course of fixation in the laboratory and, more critically, in the open field. An added complication is the ubiquity of nitrogen, as ammonia or in other forms, in living systems, which makes it difficult to decide what fraction of ammonia measured actually represents fixed nitrogen. Put another way, fixed nitrogen can simply get lost in proteins, nucleic acids, and other biological materials that contain nitrogen. What was needed was a quick, simple, and cheap way to evaluate nitrogen fixation by different fixers under different conditions. The acetylene test—devised and developed in the late sixties—accomplished that. In brief, a nitrogen-fixer fed acetylene will reduce it to ethylene, paralleling (and apparently using the same method) the reduction of nitrogen to ammonia—

$$H{-}C \equiv C{-}H \ + \quad H_2 \quad \longrightarrow \quad H{-}\overset{\displaystyle H}{\underset{\displaystyle |}{C}} = \overset{\displaystyle H}{\underset{\displaystyle |}{C}}{-}H$$

acetylene   +   hydrogen $\longrightarrow$ ethylene

Acetylene is the same gas used in acetylene torches, while

ethylene is a simple, flammable gas obtained from petroleum and natural gas and the same material used to create the plastic polyethylene commonly used in packaging. More to the point, mixed acetylene and ethylene are fairly easily separated by a gas chromatograph, a fairly standard instrument able to separate tiny quantities of similar gases. There is no comparable method for measuring small levels of ammonia, unfortunately.

The sensitivity of the acetylene-ethylene assay is remarkable. Hardy points out that, in principle, the assay can pick up ethylene produced by one cell of a nitrogen fixer within a few hours after it has been fed acetylene. That constitutes almost instant deliverance for researchers who spent decades struggling with clumsy, less-precise tests. "The acetylene-to-ethylene method," Hardy says, "is 10,000 times more sensitive than anything else available."

The people associated with the discovery of the reduction of acetylene to ethylene by nitrogen fixers are an Australian, Dr. Michael J. Dilworth, and a German, Dr. Robert Schöllhorn, the latter in 1966 when in the laboratory of Professor R. H. Burris at the University of Wisconsin. Hardy and his group at Du Pont were the major force in developing the assay for actual use.

The test has had a profound effect. Among other things, it has enabled the identification of unsuspected nitrogen fixers (some two hundred nonleguminous plants identified as nitrogen fixers, some of which were unknown). It has also helped eliminate imposters such as yeast, which some researchers thought was a fixer but which actually scavenges its nitrogen compounds from soil and plants.

Also, the acetylene test may be used to survey the nitrogen-fixing potential of the world's agricultural lands and crops. Hardy writes that "this assay is as crucial for the optimization of biological nitrogen fixation as soil analyses were fundamental to the development of agricultural fertilizer use." The assay is being used all over the world and is providing a direct reading of how well nitrogen fixers—blue-green algae as well as the free livers and the symbionts—do under varying conditions: changes in rates of nitrogen fixation through a season of growth; effects of different nutrients, including massive application of carbohydrates; how long after "infection" by a nitrogen fixer before ammonia appears; and so on. Looked at randomly, the data seem scattered. Assembled, they add up to a powerful insight into a process that is at the heart of our food supply. The acetylene assay represents a rather simple bit of chemistry that has become an exacting probe into the still poorly understood process of nitrogen fixation.

The test itself is simple to do. Over 30,000 assays have been done in the field and, in theory, the figure can be increased by 800 each day by a crew of four people. Mobile labs are now used. A sample of roots or soil-harboring nitrogen fixers are placed in a glass tube, which is then sealed. After about an hour, a bit of the gas in the tube is fed to a gas chromatograph, which reads off the relative amounts of acetylene and ethylene. From that data, the nitrogen-fixation rate of the fixers in the sample can be calculated.

Aside from helping agricultural experts assess the fertility of soils, the acetylene test also constitutes a "microscope" for following the workings of nitrogenase by enabling researchers to evaluate the effects on nitrogen fixation when they "diddle" with the enzyme. The quicker pace of the data now coming out about nitrogenase can be attributed in good measure to the acetylene assay.

However, no one knows how nitrogenase works, although most people in the field will not shy at taking guesses, sometimes backed by data. To go back to the metals—molybdenum and iron—contained within the two protein portions of nitrogenase, they are considered to have an important role. But the exact role remains a puzzle. "In spite of immense advances in technique," writes Professor John Postgate in *Nature*, "no direct evidence that a metal complex has been formed during biological nitrogen fixation has been published." This means that no one is yet certain exactly what happens when nitrogen encounters nitrogenase.

Postgate is assistant director of a unit on nitrogen fixation at the University of Sussex, England, where some valiant efforts have been made to probe the key reactions in fixation, particularly by the head of the unit, Professor Joseph Chatt.

Chatt and others have made a start in understanding the role of metals in nitrogen fixation by creating a variety of "complexes," where a nitrogen molecule chemically reacts with a metal, which in turn is part of a larger molecule, such as one of the two proteins in nitrogenase. It is a *complex*—a basic concept in chemistry—because the bonds holding nitrogen to the metal are not always straightforward chemical bonds but weaker bonds that can be fairly easily broken. With such a creation, a nitrogen molecule can be complexed to a metal and then recovered unchanged without too much chemical effort.

Nitrogen has been combined with a host of metals including ruthenium, vanadium, cobalt, titanium, and molybdenum—a fact known for decades. Two Canadians at the University of Toronto, Dr. A. D. Allen and Dr. C. V. Senoff, were the first to show that a supposedly inert nitrogen molecule would react with a metal to produce a combination that could be isolated for study.

This type of work has been intensively exploited and has led to a plethora of ideas about what iron and molybdenum are doing in nitrogenase. It is strongly suspected, but not certain, that iron may hold a nitrogen molecule in place and assist in the final stages of transferring the electrons needed to make ammonia. The role of molybdenum is more clouded, although work with various complexes of molybdenum with nitrogen— notably by Chatt's group at the University of Sussex—seems to indicate that the metal may help weaken the chemical bonds binding nitrogen atoms together, perhaps by pulling away the electrons binding nitrogen atoms together. This would help split the two atoms, the key step to making ammonia.

Various groups have attempted to create so-called model systems, simple atomic combinations that mimic some of the effects of nitrogenase without in any way coming close to its large complicated structure. Models are common research strate- gies—sometimes questionable—that abandon the complex realities in the hope that simplicity will produce a valuable insight.

Dr. Gerhard N. Schrauzer, at the University of California at San Diego, and his students have put together what they regard as a chemical model, or imitation, of nitrogenase. And like that enzyme, it can reduce acetylene to ethylene, and Schrauzer says it can also reduce nitrogen to ammonia, albeit to a much weaker extent. Others in nitrogen-fixing research are doubtful about the latter. His system is essentially a watery mixture of chemicals that contains molybdenum and sulfur, as well as traces of iron. Various "reducing agents" are added to provide electrons. With high pressures and an acetylene atmosphere, ethylene is slowly produced. An encouraging sign that Schrauzer is on the right track is his report in 1971 that the system seems to be stimulated by ATP, the same material that provides the energy for natural nitrogen fixation.

This model work by Schrauzer and others, such as Chatt's and Hardy's groups, including Dr. G. W. Parshall, may say something about how nitrogenase evolved from a quite simple molecule to the complex protein it now is. It may also say something about how complicated an enzyme has to be to behave like an enzyme. "What is the simplest possible enzyme?" Schrauzer asks. "When does a system start behaving like an enzyme?"

If a simple system such as Schrauzer's can produce ammonia, are there commercial possibilities? Not yet, says Schrauzer. "If we had to make ammonia with our system, it would probably cost $20,000 per pound."

But commercial possibilities may be at the end of the road for a process now being worked on by Dr. Eugene van Tamelen and his colleagues at Stanford University. What van Tamelen is after is a gentle way of not only reducing nitrogen in the air to ammonia, but of inserting it directly into molecules that contain carbon, i.e., organic compounds—bypass the middleman, so to speak, and go right on to the end product such as amino acids needed to feed the world as well as to amines, nitriles, cyanides, and other nitrogen-containing organics that will meet the demands of the chemical industry for raw materials with which to make plastics, textiles, etc. Van Tamelen reported recently that he and his colleagues successfully added nitrogen to various organic materials to produce amines and nitriles. His Russian competitors also report making amines in a similar fashion. The ultimate dream is a factory where nitrogen goes in one end and amino acids come out the other.

The approach represents a flanking attack on the Haber process. "In battling the Haber process," van Tamelen says, "we would want to meet the monster on our grounds," that is, put nitrogen directly into organic compounds, something the process can't do. The odds are considerable. The Haber process is famous and well entrenched. The capital investment as well as its relative cheapness (as long as hydrogen, a raw material, stays cheap) makes the process a formidable foe for someone with an alternative idea.

(The Haber process was not only a remarkable technical achievement for German chemistry—it marked the first time that nitrogen in the air was commercially available to man—but also kept the German war machine going. Most of the Germans' supply of usable nitrogen for making explosives came from nitrate deposits in the desert of northern Chile, and World War I cut that off. If the Haber process hadn't come along, Germany would have run out of ammunition in 1916. Ironically, Haber, a Jew, was driven into exile by Hitler.)

Van Tamelen and his colleagues at Stanford are working principally with chemicals that contain titanium, with which nitrogen molecules should form a complex that enables nitrogen to accept electrons from a forceful and insistent electron supplier, a powerful reducing agent. With that step taken, it is only a matter of adding hydrogen to produce ammonia. In the Soviet Union, a comparable effort has been led by Drs. M. E. Vol'pin and V. B. Shur of the Institutes of Organoelement Compounds, a part of the U.S.S.R. Academy of Sciences in Moscow. The Russians began reporting on their work in the Western literature about 1964.

Van Tamelen, who calls himself a nitrogen fixer, has reported the production of ammonia using ordinary air, about 78 percent nitrogen, rather than pure nitrogen.

"And this is absolutely astonishing because it means that normally inert molecular nitrogen is competing rather well with normally reactive oxygen," he says. Ordinarily, oxygen would be the first ingredient in air to react (iron rusting is a reaction with atmospheric oxygen), with nitrogen remaining stubbornly unreactive. While this feat astonishes a chemist such as van

Tamelen, it is humbling to remember that nitrogen fixers in soil easily pluck nitrogen out of the air and convert it to ammonia.

Applications of the current work on the chemistry and biology of nitrogen fixation are still more speculation than fact. Chatt, in charge of the Agricultural Research Council's (ARC) Unit of Nitrogen Fixation at the University of Sussex ("thirty-five people if you include the washers-up"), says in regard to the various reported systems for fixing nitrogen in the presence of water: "I won't be convinced until someone does it with ^{15}N." ^{15}N is a heavy isotope of more common nitrogen (^{14}N), which, because it is heavier, can be followed as it makes its way through a nitrogen-fixing system, natural or man-made. ^{15}N was used until the acetylene-to-ethylene assay came along to establish the occurrence and rate of nitrogen fixation. The reason Chatt is insisting that man-made nitrogen-fixing systems be tested with a nitrogen isotope, ^{15}N, that can be tracked is that the amounts of ammonia reported by the various groups so far are so small that contamination from air, reagents, and glassware cannot be ruled out.

In spite of these caveats, possible applications of successful work on nitrogen fixation are being bandied about. Taking a near-term view, what we learn may teach us how to help nitrogen fixers to do a better job; in short, we may be able to "domesticate" them. Further out is the suggestion that ubiquitous crops such as corn and wheat, which do not fix nitrogen, can be taught how. "Perhaps we can breed bacteria to live in the roots of these plants," Chatt says.

Hardy has his practical eye especially fixed on increasing the fixing powers of symbionts, particularly legumes such as soybean, the third largest crop now grown in the United States. Even a fractional boost in the nitrogen fixed by soybeans could mean more proteins added to the world's inadequate supplies, that is, more nutritious foods. Of course, it also means a considerable economic boost for the company that first finds out how to do it.

We're still a long way off. For instance, we don't even know the details of the intimate symbiotic relationship between plant and nitrogen fixer. A major research problem is to have a symbiotic nitrogen fixer make ammonia away from the plant. So far, no one's done it, although many have tried. Hardy has reported a significant step in that direction. Dr. R. D. Holsten and he have been able to cultivate a mixture of plant cells and microbes that fixes nitrogen. That at least gets researchers away from dependence on an intact plant and closer to a system they can watch directly, somewhat like the cell-free system devised in 1960 by Carnahan and his colleagues for the free-living microbes, which fix nitrogen without a host plant.

Aside from a promise of more fertile soil and more proteins, more elegant methods of plucking nitrogen out of the air may help reduce our dependence on fertilizers. This is no small matter. Fertilizers are costly, especially when they have to be shipped to places where local fertilizer plants have not been built. Generally that means underdeveloped countries, starved for both money and food. One sixth of the world already depends on fertilizers to make up for deficits in numbers or efficiency of nitrogen-fixing microbes, and use of fertilizer not only turns off nitrogen fixers (why should they make ammonia if it's given them in one form or another?) but soaks up other soil nutrients such as sulfur, cobalt, and copper. Replacing such nutrients is not easy and probably impossible in some areas, particularly in the tropics, which have sunshine, moisture, and land but little agriculture.

The United States and other industrialized countries are not terribly concerned now about artificially feeding their soil because they have the energy sources needed to stoke fertilizer plants. "But comes the revolution," says Leonard Mortenson at Purdue, "when the fuel situation gets to a point where we are hurting, then it might be worthwhile to have something to fall back on." That is, a way of prodding fixers, natural or man-made, to greater efforts.

On a slightly more prosaic level, the chemical industry is keeping an eye on the work of Mortenson and others on nitrogenase in the hope that they may learn something of how to make more effective catalysts. The profits and losses of chemical companies can rise and fall with the catalysts they use to control the speeds and products of chemical processes.

"If they can find out how the biological system works," says Mortenson, "they can probably mimic this in their own catalysis."

In truth, the work on nitrogen fixation is only beginning, although, as Hardy says, we now know more about nitrogen fixation than we do about photosynthesis, by which plants use sunlight to make carbohydrates.

Surprises will come. For instance, Australian scientists have suggested (and provided some evidence to back them up) that human beings can fix nitrogen, or rather that microbes living in their guts can do it for them. The discovery was prompted by a two-part puzzle: (1) certain New Guinea natives that live on a nitrogen-poor diet made up largely of sweet potatoes are really quite healthy and (2) seem, in an admittedly rough measure, to put out more nitrogen than they take in.

The puzzle was taken up by Drs. F. J. Bergersen and E. H. Hipsley, two nitrogen-fixation specialists working at Australia's Commonwealth Scientific and Industrial Research Organization (CSIRO). They found, using the acetylene assay, that intestines of these natives harbor nitrogen-fixing bacteria, which could explain the natives' healthy state in spite of a diet that is a dietician's nightmare.

But puzzles still abound. Nearby natives whose diet is just as bad but who do not eat sweet potatoes do suffer from poor nutrition. Perhaps, the Australians say, there is something "magical" about sweet potatoes.

Looked at coldly, it's not surprising to turn up fixers in human guts, where there is the kind of airless environment that those microbes thrive in. Fixers have already been reported in cows and other animals, including (unfounded, of course) whales.

Nevertheless, the Australian report is the first that says friendly bacteria within man can supply nitrogen—up to a point —when his diet lacks it.

The possibilities are worth thinking about.

9

INSECTS:

A MOLECULAR LIFE

—Nurtured in the apple orchards of upper New York State, the red-banded leaf roller's love life offers not only new clues to how we smell but how we can use sex in our struggle with the insects.

—Scientists watch winged, stingless bees raid a Brazilian hive, its occupants deranged by a chemical barrage.

—Guarded out front by cast-iron charging rhinoceroses, a Harvard biologist probes a bizarre life style for an understanding of human hormones.

—In European, American, and Japanese laboratories first-rate researchers are quietly, intensively, seeking ingredients for a new insect war.

These "coming attractions" are symptoms of a science deep in ferment, created by (1) the practical need for insecticides that are neutral to innocent creatures, and (2) the realization that insects may tell us a great deal about our world and ourselves, including communication, evolution, the wherefore of hormones, drugs, and smell.

Insect chemistry is an all-encompassing phrase that can be split into several branches, two of which—pheromones and hormones—are germane to the current excitement. Pheromones are chemical signals transmitted among members of an insect species. They help them find mates, raise alarms, signal an attack, or mark the way to food.

Hormones are cousins to pheromones, providing communication between cells as do pheromones between organisms. An insect's dependence on hormones may seem surprising. Yet hormones of insects govern an incredible life style—a metamorphosis that enables an insect to survive the seasons, living long enough to find a mate and renew the cycle. For example, a moth within a year passes through a succession of guises—an egg, a voracious caterpillar, and a pupae, or winter form, protected by a cocoon of spun silk, finally becoming an adult, a moth—a reproductive machine that never eats and lives only long enough to mate and continue the cycle. Within the past decade—and increasingly within the last few years—work on hormones governing metamorphosis has crystallized into a totally new approach to insect control, one that is harmless to other animals, even harmless to the "good" insects, including a product that disappears after it has done its work; in short, a truly scientific alternative to DDT and its counterparts.

Odd realizations have dropped out of the recent work on insect chemistry. For instance, inadvertently we've probably adopted some of the chemical signals by which insects communicate with each other: Shaving creams, body deodorants, facial lotions, etc., may contain some of the chemical that insects depend on for their organized life. "The very sweet odors of lemon and lime," says an entomologist, "are primary, important, and critical trigger compounds employed by many species of bees."

Whether cosmetics may disturb the chemical harmony of bees probably means little to the apple growers of upper New York State. What may mean something to them is that the material male and female red-banded leaf rollers find each other by has been identified, as have the attractants of the oblique-banded leaf roller, codling moth, and oriental fruit moth. All are orchard pests, chomping their way through groves of apple, peach, and other fruit trees.

The red-banded leaf roller is found mostly in the eastern part of the United States, thriving in part because DDT campaigns against the codling moth have also killed off many of the leaf roller's natural enemies. The leaf roller does its damage when it is in the caterpillar, or larval, stage; there are two larval generations each year, with the second generation doing the apple chomping. In June or July the moth, or adult, form of the red-banded leaf roller emerges, with its only purpose now being to find a mate. The female roller's chief tool in that mission is a chemical scent—a sex attractant—it sends out to draw a male. In 1968, that sex attractant was isolated, identified, and synthesized by a team of scientists at Cornell University,

Red-banded leaf roller moth. *Courtesy: Wendell Roelofs, Cornell University*

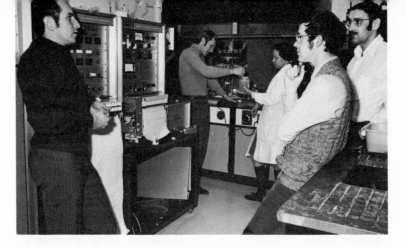

"Attractant" chemists at Cornell University. *Left to right:* Dr. James Tette, Dr. Wendell Roelofs, Dr. Ada Hill, Dr. André Comeau, and Dr. Heinrich Arn. *Courtesy: Wendell Roelofs, Cornell University*

led by Dr. Wendell Roelofs, a young and modish organic chemist. Roelofs and his colleagues work at the New York State Agricultural Experiment Station, a unit of Cornell University located in Geneva, New York.

"Isolated, identified, and synthesized" glosses over a great deal of hard work and considerable original thinking. The moths were raised on a mixture of apple cider and alfalfa concocted at Cornell, and females then separated from males by their different genitalia. The sex attractant is located in the tip of the female abdomen, and the tips of some 40,000 females were clipped, mashed, and extracted with various liquids such as ether. They were then put through other operations designed to provide progressively purer amounts of the leaf-roller sex attractant. Roelofs and his colleagues introduced an olfactometer—ten live male moths that responded to a whiff of the attractant by fluttering their wings, trying to crawl up the sides of their cages, and flying toward the source of the scent. "So the males are the instruments used to tell us where the active compound is," Roelofs explains.

The final and critical purifications were done by various forms of chromatography, a technique for separating closely related chemicals by their differential flows through materials such as paper, a host of resins, and even fine earths. Once a pure material was in hand—confirmed by male moths fluttering appropriately—Roelofs and his colleague, Dr. Heinrich Arn, identified the attractant's structure. That effort took two directions: (1) measurements with various instruments, such as an infrared spectrophotometer that could provide information comparable with criteria taken from molecules whose structure was already known, and (2) functional group analysis, that is, a search for specific chemical features of the molecule. For instance, the researchers suspected that the attractant of the red-banded leaf roller would contain at least one double bond between two carbon atoms (a carbon atom may be joined to other atoms by one [C-X], two [C : X], or even three [C ⋮ X] chemical bonds).

To a chemist a double or triple bond between two atoms implies that they can react fairly easily with other chemicals. So Roelofs and company, using a standard technique in organic chemistry, exposed the attractant to hydrogen gas in the presence of a catalyst, usually platinum, the expectation being that some of the hydrogen would be taken up by the two double-bonded carbon atoms:

$$-\overset{|}{\underset{}{C}}=\overset{|}{\underset{}{C}}- \ + \ H_2 \ \xrightarrow[\text{catalyst}]{} \ -\overset{|}{\underset{H}{C}}-\overset{|}{\underset{H}{C}}-$$

The uptake of hydrogen did confirm the presence of a double bond. These and other considerably more complex tests narrowed the structure for the sex attractant of the red-banded leaf roller to one of two possibilities, *cis* or *trans* 11-tetradecenyl acetate:

The sole difference between the two is geometry. A double

bond can lock two chains of carbon atoms into two distinct forms. In the *cis* form the carbon atoms (the underlined) are on the same side of the double bond. In the *trans* version they point in both directions. The difference is more than a chemical nicety. In the world of biology, these different chemical geometries can decide if a molecule will be active in the body or not, that is, will the molecule do any "useful work."

Roelofs and Arn first synthesized both the *cis* and *trans* forms of the attractant, using what they call a "one-pot reaction sequence," just one combination of off-the-shelf chemicals. The product, a mixture of the two forms, *cis* and *trans*, was then chemically separated. The *cis* form was the active material, the true sex attractant.

"The synthetic attractant passed the ultimate test," Roelofs and Arn reported in *Nature*, "by attracting more than 3,000 male red-banded leaf roller moths to traps hung in apple orchards during a brief flight period. The *trans* isomer caught no moths."

Parenthetically, it might be noted that the history of sex-attractant research is marred by some questionable work. The structure reported for several sex attractants, including those of the gypsy moth, American cockroach, and spruce budworms, was wrong. A synthetic version of the supposed gypsy-moth attractant—called gyplure—was even field tested in the early sixties at some expense and found to be inactive, to the considerable embarrassment of the United States Department of Agriculture. The sexual behavior of an insect in captivity may be quite different from what it does in the field, and researchers have come to grief in part by relying on laboratory responses of their insects instead of actually trying out an attractant in the open air. As Roelofs and Arn somewhat acidly commented in their *Nature* paper, "reports on insect attractants are numerous, but few actually reveal the structure of a compound which is active outside the laboratory." A new structure for the sex attractant of the gypsy moth was reported in 1970 by USDA chemists and found to be active in the field.

While their synthetic attractant, which the Cornell group called RiBLuRe, did attract male moths in the field, it was apparent that the call of the live female was considerably more alluring; more males went to her scent than to the test-tube product. Why? A clue came when Roelofs and Dr. James P. Tette identified the sex attractant of the *oblique*-banded leaf roller and found it to be the same as its red-banded cousin. Since the two species didn't mate even though they used the same attractant and flew in the same fields, it means that other factors aside from the raw attractant were involved.

More or less by intuition, the Cornell people, particularly André Comeau, found that adding various secondary chemicals to the pure sex-attractant could raise or lower its potency. Curiously, one fairly simple chemical, dodecyl acetate, increases the potency of the attractant for the red-banded leaf roller while weakening its attraction for the oblique-banded leaf roller. Aside from raising interesting questions about insects and their evolution, this discovery that attractants can be fine-tuned with secondary chemicals represents another approach to controlling one particularly pestiferous species without harming others. The synergistic combination of dodecyl acetate and the attractant of the red-banded leaf roller was some thirty times more attractive to the males in the open field than was the live female.

"This represented the only case," says Roelofs, "where an attractant mixture has been competitive enough with female moths to be used in a control situation."

Along with an effective attractant, better traps were also developed, largely with the help of the 3M Company in Minneapolis, which supplied portable traps lined with a sticky material called Tanglefoot that could be hung on trees and unfolded.

A small capsule of polyethylene plastic released RiBLuRe in just the right amounts to attract the male to his sticky fate; too much attractant repels the males. About ten milligrams, or the equivalent attractant of some 30,000 females, was used for each trap.

Field tests took place on a twenty-acre orchard bordering Lake Ontario. The love-baited traps, reports Roelofs, completely controlled the red-banded leaf rollers that appeared in the spring in a typical commercial orchard. In a heavily infested orchard, the competition of live females was simply too much and many fertile eggs did get laid. Nevertheless, the success in moderately infested fields proved that sex attractants can be valuable in a control program; certainly, they can be used to eliminate survivors of a conventional spraying program.

Roelofs has an alternative—although untried—technique for controlling insects, a 180° switch that illustrates their highly selective "noses": infuse the orchards with inhibitors, materials that block the male's ability to smell the scent of the female, putting them somewhat in the position of a lover with a cold. Curiously, one inhibitor turns out to be the *trans* form of the natural attractant, while another inhibitor differs only in that its double bond has been shifted to two other carbon atoms.

Roelofs and others would like to know more of insect selectivity, partly because they're curious and partly because they may learn something about how we smell, a somewhat confused subject at the moment.

The most intensive work on how insects smell, or olfaction, has been done by Dr. Dietrich Schneider, a director of the Max Planck Institute for Behavioral Physiology in Germany. Schneider has outlined what happens when an insect smells something. Sensilla, or sense organs, located on antennae, hairs, etc., receive molecules which then travel through fluid, or sensillum liquor, to reach the receptors, nerve endings where the transported chemical information is transduced into electrical patterns for transmission through the nervous system, as in humans. How that transduction is done is unknown, both at insect and human levels.

Sensilla are actually clusters of two to three cells and apparently are unique: some respond only to one type of molecule, while neighbors respond to a different type. The number of sensilla assigned to a given purpose seems to depend on what is important to the insect—a system of olfactory priorities, really. In one type of moth, about 60 to 70 percent of its sensilla cells respond only to sex attractants, while the remainder, those indicating food, prey, danger, etc., respond to a variety of other chemical cues.

The sensitivity of an insect's nose is somewhat astounding. Only a few molecules within the immediate flying space of an insect will produce a response. Schneider has measured insect response in several ways: by using sex attractants that are radioactive so that their movements can be followed, and by hooking dissected antennae to an electrical circuit. Presumably in the same way as when attached to their original owners, the isolated antennae respond to varying amounts of attractants and signal the intensity of their responses on an oscilloscope. These are what Schneider calls electroantennograms or EAGs, like electrocardiograms (EKGs), which measure the condition of our hearts.

These EAGs make quite nice chemical instruments, Roelofs has found. He has used the antennae of the red-banded leaf roller to check the position of double bonds in unknown materials. He blows a whiff of the stuff across the sensilla, or sense organs, of a wired antenna. If the double bond is in the same position as that of the natural attractant, there is a strong signal on the oscilloscope; if it is in a different position, the signal is weak.

"This actually becomes the most sensitive bond-finding instrument we've ever devised," Roelofs points out. "And because the male moths are a million times more sensitive than our gas chromatograph, we can work with very small quantities."

Related to this work is a very basic question: How do receptors—the interface between the insect's environment and the internal circuitry of its nervous system—discriminate between molecules that chemists have difficulty telling apart? To put it more specifically, how does the "nose" of the red-banded leaf roller moth discriminate between its sex attractant and sex inhibitor; why do almost identical materials produce such radically different behavior? Another puzzle is to account for the ability of some materials discovered by Roelofs to increase the potency of the natural attractant.

Roelofs and André Comeau have offered some answers, based in good part on what has been learned in the past few years of the flexible responses of various proteins to the molecules they encounter. Proteins such as in enzymes or receptor sites can change their shape in part according to the molecule

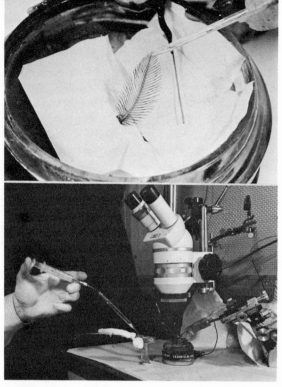

Experiments with insect antenna connected to electrode (*top*); "puff" of odor injected into airstream passing across antenna (*bottom*). These experiments help identify structure of attractants and offer clues to the mechanism of smell. *Courtesy: Wendell Roelofs, Cornell University*

encountered, much as a glove will adapt to the hand it covers. This is a basic idea first suggested by Dr. Daniel E. Koshland, Jr., of the University of California at Berkeley, mentioned earlier in the discussion of ribonuclease.

Roelofs and Comeau suggest that inhibitors can block the effects of natural attractants because they can occupy the same places in receptor sites; they're similar enough to the real article to fit into the same space but different enough to be useless in starting the chain of happenings that tells a male to start flying for love and the species.

"The inhibitory chemicals possess strong affinity but no intrinsic activity" is how Roelofs and Comeau put it. What about the synergists, materials that considerably increase the potency of the synthetic duplicates of the natural attractant? The matter is somewhat clouded, but one reasonable explanation is that these synergistic molecules attach to regions bordering the active site of the receptor protein, producing what Koshland has called a "cooperative effect." Active sites are the regions in a protein where the attractant molecule lands.

Because of this cooperative effect, the shape or conformation of the receptor protein is changed, but no signal can be transmitted until the main actor—the attractant molecule—arrives, somewhat like a car engine but which won't turn over until someone turns the key. The specific effect of the conformational changes brought on by the synergists in this situation is to amplify the effects of the attractant, thereby raising its potency.

Much of this is work still in progress, with Roelofs and his colleagues throwing off new ideas and exploring new directions, all based on the love perfumes of pests that plague New York State's apple orchards. A sample of future directions: Work on how slight alterations in molecular structure can affect the behavior of an insect may be applied to the problem of designing more effective drugs. Roelof's chemistry can also probe insect evolution. For instance, insects so alike in appearance and habit as to appear to be members of the same species actually use different sex attractants, and, therefore, are different species.

The kind of work Roelofs and his colleagues are doing represents one corner, albeit a very important one, of a very large and partly explored territory—the chemical communication of insects. Because of our stronger reliance on what we can see and hear, the kind of molecular dimensions insects live by is difficult to grasp.

"It is difficult for human observers, being exceptionally visual and auditory organisms, to appreciate the predominantly chemical *Umwelt* in which so many other animal species live," writes Dr. Edward O. Wilson of Harvard University.

Wilson is professor of biology at Harvard and famous for his detailed exploration of the various ways in which insects—particularly social insects such as ants, bees, and wasps—communicate through chemicals. Perhaps more than anybody else, he has tried to define that chemical language—through densities of trail odors, intensities and lengths of responses, and insect interpretations of various combinations and concentrations of different chemicals.

Wilson's social insects operate by necessity in dark corridors, dependent almost exclusively on what their noses tell them—the presence of a mate, of food, danger, or the trumpet call for an attack. Insects also practice effective chemical warfare on each other. For example, some slave-making ants use as their secret weapon a remarkable accumulation—sometimes up to 10 percent of their own weight—of what Wilson and Dr. F. E. Regnier of Purdue University call "superpheromones." These don't evaporate as quickly as other pheromones and when discharged at victims, throws them literally into a tizzy. Wilson calls these superpheromones "propaganda molecules" because, like any enemy propaganda offensive, they immobilize a population.

About six different ant species practice slavery. They raid the nests of other ants and steal their pupae; when these pupae "hatch," knowing no other home, they will share the work of the colony. For some species, slaves are literally part of survival—their masters have mandibles adopted for raiding and killing but not for chewing food and must therefore depend on their slaves to chew for them.

The raid of these slavers amounts to a rout: guard ants flee, others scurry about in apparent utter confusion, and even hours after the slavers have left, the survivors are still reluctant to return home. A Frenchman, Pierre Huber, discovered ant slavers in 1810 and in his report (quoted by Wilson and Regnier) remarked that "one of the principal features of the wars on the ash-colored ants seems to be of exciting fear, and this effect is so strong that they never return to their besieged nest, even when the oppressors have retired to their own nests; perhaps they realize that they could never remain in safety, being continually liable to new attacks by their unwelcome visitors."

Apparently, the raid begins when scouting ants find a nest of potential victims. The scouts scurry home, laying an odor trail that will be retraced by a full raiding party (in some species, already-domesticated slaves are never permitted on raids and are thoughtfully left behind). Some killing takes place, but most of the victims are simply scattered by the propaganda molecules. Wilson and Regnier, by collecting victims after an attack, found that these had been sprayed with substantial amounts of chemicals the slavers carry in little reservoirs called Dufour's glands.

"We feel certain," they wrote in 1971 in *Science*, "that this accounts not only for the disorientation observed in many defenders during the raids but also to some extent for the panic and rapid retreat displayed by the slave-species colonies and the relative ease with which their nests are breached by the slave-makers."

These raiding weapons apparently also help the slavers to defend themselves when attacked. In an experiment in which the slaves were picked at by a cotton swab, they sprayed the swab with an irritating mixture of materials, probably identical to the propaganda molecules.

Much of the work identifying the chemicals—a mixture of acids and esters (a combination of acid and alcohol)—has been done by Drs. G. Bergstrom and J. Lofquist in Sweden. What

Two slave-making ants attacking a defending worker during an artificially induced raid. *Courtesy: E. O. Wilson, Harvard University, and Science*

these materials are is still uncertain, although their basic structure seems remarkably similar to the sex attractant of the red-banded leaf roller identified by Roelofs.

These chemical muggings of ants are by no means unique. Some varieties of stingless bees found in tropical regions such as Brazil use gas warfare to gain entry into the nests of other bees. These robber bees lack a corbicula, or pollen basket, and must perforce steal food supplies gathered by fellow bees.

Precisely how that is done has been worked out in a joint effort by Murray S. Blum and R. M. Crewe of the University of Georgia; M. M. Walker, L. H. Keith, and A. W. Garrison of the United States Department of the Interior; and W. E. Kerr of the University of São Paulo in Brazil. The group discovered the chemical thievery practiced by the robber bees somewhat indirectly; they had identified the chemicals used by one of the victims—also stingless bees—to lay scented trails to food, and these chemicals turned out to be the same materials used by robber bees.

The victims, like other social insects, lay periodic odor trails along a flight or crawl path. The trails attract, or recruit, other workers, and soon an exodus to the food is underway. Each worker when he finds the food lays down more of this trail material, whiffs of fairly volatile stuff, reinforcing the lure of the food and attracting more workers. As food is depleted, disappointed stragglers stop the reinforcing process. Fairly rapidly —sometimes in minutes—the trail substances evaporate.

The trail substances of these bees is citral, found in many plants and best known to organic chemists as the starting point for synthetic vitamin A. Citral from lemon-grass oil is used industrially in perfumes and flavoring agents. Citral is actually a mixture of two materials—geraniol and neral—that differ only in their geometry, that is, the spatial arrangement of their atoms (as the on-off attractants for the red-banded leaf roller).

Blum and his colleagues confirmed the citral connection in several ways. A droplet of citral on a stick attracted the bees, while citronellal, very similar in its chemistry to citral, did not attract, again confirming the acute sensitivity of insect noses. Interestingly, when a stick heavily coated with citral was used, the bees attacked it; apparently in low concentrations, citral guides the way to food, whereas in high amounts it is a tocsin for attack.

"Since the generation of an alarm signal can be achieved by the same compound that functions as a trail pheromone," Blum and his colleagues write, "workers of *T. subterranea* [the victims] have increased their information output without requiring any increase in their natural products repertory."

This "parsimonious utilization" makes sense. A mild trail laid down by a few bees is all that is needed to find food. When excited or disturbed, the bees will empty their sacs of citral, producing an immediate and high concentration in a small area, and that is the signal for battle.

However, this rather sophisticated chemical language, such as used in food gathering, breaks down when robber bees—one type is formally known as *Lestrimelitta limao*—attack: A scouting party of robber bees enter the hives of their victims and are instantly killed. In dying, they release their citral, which attracts a swarm of robber bees. A raid begins, marked by a barrage of citral. As with the raids of the slavers, the careful social order of the bee victims breaks down, and they are unable to mount any sort of defense. But while citral disrupts the life style of victims of *Lestrimelitta* it has little or no effect on other, quite similar species of stingless bees.

How do stingless bees defend themselves against more conventional attacks? Quite effectively. They have powerful mandibles and once they grab hold of an enemy's hair, ears, snout, or other insects, they won't let go. They can even smother an intruder, and some varieties can let go with a mixture of material so irritating that the Brazilians call them fire defecators.

As exciting as this and other work on insect pheromones is, it is being matched by advances in our understanding of how insect hormones work.

Enough is now known about insect hormones—how their chemical structures relate to what they do—that chemists can make subtle changes in the molecular structure of natural hormones and produce materials that derange the metamorphosis of one group of insect pests, while leaving the others alone.

"One would have to search long and hard to find a clearer example of the strange and sometimes wonderful fruits of the untainted vintage of pure research," notes Dr. Carroll Williams of Harvard University. Williams and a few other people—notably Sir Vincent Wigglesworth in Great Britain and Dr. Adolph F. J. Butenandt of Germany—are largely responsible for what we now know of the chemical cues that control insect metamorphosis.

Three insect hormones are known—brain hormone, ecdysone, and juvenile hormone. A job of the brain hormone is to turn on the glands that produce ecdysone, the growth or molting hormone, and possibly those that make juvenile hormone.

Ecdysone controls the division of the insect's cells and triggers molting—the periodic removal of the insect's hard outer coat, or molt, when the insect begins to outgrow it. This is the process of ecdysis, or getting out, which is why we call stripteasers eydysiasts and the molting hormone of insects ecdysone. Juvenile hormone is intriguingly different. Its presence or absence dictates whether or not the insect will reach the next metamorphic level, the next change in form. Essentially, too much juvenile hormone will keep an insect from growing up, so quite properly, it is the juvenile hormone or, as some like to call it, the Peter Pan hormone. A caterpillar given too much juvenile hormone will not pass to the pupal stage but will repeat the caterpillar stage; a pupa given juvenile hormone remains a pupa, never becoming a moth. An adult moth, because it is the end product, is unaffected by juvenile hormone.

That we now know a great deal about juvenile hormone—and indeed that a new generation of pesticides is almost upon us— is due in good measure to a 1956 discovery by Williams (now Benjamin Bussey Professor of Biology at Harvard) that the male cecropia moth, a common, harmless, and rather beautiful species, thoughtfully stores a generous amount of juvenile hormone, JH, in its abdomen about a week before it dies. A close relative, the male cynthia moth, does the same thing. Only these two insects seem to do this, which is why almost everything we know about juvenile hormone comes from them.

Williams had extracted a bit of JH with ether, swabbing

the liquid on the cuticle of a pupa. This produced a hybrid of pupae and adult moth, a chimerical creation that could not survive. "Therefore," Williams wrote, "in addition to the theoretical interest of the juvenile hormone, it seems likely that the hormone when identified and synthesized will prove to be an effective insecticide. This prospect is worthy of attention because insects can scarcely evolve a resistance to their own hormones."

Juvenile hormone was actually identified and synthesized some ten years after Williams's discovery by Professor Herbert Röller and his colleagues at the University of Wisconsin (Röller has since moved to Texas A. & M. University). Röller's achievement was considerable, not only in what it did for insect chemistry but for its display of the powers of microchemistry: for a rather complex identification task he had only about three hundred micrograms, barely enough to see with the naked eye.

The structure of juvenile hormone turned out to be quite unusual when compared to other materials that are biologically active. The formal chemical name for the juvenile hormone of the cecropia moth is methyl *trans, cis*-10-epoxy-7-ethyl-3, 11-dimethyl-2, 6-tridecadienate. To a chemist, juvenile hormone is a rather complex variant of a fatty acid (because the material dissolves in fatty liquids). A chemist can also appreciate that there are some sixteen different isomers of juvenile hormone; that is, they all have the same atoms linked in the same order but differ in the directions those atoms point in three-dimensional space. It's somewhat like a twist toy that never changes its basic structure but takes on a myriad of shapes in a child's inventive hands.

Röller and his people synthesized a mixture of these isomers, and (no mean accomplishment) were able to separate out the one variation that was the active hormone, one that was properly suppressive of the growing up of a number of different insect types. Since that time, various groups have found ways to get the juvenile hormone directly, without having to contend with a number of false variations. Such stereospecific syntheses have been devised by groups led by Dr. J. B. Siddall at the Zoecon

Corporation in Palo Alto, Dr. William Johnson at Stanford University, and Dr. E. J. Corey of Harvard. Corey's and Williams's labs at Harvard are separated only by Frisbee Court, and the two have a close-knit collaboration. "They know how to make them, we know how to test them," Williams says.

Curiously, other people have found materials that mimic juvenile hormone in effects on insects and molecular shape but differ in the atoms that compose them. For example, a group in Czechoslovakia, whose scientists have made a considerable contribution to insect chemistry and biology, found that some peptides, or small proteins, although chemically dissimilar from the natural hormone, repressed the maturation of some insects; they had juvenile-hormone activity.

The implications, aside from opening up new routes to JH insecticides, are that the effects of the hormone are based on their ability to fit into appropriate spaces on a receptor site; more specifically, juvenile hormone sits on a switch that allows the genetic information needed for movement to the next level—pupa or moth—to be used.

"We feel that the juvenile hormone when it is present prohibits a cell from turning on any new genes," Williams says. "But it does not interfere in any way with the use and reuse of genes that have already gotten turned on." While the idea is in tune with current concepts of how genes are switched on and off, the details of the process are still in the "arm-waving" stage.

But once the genes are turned on, allowing synthesis within the insect's cells of the proteins they need, the insect can grow into whatever form is next. And that growth is paced by ecdysone, the growth and molting hormone. What we know chemically of ecdysone is due in good measure to two German chemists—Drs. Adolph Butenandt and Peter Karlson. Butenandt is the 1939 Nobel Prize winner in chemistry for his work on human sex hormones. (He could not accept the prize until after the war.)

Just before Williams's earlier discovery, Butenandt and Karlson had squeezed about twenty-five milligrams of pure ecdysone from a ton of silkworms. Williams confirmed that their hard-won drop was ecdysone by noting its molting effects on insect development. In the mid-sixties—just before the structure of juvenile hormone became known—the molecular structure of ecdysone was deciphered by European chemists. An unusual feature of this work was the first use of X-ray crystallography to identify the chemical structure of an unknown material.

A fascinating dropout of this research was the chemical similarity of ecdysone to cholesterol. Insects need cholesterol to live and include it in their diet, not being able to make it as we can. Apparently, one use insects make of cholesterol is to manufacture ecdysone. That would seem to eliminate ecdysone as a basis for a general insecticide: the ubiquity of ecdysonelike materials makes it likely that whatever variant affects insects will also affect higher animals, including man.

The actual synthesis of ecdysone in the sixties was a hotly competitive matter. Several groups succeeded: one at the Syntex Corporation in the United States; another group of chemists from two European drug companies, Schering and Hoffmann—La Roche; and, two years later, a Japanese group. Two insect ecdysones have now been identified—alpha and beta ecdysone —the two differing only by a hydroxyl group, that is, a molecular fragment of one oxygen and one hydrogen atom. More ecdysones have been found in other creatures, including crustaceans such as the fiddler crab and molting shrimp.

Recently the bizarre discovery was made that over thirty different types of plants—ferns, evergreens, and the like—produce close mimics of natural ecdysone. Collectively, these mimics are called phytoecdysones, and some of them are so much more potent than the insect's own ecdysone that Williams calls them "superhormones." Credit for the discovery of some of these goes to Japanese scientists, principally at Tohoku University and the Takeda Pharmaceutical Industries.

The finding that plants were making ecdysonelike materials perked up this section of insect chemistry. "The synthesis of ecdysone was so difficult and the yield so small," Williams writes, "that it seemed as though only vanishingly small amounts would ever be available for study." Williams points out that while Butenandt and Karlson needed a ton of silkworms to get a speck of pure ecdysone, material with equivalent effects on insects can be gotten from about an ounce of the leaves and roots of the yew tree.

The immediate question is why do plants make phytoecdysones, presuming there has to be a why. Williams has tried various phytoecdysones on growing insects in the laboratory and found that they will derail the careful schedule of sequential events needed for proper growth; the result, inevitably, is a dead insect. And Professor Lynn Riddiford ("the only female biology professor Harvard has," Williams says) found that very tiny amounts of a phytoecdysone—one part in a billion—in a silkworm's diet will mess up its development. Williams feels that phytoecdysones are the plant's weapons in their perennial battle with the insects.

"We think that the plants have not gone to all this trouble for nothing," he says. "We think they've made these things as an extremely sophisticated self-defense against insect predation."

Others aren't so sure. Two researchers at the Anti-Locust Research Centre in London found that locusts fed on bracken, a plant that contains phytoecdysone, not only developed normally but excreted whatever ecdysone they ate. And silkworms are grown on mulberry leaves, which also contain phytoecdysones.

A parenthetical story Williams likes to tell is of the insect-free Río Negro, a river in southern Brazil. The river periodically overflows, flooding about a half million acres of vegetation, presumably extracting a rich assortment of juvenile hormone-like materials as well as phytoecdysones. Williams, who has visited the region, reasons that there are no insects on the Río Negro because they are literally flooded by their own hormones.

"So people like to live on the Río Negro because they aren't going to get zapped by the mosquitoes. But it's such an impoverished place that even though you may not get malaria, you're going to starve to death."

Even though ecdysone is an unlikely candidate for insecticides for reasons mentioned earlier, Williams sees it as providing a model for a general theory of how hormones work. A central problem in contemporary biology is to explain how hormones, often rather simple molecules, can govern and mediate a host of complex processes. Recently Williams and two colleagues, Dr. Tetsuya Oktaki and Dr. Roger D. Milkman, have taken a close look at how ecdysone works in flesh flies. These were picked because they are fairly large and because their metamorphosis into the pupal stage can be closely controlled.

A flesh-fly pupa forms a puparium, a hard outer coat that protects the pupa much as a cocoon of spun silk protects the changeling caterpillar. Ecdysone guides the creation of the puparium. But the three men found that ecdysone, whether natural or injected, seems to "disappear" before the puparium begins to form. It wasn't merely a matter of the ecdysone breaking down with time. If they worked with larval blood or mashed flesh flies, the ecdysone remained. Complete cells were needed to make ecdysone disappear or, more properly, inactivate it.

With the fact established that a hormone—ecdysone—disappears before its effects are seen, Williams and his colleagues proposed that ecdysone's role is finished as soon as it has reacted with a number of "primary receptors," whatever they may be.

"As a result of this primary reaction," they wrote in the *Biological Bulletin,* published by Harvard, "a concatenation of biochemical and biophysical events is set in motion which comprise the covert effects of the hormone. The latter undergo spatial and temporal summation within the target organs and finally trigger the overt effects," i.e., the initiation of molting or metamorphosis. Ecdysone, a hormone, triggers a series of hidden events that are eventually summed into visible changes in the life style of an insect.

"It has not escaped our attention," they added, "that this conception of the dynamics of ecdysone action may be applicable to hormones in general."

Williams now suspects that the actual role of ecdysone may be to assist a "macromolecular factor"—probably a protein—into the cells of the insect. That assistance is reminiscent of insulin, whose role may be to "shoehorn" the sugar glucose into cells.

Blatantly missing from this talk of hormones and pheromones, robber bees, and telltale cecropias is the excitement sweeping through the circles searching for new ways to control the bugs. Within the past year, that excitement has crystallized into a realization that a new generation of pesticides based on the biology and chemistry of juvenile hormone may be near.

To date, an unknown but substantial number of chemical variants of natural juvenile hormone that act on specific insect pests have been created in chemical laboratories. Some have been made at the Institute of Entomology in Czechoslovakia and some by United States Department of Agriculture chemists but most by a number of companies hotly pursuing the half-billion-dollar market in insecticides. Notably among those are the Zoecon Corporation and the Stauffer Chemical Company in the United States; Schering and Hoffmann-La Roche in Europe; and the Takeda Pharmaceutical Industries in Japan. It is no accident that several companies are drug houses (Zoecon is a spinoff from Syntex). Both drug and juvenile-hormone research applies specialized knowledge of how molecular structures relate to biological effects.

These companies, and others, met in Basel in the summer of 1970 and reported—albeit guardedly—on their field trials of various chemical variants, or analogues, of juvenile hormone. Williams was impressed. "We're at the point where we're going to get products," he reports. "There were some very encouraging results in those practical field tests."

But details are scarce, with each company—for sound commercial reasons—refusing solid details. Williams himself has to be guarded because he is a scientific advisor to Zoecon, a company that was set up by Syntex for the express purpose of finding, developing, and marketing a new generation of pesticides based on an insect's own chemistry. Exactly what Zoecon and other companies will come up with is difficult to pin down, but some educated guesses as to possibilities and problems are possible.

The JH analogues probably will be used as sprays in fairly large-scale programs that may cover a county, the agricultural part of a state, or even an entire region. The expense and sophistication required will be such that a farm-by-farm approach will be ruled out. They probably will be used first in situations where conventional insecticides, for ecological or political reasons, cannot be applied.

One likely exception may be the use of the new pesticides in storage bins or warehouses where foods are stored and insect pests thrive; conditions can be better controlled, simplifying the use of biologically sophisticated, sometimes sensitive, chemicals.

Sprays can be used because juvenile-hormonelike materials, unlike ecdysones, can seep through the cuticle, or outer coat, of insects. This, incidentally, provides another lever for fine-tuning the specificity of juvenile-hormone analogues because cuticles differ from species to species; analogues can probably be designed that will penetrate one type of cuticle and not another.

A glimpse into what Zoecon is up to was provided late in 1971 by *Chemical* & *Engineering News* as it reported field trials on mosquitoes of two JH mimics similar in chemistry to natural JH but up to 1,900 times more potent (in the laboratory) and five times more stable than any other compound tested. One compound, according to the magazine, in small field trials gave 99 percent control of a mosquito species *Aedes nigromaculis,* said to be "almost totally resistant to known conventional pesticides."

In addition to materials that derail the development of an insect because they mimic its hormones, materials may be used that can block the action of the natural hormones, either juvenile hormones or ecdysone. On paper that's a good idea, because it may be simpler to block a process than try to imitate it.

Dr. Koji Nakanishi, who led the Japanese effort in the insect-hormone field while at Tohoku University and is now at Columbia University (and a scientific advisor to Zoecon), has already found materials that block the action of certain ecdysones—insect-molting inhibitors, in short.

How will these analogues (and probably the inhibitors) be applied? Curiously, and somewhat ironically, with the same sort of spraying equipment that has been used to apply DDT.

"They have exactly the same solubility properties as DDT," Williams points out. "They are insoluble in water, and they are soluble in all organic solvents. So the same technology developed for DDT can be used to disseminate these things."

Now for the problems. The biggest—certainly from the standpoint of Zoecon and its competitors—is proving to the United States Food and Drug Administration that the new generation of pesticides it would like to throw against insect pests does no harm to higher animals, including man, and will vanish from our environment after a decent interval. In an enlightened age, when the cyclamate business and similar brouhahas still reverberate down the government-gray halls at FDA, proving the safety of the JH analogues, particularly the safety of exposing a population to low doses over a number of years, is likely to be a long and costly business. Dr. Carl Djerassi, a man who carries many hats including professor of chemistry at Stanford University and president of Zoecon, pointed out in *Science* that were the perfect human contraceptive to be found now, it would take decades and millions of dollars for it to clear government protocols.

Toxicity tests so far indicate no harm to vertebrates, according to Williams. The people at Zoecon don't see anything in the chemical structure of the JH analogues that might disturb mammalian biochemistry.

They recently supported that supposition in part by force-feeding a group of mice massive doses of a natural juvenile hormone, as well as a very similar analogue, and found no adverse effects whatsoever. However, Drs. John B. Siddall and Michael Slade, of Zoecon, who reported this experiment in 1971 in *Nature,* write that these results "indicate only that large quantities of an insect hormone and an analogue can be tolerated on acute ingestion by one mammalian species." The issue of toxicity, particularly long-term safety, remains open.

The nontechnical but nettlesome problem of what to call this new generation of pesticides seems to have been solved. Zoecon issued a call for possible names in *Scientific American* and got some 2,000 suggestions, including Bugoff, Frigid Nit, Hector: The Vector Defector, Mate-Abate. Slug-A-Bug, and Stud-Dub. The winning entry was Entocon.

Returning to technical problems, there are several weaknesses of JH analogues that remain to be solved. For instance, they break apart too quickly when they contact plants, so a way will have to be found to protect the JH analogues from the corrosive effects of plants.

Concentrations needed under various field conditions are still unclear. Also, costs, at least initially, may be formidable, especially in comparison with the cheap effectiveness of DDT and other pesticides of its generation.

However, the clock is ticking for the latter and many will go. DDT has already been constricted drastically, and some insects —for example, the gypsy moth now chomping its way through forests along the East Coast of the United States—are having a renaissance.

As Williams says, "You're jolly well going to have to control the insects. Otherwise, we all can go back to living in caves somewhere."

10

RUSSIAN WATER

"Why should I bother with made-up games when there are so many real ones going on?" Felix Hoenikker once asked. Fair question, especially for Hoenikker, a Kurt Vonnegut, Jr., creation supposed to have invented a substance called ice-nine that could freeze the world's waters. Ice-nine is imaginary, but it has a counterpart in the real world that would have delighted the fictitious Hoenikker. The counterpart is a strange material with strange properties, the strangest, perhaps, being the guerrilla warfare it set off in one corner of chemistry.

Its labels are plentiful—anomalous water, water two, ortho water, superwater, Russian water, polywater, and (inevitably) weird water. Whatever it's called, the stuff has polarized scientists into two extremes—either it is a new form of water, or it is simply dirty water, contaminated by various impurities that might account for a rich assortment of properties. The situation has taken on the aspects of a French farce with various actors entering and exiting in rapid succession, making their declarations, suffering ridicule, and, perhaps, bestowing their attentions on mythical material. And, as in all good farces, there is a darker side: blood has been spilled, several reputations are in the balance, and there are offstage whispers of deceit.

What is anomalous water? It is material—*perhaps* pure water—formed in hair-thin tubes of quartz that neither boils nor freezes at reasonable temperatures, has a consistency somewhere between heavy oil and molasses, is considerably denser than plain water, and displays none of the normal signs of water to the various instruments chemists use to decipher molecular structures. Anomalous water, some argue, is simply water, but water in which individual molecules are bound together by novel chemical bonds to form sheets of tightly woven water molecules joined at various points. The result is a three-dimensional network of many molecules, or polywater (poly=many).

Counterpoising this minority view are a growing number of people who see a host of impurities that may account for some—perhaps all—reported properties of anomalous water.

How much exists? "Enough for about fifteen articles," Dr. Boris Deryaguin, the codiscoverer of anomalous water, told his Soviet colleagues. They didn't see the humor. In all, the world's supply probably amounts to about a drop or two, divided among some thirty laboratories on three continents. And that is the crux of the problem. No one—believer or nonbeliever—has enough to assess all the properties of the anomalous water he has made and have enough left over to probe its molecular structure. No one has enough to make a kill. While lip service has been given to the possibility of pooling efforts—especially among pro and con groups—it hasn't happened. "They'll give you some phony technical reason, but it's politics," says one chemist. Natural reluctance to send uncertain samples to other, sometimes competing, laboratories is perhaps the fairer reason.

Also stirring this test-tube tempest is the inability of researchers on both sides of the fence to repeat many of their results from week to week. Anomalous-water production fluctuates for apparently mystical reasons. Measurements done on one sample cannot be repeated with another. Impurities seen in one batch of samples are replaced by something else in the next. The result has been, necessarily, a plethora of one-shot experiments: experiments that cannot be repeated but are nevertheless published. Inevitably, confusion among participants (and innocent bystanders) has resulted. Those who disagree wonder if they are arguing about the same thing. One man's polywater may be another man's pollution.

The recipe for making anomalous water is simple, although the product is highly variable both in quantity and quality. It was first deliberately made in the early sixties by N. N. Fedyakin, a young chemist then working in relative obscurity at the Institute of Light Industry in Kostroma, a town on the Volga about two hundred miles northeast of Moscow. Fedyakin wanted to know how water would act when it was trapped in glass tubes of various sizes, some as thin as a human hair. His curiosity was whetted, in part, by 1928 experiments at The Johns Hopkins University that indicated that water trapped in thin tubes, or capillaries, didn't seem to have the vapor pressure that equations said it should. (Vapor pressure is the pressure created by molecules evaporated from liquids and solids.) Fedyakin found that normal water simply forced into capillaries behaved normally. But he found that if he sealed some water in a capillary without completely filling it and left it alone for a while, a second column of water formed in the empty portion of the capillary—what Fedyakin appropriately called "offspring water." It appeared to be thicker than the "mother water" and had a lower vapor pressure. Deryaguin heard of this and immediately invited Fedyakin to join his laboratory in Moscow. It was the sort of invitation that a young chemist dreams about. Boris Deryaguin is one of Russia's great chemists. His reputation is such that even his opponents—in and out of Russia—speak of him with awe. "I personally would be willing to sacrifice even certain foundations of physics for his sake," declared one of his colleagues in the Soviet Academy of Sciences during a heated review of Deryaguin's work and claims.

Since 1934 Deryaguin has directed the laboratory of surface forces at the Institute of Physical Chemistry on Lenin Prospect in Moscow. His work borders on the area between physics and chemistry and centers on the interaction of solid and liquid surfaces. Lubrication, adhesion, and friction are all touched by his basic research. The Russian photographic industry benefited directly from his basic work on how photographic emulsions spread on film. Recently his laboratory reported creation of very tiny diamonds by using normal pressures rather than the brutal pressures applied by American diamond makers. That work, put down by his United States counterparts, was labeled a major scientific discovery by the U.S.S.R. Council of Ministers.

Deryaguin directs—reportedly with an iron hand—the work of about seventy researchers. A small contingent was put to work in a twenty-by-thirty-foot laboratory to see what Fedyakin had wrought. Deryaguin and many of his colleagues had a subtle reason—aside from its oddness—for their intense interest in off-spring water. Some Russian chemists believe that surfaces of solids play an important role in the formation of new materials, and that this so-called ordering effect extends well beyond the first few layers of the material actually in contact with the surface. It is a controversial argument, not accepted in the mainstream of physical chemistry. Fedyakin's water seemed ideal proof that "long-range ordering forces" do exist. Too ideal and too convenient, think some of Deryaguin's opponents.

New methods were devised in Moscow to make the strange water, primarily to simplify running a cleaner experiment. Rather than sealing water in a capillary, several hundred capillaries were suspended over a dish of doubly distilled water and the whole arrangement installed in a glass vessel from which air could be pumped out. Deryaguin reports that within ten to thirty minutes columns of anomalous water could be seen. This method of producing anomalous water is now used universally by believers and nonbelievers alike. Occasionally salt is added to the water to control the relative humidity in the glass vessel. But for unknown reasons it takes most people a day or even a week, rather than minutes, to make anomalous water.

Both quartz and Pyrex capillaries are used. Quartz is a crystalline form of silicon dioxide, that is, silica, or common sand. Pyrex, a high-melting glass made mostly from quartz and also containing boron, is a borosilicate. For uncertain reasons, Pyrex capillaries seem to improve the yield of anomalous water. In a typical run, several hundred carefully cleaned capillaries are used, air is pumped out, and, after a few days, the capillaries are carefully examined—a procedure that costs time, patience, and considerable eye strain. Contamination is almost inevitable. "The whole business of handling it without getting your fingers all over it is not a trivial matter," comments Dr. S. Barry Brummer of Tyco laboratories in Waltham, Massachusetts. The total product of any one run is small and tends to fluctuate. Five to 10 percent of several hundred capillaries may have some anomalous water in them. And of that, about 90 percent is plain water that must be evaporated to recover the residue, polywater, that some proponents believe is the reason for the anomalous character of water. All this is discouraging, says Brummer, an agnostic in this business. "You have to process several thousand tubes to get out a few micrograms or two of material."

Deryaguin, quite possibly because he lacked the equipment, never analyzed the structure of what he had but thoroughly analyzed its properties—one of his scientific fortes. Specialized equipment, scarce even in the United States, is needed to analyze microscopic specks of questionable matter. Deryaguin

Material (indicated by arrows) in capillary that may be anomalous water. Glass wall is one five-thousandth of an inch thick. *Courtesy: Purdue University*

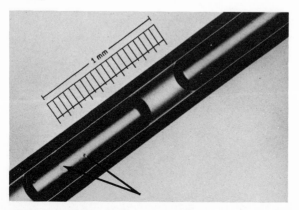

probed the properties of his creation in fairly direct, classical fashion. He measured its density, for instance, by plunking a tiny drop of anomalous water in a liquid that varied in density from top to bottom. The drop stopped when it reached its own density.

Word of the Russian water seeped slowly to the West. Deryaguin complained to a Western visitor of his difficulties in publishing outside Russia. However, he did make some trips outside the Soviet Union, including one in 1967 to the United States, where he reported his new water. Interest began to rise. Deryaguin was simply too good a scientist to ignore. His Boswell was Dr. R. A. Burton of the London branch of the Office of Naval Research (ONR), who began reporting on Deryaguin's work in the gossipy but informative *European Scientific Notes*, published by ONR. Deryaguin sent a sample to a famous English crystallographer, Dr. J. D. Bernal. But it was Dr. B. A. Pethica and his colleagues at the Unilever Research Laboratories in Britain who gained a permanent footnote in the saga of anomalous water by apparently being the first Western scientists to repeat Deryaguin's experiments. Several groups, primarily industrial, jumped in unannounced, spurred in part by a feeling that the Russians really may have something, perhaps as large a jump in the microworld of molecules as they had with Sputnik I into space. American scientists plunged in belatedly, but with vengeance, in an article in *Science* simply titled "Polywater." They confirmed that Deryaguin really had something, and provided data on the molecular structure of polywater, which they used to propose an audacious explanation for polywater's properties. Four authors signed the paper, two from the United States National Bureau of Standards (NBS) and two from the University of Maryland. That was in 1969. A year later, only one coauthor, Dr. Ellis Lippincott of the University of Maryland, remained a declared believer, while another, Dr. Robert Stromberg of NBS, told reporters that "on the basis of new evidence, there is serious doubt that a polymer of water exists; it may very well be due to contaminants."

The heart of the "Polywater" paper was an analysis of the odd water by a truly unique instrument called a double beam microscope spectrophotometer. Only two exist, one in Lippin-cott's lab, where it was built in the early sixties, and another at the nearby NBS laboratories. Essentially, a microscope is coupled to an infrared spectrophotometer, with accessories added to assure the adequate transmission of light from the microscope to the light detectors in the spectrophotometer. As the name implies, the spectrophotometer transmits infrared light through a sample. Chemical bonds—depending on whether they are vibrating, stretching, or twisting—will absorb infrared radiation at various wavelengths. By smoothly varying the wave-length of the radiation, a researcher will obtain a spectrum that tells him how much infrared radiation is being absorbed at different wavelengths. Then by comparing this spectrum of an unknown sample against reference samples of known mate-rial, he can identify his sample.

In any case, the IR (infrared) spectrum depends on the type of bonds being scanned, some having an effect at particular wavelengths, while others are "invisible." Water, for instance, has an O-H (oxygen-hydrogen) stretching band at a particular point in the IR spectrum that is an almost notorious hallmark of its presence (notorious because most IR spectroscopists are anxious to keep water out of their samples since it may obscure the spectrum). Lippincott and company, however, using their novel instrument, looked for water and didn't see it.

"Here we started with presumably nothing but water," Lippin-cott points out, "and, by golly, these water bands disappear. That was highly unusual."

The infrared spectrum obtained by the NBS–University of Maryland group has been one of the few fixed points in the anomalous-water story. Other groups—those who saw impurities and those who didn't—have gotten similar spectra with their samples.

The same thing cannot be said of the Raman spectrum the group took of their samples. A Raman spectrum, named after the Indian scientist C. V. Raman who found the effect, is a measure of the light scattered at particular wavelengths by a molecule. Lippincott and his colleagues were able to get a Raman spec-trum of only one sample. All the others were burned by the

laser beam that provides the intense light source needed by a
Raman spectrophotometer. Why this happened is another part of
the mystique of polywater, but the group—probably to their
regret—published it anyway.

Their failure to find water or a significant amount of impurities led the quadriad to propose their strange, and still controversial, structure for the Russian discovery. It was based in
part on an intuitive guess made by Dr. Stromberg, a polymer
chemist, when he first heard Deryaguin describe his water at a
conference in New Hampshire. The four cosigners of the *Science*
article—perhaps with a thought to Caesar at the Rubicon—
proposed that Russian water was really a polymer of water.
"The properties, therefore, are no longer anomalous," they wrote,
"but rather those of a newly found substance—polymeric water,
or polywater." It was a meaty statement, a red flag to many
who bridled at being asked to accept a rather heretical beast
into the orthodox world of chemistry. (Polywater is now considered the concentrated form of anomalous water. That is,
anomalous water is a mixture of polywater and plain water.)

There was certainly a great deal to be swallowed if polywater
was to be given any legitimacy. A new type of chemical bond
had to be invoked to support a polywater structure. "The . . .
spectra are consistent with a structure having previously un-
recognized bonding for a system containing only hydrogen and
oxygen atoms," Lippincott et al. wrote in *Science*. They proposed a network of water molecules stabilized by unique and
very strong hydrogen bonds.

Hydrogen bonds, introduced to chemistry about 1912, help
explain the properties of plain, watery water and may explain
the odd features of polywater. Hydrogen bonds, as the name implies, involve hydrogen atoms. Normally a hydrogen atom will
share its single electron with another atom to form an old-
fashioned, run-of-the-mill chemical bond. However, when a
hydrogen atom is trapped between atoms that have a very
powerful attraction for electrons (i.e., strongly electronegative
atoms), the single electron is shared only to a small degree with
the second atom. Accordingly, a second bond is formed considerably weaker than a normal bond but strong enough to have

a significant effect on properties. Water molecules are linked by weak hydrogen bonds that are formed as a hydrogen atom of one molecule cozies up to an oxygen atom of a neighboring molecule. It is these hydrogen bonds that help explain ordinary water's odd properties—odd in the sense that a molecule of its size and apparent simplicity doesn't behave the way that chemical theory predicts it should: it is a liquid, whereas it should be a vapor, freezes at too low a temperature, and should boil at about half the temperature it actually does. The hydrogen bond is one of several little tricks of nature that make the life we know possible on this planet. (A caveat: hydrogen bonds do not explain *everything* about liquid water, whose exact nature still continues to elude physical chemists.)

Normally, hydrogen atoms are closer to their "home" oxygen atoms than to any other neighboring atoms they happen to join up. That accounts for the relative weakness of conventional hydrogen bonds. Lippincott and company proposed a symmetrical hydrogen bond for polywater, one shared equally between oxygen atoms. The result was an unusually strong bond that could explain the ability of polywater to remain intact at temperatures of 1,000°F. "The strength of these bonds could account for the remarkable ability of this material to stand rather extreme temperatures," Lippincott confirms.

Symmetrical bonds are known in various materials, including some fluorides. But for common water it was a heretical suggestion. This heat-stable hydrogen bond was the key ingredient in the proposal made by the NBS–University of Maryland group that the anomalous properties seen by the Russians were caused by water molecules bonded into a polymer.

Their paper had a schizoid quality. Really two papers, one fairly orthodox, the other radical in the extreme. The first part —measurement of the infrared spectrum of polywater—has been accepted in part because others have been able to repeat it. Lippincott had his unique instrument on which he and his colleagues were willing to stake their considerable reputation. The second part—the proposal of a polymer of water based on rather strange hydrogen bonds—raised hackles, largely because of its ad hoc quality, a necessity for a novel kind of chemical bond.

Reaction was mixed—excitement, amusement, and scorn from various sectors of the scientific community. It was heady stuff and a heady time. Anomalous water suddenly had a dramatic name, dramatic structure, and the confident tone of an article that appeared in a respected journal written by competent scientists from well-regarded institutions. Possible applications were bandied about: the perfect antifreeze; an ideal high-temperature lubricant; furniture made with water, etc. There was even talk of possible danger. A physicist, Dr. F. J. Donahoe of Wilkes College in Wilkes-Barre, Pennsylvania, wrote to *Nature*: "I regard the polymer [of water] as the most dangerous material on Earth." Donahoe's hyperbole was nurtured by a fear that a seed of polywater might polymerize normal water, perhaps turning the world's ocean into a jellylike mass useless to everything, including life.

Lippincott and Stromberg sought to reassure him: ". . . there is no evidence that the material is dangerous. The evidence indicates that the polymer does not nucleate liquid water to form the polymer. . . . In fact, one of the difficulties in the preparation of polywater is to separate the polymer from normal water which is frequently mixed with it."

This was mid-1969, a wonderful time for the polywater group, who had played an important part in unraveling one of the new and great finds of science. A possible Nobel Prize for Deryaguin was suggested. A year later, all was chaos as one group after another made their own polywater and found a mother lode of impurities ranging from expected items such as sodium to more disturbing things such as boron, sulfates, nitrates, carbon, and even evidence of human sweat.

But the report of dirt in polywater, if one is reasonably objective, is not too surprising. Just from a logistical point of view it is terribly hard to work with hundreds of capillaries, a few of which contain some interesting material that, in turn, must be condensed, and then expect extremely powerful instruments to turn up nothing suspicious. The central point is whether the impurities found can explain the properties ascribed to polywater, including the reasonably solid infrared spectrum first reported by Lippincott and his colleagues. That issue has in part been clouded by the hard attitude of Deryaguin toward the impurity faction. "I'm not responsible for the work of others" is a typical comment. His impatience with the counter-arguments, or alternative explanations, of Soviet critics has even been criticized by his colleagues in the U.S.S.R. Academy of Sciences, judging by an account that reached the West. "We see an unhealthy attitude on the part of Deryaguin toward his critics," said A. S. Nesmeyanov. "But even though the doubts of his critics are legitimate, we see only a friendly attitude toward Deryaguin," he continued. Deryaguin gave little ground: "I have the advantage of having available all the facts and therefore do respond rather sharply to the critic who ignores these facts." Deryaguin's attitude is understandable. He is the master at making anomalous water, having had almost a decade of practice and having devised unique equipment to insure the utmost cleanliness. Moreover, Deryaguin will be the heaviest loser if the decision goes against him. Yet, some of his counter-arguments are weak since he himself has done little thorough searching of his samples for possible impurities.

"I wish Deryaguin would back up his claim with good analytical evidence," says Dr. Denis L. Rousseau of Bell Telephone Laboratories. Rousseau, a young physical chemist specializing in Raman spectroscopy, together with Dr. S. P. S. Porto of the University of Southern California, laid down the first gauntlet to the polywater hypothesis in an article in *Science* in 1969 (by now the unofficial polywater journal) entitled "Polywater: Polymer or Artifact?" They came down heavily in favor of the latter. "Our evidence," Rousseau and Porto concluded, "makes it extremely unlikely that the recently reported polymer of water exists." They prepared polywater samples which had essentially the same IR spectrum that Lippincott et al. reported, meaning they *should* be working with the same sample. But when they analyzed the residue remaining after evaporation—nominally, the polywater—with an electron microprobe and other analytical instruments, they found a significant amount of impurities. They found sodium wherever they found oxygen. They found other worrisome things: potassium, sulfate ions, evidence of chlorine, a significant amount of carbon, a bit of boron, and so on. Interestingly, they found little silicon, weakening the later argument of some—notably in England and

Australia—that polywater was merely a lot of dissolved quartz or silicon dioxide.

In perhaps the unkindest cut, Rousseau was able to partly match the spectra obtained by himself, Lippincott, and others with sodium lactate, which Rousseau calls the "primary organic constituent of sweat."

With the Rousseau-Porto papers, other foes began to pop up, many of them confirming in one fashion or another that there were substantial impurities in *their* samples. To date, at least in the West, no pro and con polywater laboratories have exchanged samples to let the other side have a go. Boris Deryaguin, however, submitted almost thirty samples of his anomalous water to one of Russia's leading analytical chemists, V. L. Tal'rose of the Institute of Chemical Physics of the U.S.S.R. Academy of Sciences. Tal'rose used a mass spectrometer on Deryaguin's samples and found phospholipids, a combination of phosphate and a fatty material, which, like the sodium lactate that Rousseau may have found, could come from human sweat. Moreover, Tal'rose failed to find any signs of a polymer of water molecule, nor did he even find signs of just two or three water molecules linked. However, Deryaguin argued that the technique of mass spectrometry—in which molecules are broken apart by an electron beam and the fragments individually identified—had destroyed any water polymers. Deryaguin acknowledged the impurities noticed by Tal'rose and, in a rather paradoxical defense, denigrated any conclusion based on an analysis with a mass spectrometer simply because they were done with impure samples!

Other critics appeared. Drs. S. W. Rabideau and A. E. Florin, both at the Los Alamos Scientific Laboratory, made polywater using extreme care to keep out contaminants and still found about 5 percent boron and 6 percent sodium in their samples, many of whose properties were similar to those reported for polywater. They made a strong case that polywater is a combination of water and sodium tetraborate, and showed that the infrared spectrum of polywater and sodium tetraborate are similar in several respects.

A different tack to the polywater puzzle was taken by Dr.

Robert Davis of Purdue University, who used a relatively new technique called ESCA, or Electron Spectroscopy for Chemical Analysis. The peculiar advantage of ESCA is that it not only detects elements but also is able to say something about their chemical environment, that is, what other elements they are surrounded by and attached to. Other techniques such as electron microprobes say little about the kind of company a particular element is keeping. ESCA, as the name implies, analyzes shifts in electron energies of various elements as they are sprayed with X rays. These shifts are strongly dependent not only on the element itself but the effects of surrounding atoms. Davis, working with Rousseau and Dr. Robert Board of the Hewlett Packard Corporation, found that all of his anomalous-water samples and those prepared at Bell Labs contained such things as sodium, potassium, sulfate, nitrates, borates, and so on. The largest single impurity, according to Davis, was most often sodium. With ESCA, Davis postulated a link between the organic carbon in his samples and specific compounds such as acetates and lactates.

A nicety which has become important recently in the polywater tempest is that to obtain an infrared spectrum on the polywater samples, Lippincott, Rousseau, and others had to remove traces of ordinary water. In effect, they concentrated their strange water and actually measured the properties of residue. Deryaguin and his proponents increasingly argue that in concentrating the material, its nature was changed, and, most importantly, that the effects of impurities became significant. Others argue that the effects of concentration on the chemical bonds should be nil. Also, it might be said that as late as March 1971, in *Scientific American*, Deryaguin did not make an explicit distinction between the polywater residue analyzed by Lippincott, etc., and his concept of what he (Deryaguin) had found— what he calls water II.

The issue remained polarized about the believers and non-believers—those who were ready to consider seriously a polymer of water and those who dismissed it as a mixture of various contaminants. The unfortunate part is that for a variety of reasons—some very human—the central issue of Deryaguin's water was not being met. An anonymous Russian colleague put it this way: "The opposition is all very well, but no one has said what it is that Deryaguin has observed. Water columns having anomalous properties really exist—I have seen them with my own eyes. This means that this fact must somehow or other be explained. And no one, unfortunately, can yet do this."

That was said in June 1969 at a meeting of the Division of General and Engineering Chemistry at the Academy of Sciences, where Deryaguin gave a report on his work. A year later, Deryaguin was at Lehigh University in Bethlehem, Pennsylvania, to keynote a full-day symposium on his anomalous water.

Between those two meetings, the impurity faction had grown in number, both in Russia and the West, although no one could yet fully explain the strange stuff in Deryaguin's capillaries. It was hoped, fervently by some, that the Lehigh meeting would settle the issue. It didn't. "The issue won't be settled here today," declared Dr. Frederick Fowkes, chairman of the chemistry department at Lehigh, at the outset, and the day's proceedings bore him out. The Lehigh meeting was marked by a fast-moving parade of pro and con water men presenting data and stating their positions, although a few waffled a bit. There were a few major surprises, including an apparent ace served up by Deryaguin at the outset. Speaking softly in a heavy Slavic accent, he reported that he and N. V. Churayev, his laboratory chief, had successfully distilled anomalous water, and that the distillate —the portion recovered after the original sample was evaporated and condensed—retained most of its anomalous properties. And when heated over 1,000° F., the stuff apparently broke apart, enabling Deryaguin to recover normal water. Thus, in one fairly simple experiment, Deryaguin could claim to have put a large hole in his opponents' case for contaminants. Any impurities would, by definition, be left behind in any distillation. Therefore, anomalous properties, if they were due to impurities, should have vanished with them. That they didn't was an impressive new piece of evidence for Deryaguin's side.

However, not all at the meeting were sure "distillation" in a wire-thin glass tube could be compared to the usual type of distillation in laboratories where the apparatus used and the amounts distilled are infinitely greater. Rabideau suggests the possibility that the water may have moved as a film along the wall of the capillary, carrying impurities with it, or that the impurities may somehow have been transported with the water vapor, or even that the entire distillate may have moved as a "slug," from one end of the capillary to the other.

Denis Rousseau also threw a new chip into the pot by reporting that he had obtained very similar IR spectra with anomalous samples made from heavy water and normal water. In heavy water, a heavier isotope of hydrogen—deuterium—is used in place of the lighter hydrogen atoms. Because of the exquisite sensitivity of hydrogen bonds, the use of the heavier form of hydrogen by Rousseau should have produced a different structure and different infrared spectrum. That it didn't weakened the case for a polymer of water. However, Rousseau based his report on only one sample. Lippincott tried the same experiment and reported that he was not able to make any anomalous water starting with heavy water. Brummer at Tyco Laboratories repeated the same experiment in 1971 (he had already *exactly* duplicated Deryaguin's results using ordinary water!) and was also unable to make any anomalous water. These failures, in a negative way, are points for polywater; researchers *should* have difficulty making polywater with heavy water because of differences in hydrogen bonding. A Mexican standoff.

Other items of interest popped up at Lehigh. Dr. Robert Stromberg, a coauthor of the original "Polywater" paper, confessed an increasing skepticism, partly based on his own experiments. He found, for instance, that the purer his quartz capillaries, the lesser the chances of forming anomalous water. "If these results are true," he told reporters, "it means one of two things: either we need something like sodium to initiate and stabilize the material, or it means that we had no contaminants and, therefore, we were unable to collect contaminants and wash them into capillaries."

In all, the day went against the pro-polywater faction, a tired Ellis Lippincott acknowledged over drinks in the early hours of the morning. And, during the symposium, one participant said that he felt that "he was taking part in a public hanging." This was Dr. Leland Allen, professor of chemistry at Princeton University, who had never tried to make any polywater but nevertheless had become a central, at times controversial, figure, in the debate. While believers and nonbelievers, between immersion in their laboratories, have hurled data at each other, Allen at Princeton and some others have tried to build a theoretical case for or against the existence of polywater. It is the unique beauty of science, which baffles and sometimes infuriates laymen, that the Princetonians tackled their beast in two theoretical ways and came up with two answers—yes and no. Yes, they reported, the stuff could exist, but, sorry, its actual existence was highly improbable.

The now-you-see-it-now-you-don't arguments were put together by Allen and his graduate student Peter Kollman, with the considerable aid of a Princeton computer running to the tune of $5,000 a month. The two essentially tried to find out if electrons could be distributed in a way compatible with chemical logic from which a structure could be put together that explained the reported properties of polywater. That goal would probably terrify most theorists, who have difficulty understanding one or two properties of infinitely simpler materials than polywater. "There are twenty to thirty properties attributed to this material," Allen points out, "in contrast to most scientific phenomena where you are fighting to understand two or three properties."

The theoretical probing into polywater rested basically on the work of Edwin Schrödinger, a German physicist, who produced a set of equations that, given only the nuclear charges and the number of electrons, enabled one to predict the probable location and behavior of electrons. These equations are the foundation of quantum, or wave, mechanics. By using Schrödinger's wave equations to calculate "waves of probabilities" for electrons, theoretical chemists can build a case for the existence or nonexistence of molecules and help explain various properties turned up by chemists in the laboratories. Needless to say, these calculations are terribly complicated even in the computer age.

Allen and Kollman tackled a structure whose properties were

rather nebulous and whose very existence was in doubt. To get anywhere at all, they had to make a series of approximations—simplifying assumptions that help bypass theoretical ground computers can't touch.

Allen and Kollman used two different levels of approximation, one fairly crude, the other considerably finer. With the cruder, so-called semi-empirical approach, results could be obtained for a system containing over one hundred atoms. The two chemists used some of the known properties of polywater as suggestive clues to likely structures. Calculations then were used to flesh out this structure and verify its possible existence. The Princetonians were in the position of architects given the materials available for a house and asked to produce a design that used all those materials, no more and no less. They produced a molecular structure of layered sheets of oxygen and hydrogen atoms interconnected at periodic points. The fundamental units from which the sheets were created were hexamers, cyclic arrangements of oxygen atoms held together by intervening hydrogen bonds. Fifty or more water molecules form a series of layered sheets, or "microcrystallites." These free-swimming microcrystallites, or water clusters, could explain many of the properties of anomalous water, or its concentrated form, polywater, according to Allen and Kollman. The leitmotiv, of course, was the symmetrical hydrogen bond proposed by Lippincott and company.

The Princetonians added their own name to the anomalous-water thesaurus—cyclimetric water, from cyclic and symmetric. The name remains a footnote.

Other theoreticians and physical chemists had strong reservations about the existence of polywater. Linus Pauling dismissed it, according to his son-in-law, Professor Barclay Kamb of the California Institute of Technology, himself a theoretician and nonbeliever. Dr. Walter Kauzmann, a colleague of Allen at Princeton and a world authority on water structure, didn't believe in it. Another liquid man, Dr. Joel Hildebrand of the University of California at Berkeley, wrote in *Science* in 1970 that "we are skeptical about the container whose label bears a novel name but no clear description of its contents. . . . We are suspicious

Original polywater model—"cyclimetric water"—proposed by Leland C. Allen and Peter Kollman of Princeton University. Oxygen is in black, hydrogen in white. *Courtesy: Leland C. Allen, Princeton University*

of the nature of an allegedly pure liquid that can be prepared only by certain persons in such a strange way."

Allen isn't surprised that most scientists scoff at polywater. "If a vote were taken among the nation's leading scientists," he says, "you'd find that 95 percent didn't believe it." To that not-so-silent majority must be added Allen and Kollman, who, after a period of agonizing reappraisal, now think that "the existence of anomalous water is highly unlikely."

The reasons are again complex. They are based on finely detailed calculations they made of the probable formation and existence of the hexamer of oxygen and hydrogen atoms that is the basic unit in their cyclimetric water. These were *ab initio* calculations, or "from the beginning." These calculations, the two say, are "the most rigorous and accurate that can be carried out for the smallest representative piece of material within the present state of technology."

When the two looked at their *ab initio* results, they saw several serious weaknesses in the case for polywater: (1) the bonds needed to hold the hexamer together were much less stable than normal hydrogen bonds; (2) there were no barriers that would stop a symmetrical bond from transmuting to the more probable asymmetrical bond that holds plain water molecules together; and (3) it was difficult to justify any of the various formation schemes proposed for polywater.

The question, says Allen is how metastable can it be and still exist. "You are in a never-never land where you get a nondecomposing material that is acknowledged to be metastable." A metastable state, simpler to explain with an analogy, is a rock balanced on the lip of a hill. It doesn't take much to get it moving.

Allen tends to be philosophical about his conversion. "This is theory on the firing line," he says. He believes that theorists must help chemists working in the laboratory while they're still gathering data and groping for an explanation. Experimentalists aren't always appreciative. "When I see a theoretical paper, I have a big yawn," says one.

What then is polywater? Allen now believes it to be a very small amount of silicate plus a larger variety of other impurities such as carbonates, nitrates, borates, or still others.

A 1971 article in *Nature*, "Polywater and Polypollutants," by a group from Birkbeck College, University of London, cited a number of possible impurity sources and pointed the finger at contaminants inherent in the apparatus needed to make polywater: greases between glass joints; leftover residues from cleanup of the apparatus; oil vapors from the vacuum pump; dust particles; trapped gases such as carbon dioxide, and so on.

But the issue is still not settled. Deryaguin's observations—particularly his claimed ability to distill anomalous water and retain most of its properties—must be verified or explained. And if the issue of polywater—polymer or contamination—is finally to be settled, fairly large amounts must be made, enough anyway so that properties and structure can be analyzed, with enough left to pass on to other laboratories. Several groups are making the attempt. Notable is the effort of Dr. Frederick Fowkes of Lehigh University. Fowkes, a 95 percent believer, is probably the closest to Deryaguin of any of the anomalous-water group. He has visited him in Moscow and has had him to his home on at least two occasions. What Fowkes has tried to do is mass-produce anomalous water—initially on alternate Saturday afternoons—by condensing water on ultrapure quartz powder (sand). At the Lehigh University meeting, Fowkes displayed a viscous liquid with a relatively high boiling point that, when evaporated, sometimes leaves a residue of what may be a polymeric material. "Is you or is you ain't my baby," Fowkes asked at the Lehigh meeting, and the prevailing feeling seemed to be that it ain't. "We've tried to repeat the work," says one researcher, "and all we do is dissolve a hell of a lot of silica." Fowkes was understandably reticent on the exact conditions he is using for his attempt to mass-produce anomalous water. He is content to say that he is trying to bring sodium ions to the surface of the quartz powder. Sodium ions, believers think, may have a crucial role in the formation of anomalous water, either as a catalyst or as a necessary ingredient.

The polywater episode is distasteful to some scientists. "I think people get upset because it's water," says Brummer of Tyco Laboratories. Others are disturbed by some apparently sloppy lab work. Errors have been made. "All of us—myself included—tried to rush things," says Rousseau. Groups published results that they themselves could not repeat, much less their colleagues. Measurements of properties were taken on different forms of the material—anomalous water, or water two, in some cases, polywater, the concentrated form, in others, and various points in between for still others. The result has been little agreement on what constitutes admission to the club for a particular sample. Well-intentioned people who found impurities in their samples were attacked for unclean methods. In Deryaguin's case a Soviet colleague told him, "It was incautious . . . to publish these results immediately."

The issue will certainly be settled, probably when enough is made so that everyone—pro and con—can have a go.

"Science is pretty conservative, and it has to be," Brummer says, "but in the end when something is true, it finally hits us on the head and says it's true."

11

THE

POLLUTED

OCEANS

Notwithstanding what we have still to learn of proteins and nitrogen fixers and the puzzles of aging and subterranean neutrinos, the oceans remain man's most uncomfortable outpost—a last frontier for science. We do not understand the oceans—the nature and behavior of seawater; what happens when ocean meets air; and how the chemistry of the oceans affects the life these waters nurture. We know more about ocean bottoms than their overlying waters.

These gaps point to a deeper significance than simply the

drive to know: the oceans are being polluted at an increasing rate, and we do not know the consequences.

The annual amounts of lead and mercury now being added by man to the oceans are approaching the levels added by natural weathering of the continents; the hydrocarbons from spilled oil are reaching the level of natural hydrocarbons from decay of plant and animal life; some 25 percent of all DDT ever made is now in the oceans. Pesticides from Africa follow the winds and appear in the Bay of Bengal off the Indian Ocean and the Caribbean. Pesticides sprayed in a Kansas cornfield turn up in glaciers in the Northern Hemisphere within a year. Any competent analytical chemist can find man-made radioactivity in water taken from any ocean.

The point of this bill of particulars is obvious: wastes going into the ocean are reaching astronomical levels, and to talk of local pollution problems makes no sense—the lead pouring out of tailpipes and into New York City air may settle down in fertile fishing grounds in the North Sea.

Thor Heyerdahl brought back samples of polluted water plucked from the Atlantic on his transoceanic voyage in a papyrus boat. While the stuff was abominable and interfered with shaving, bathing, and other amenities, ocean scientists are more concerned about pollution that is less visible but more insidious, certainly more inimical to life in the seas. This includes toxic metals such as lead and mercury, suspect materials such as DDT and similar chlorinated hydrocarbons (a compound of hydrogen, carbon, chlorine), uncertainties such as oil, and the localized problems of deliberate ocean dumping of wastes. Weaving through this litany of pollutants is the chorus of ignorance—the now almost desperate need to understand the natural oceans, to have a base line against which to assess man's "chemical invasion of the oceans."

"To understand the fate of these substances, we must understand the natural chemistry of the oceans," says Dr. Edward Goldberg, a leading chemical oceanographer and professor of chemistry at the Scripps Institution of Oceanography of the University of California.

Antoine Lavoisier, a French chemist, codiscoverer of oxygen, guillotine victim, and one of the first to analyze seawater, remarked (quoted by Goldberg): "Seawater results from the rinsing of the whole surface of the earth."

The oceans are indeed a haven for, and reflect the rubbings from, the lands, delivered by rivers, glaciers, rainfall, etc. Virtually every element is in the sea and at least two (bromine and iodine) were first discovered there. Seawater no matter where you look is largely a solution of sodium chloride, or table salt, with a trace of magnesium sulfate and a pinch of virtually every known stable element. The proportions of the different salts tend to be constant from ocean to ocean, indicating that the seas are well mixed.

With that cursory outline of seawater, it must be pointed out that chemists don't understand it. More specifically, they don't understand the interaction of seawater with its boundaries— air, the bottom sediments, and life.

"A sample of seawater is basically a dull thing," says a chemical oceanographer and sometime sculptor, Dr. Ralph Albert Horne of the Woods Hole Oceanographic Institution on Cape Cod. "But there's all kinds of interesting chemistry which goes on in the interaction of the sea with the atmosphere and that of the seawater with the sediments beneath."

But these interface processes can be extremely difficult to study. How does a chemist, or any scientist, for that matter, study what goes on between the air and the surface of the sea without in some way imposing an artificial situation that may twist his data? Yet it is precisely this kind of knowledge that we need if we are going to understand such things as the effects of an oil slick on natural processes—photosynthesis or sea-air weather, for example.

What complicates the efforts to understand sea chemistry is that it is often agonizingly slow.

"A chemist in the laboratory considers a reaction slow," Goldberg explains "if it takes place in a matter longer than a day; it's fast if it occurs in milli- or microseconds. . . . However, the marine chemist looks at reactions that take place over geological time periods; hundreds or thousands or millions of years are often necessary to produce discernible amounts of materials."

By example, tiny nodules, composed of manganese and iron

and varying in size from tiny marbles to large baseballs, are scattered on the ocean floor. These nodules grow by accretion of material from seawater at the rate of a tiny fraction of an inch every *thousand* years.

Fortunately there are interchanges, or shuttlings, of materials between the seawater and its boundaries at top and bottom that are fairly fast and measurable. For instance, by analyzing seawater taken from various depths and locations, chemists have been able to measure the interfacial exchanges of oxygen isotopes and radioactive elements such as thorium between seawater, sediment, and the atmosphere. The result has been a growing knowledge of how fast top water sinks, bottom water wells up, and so on.

Some notable progress has been made. For instance, marine chemists can now calculate with a fair degree of accuracy how long on the average any particular element is likely to remain in seawater before it departs either by precipitating to the bottom or flying off in the atmosphere. This is the "residence time."

As one would expect, residence times fluctuate widely. Things like sodium, potassium, and magnesium ions remain in ocean water for hundreds of millions of years before being removed in one fashion or another, while elements such as thorium and lead leave—generally by precipitating to the ocean bottom—in a few hundred years. Lab analysis shows that an atom of titanium plunked into the ocean should remain for some 1,600 years; aluminum about 1,000 years; copper some 10,000 years, and so on.

Various factors influence residence times. The saltiness of the water through which a particle passes will influence the water's chemical makeup—what elements it does or does not pluck from seawater. Also, it is now clear that residence times are actually a matter of total-earth chemistry rather than simply the chemistry of seawater. Two factors basically clock residence times: the rate at which any particular element enters the oceans and the rate at which this element interacts with clay minerals on the sea floor.

For example, the residence time of potassium ions depends

quite directly on the chemical transformation of two clays, illite to kaolinite. Sodium depends on a slightly different clay chemistry, the transformation of soda-montmorillonite to kaolinite and quartz, and magnesium on the transformation of chlorite to kaolinite and quartz.

While all this is very nice, it also illustrates the complexity of seawater chemistry because the transformation of these clay minerals on the ocean bottom, which directly controls the levels of sodium, potassium, and magnesium, also controls the levels of calcium in seawater. That, again, might be considered academic but for two points: (1) the sea creatures that construct shells need the calcium for raw material; and (2) calcium reacts reversibly with carbon dioxide from the atmosphere to form calcium carbonate. This simple reversible reaction makes it possible for the seas to soak up and store carbon dioxide and regulate the amount of carbon dioxide in the atmosphere that sustains life on earth.

While we have a great many details on this or that facet of sea chemistry, many are assemblages of scattered, random information, often gathered as footnotes by expeditions that had other purposes in mind. Nevertheless, ocean scientists have created some "models" of the ocean, conceptions that more or less fit known facts but incorporate a good deal of very educated guessing.

"The simplest models consider all oceans as one," Goldberg explains. "That is, the Pacific, Atlantic, Arctic, Antarctic, and Indian Ocean are lumped together as one gigantic ocean, the world ocean. We can sophisticate this model by saying the ocean consists of two parts, an upper mixed layer and the deeper ocean. We can then go to more and more complicated models where we actually divide the world ocean into its five components. But our sampling data is so sparse that as we go to more and more complicated oceans, our paucity of data does not allow us to make rigorous interpretations or studies."

In other words, when it comes to the type of questions being raised out of concern for the oceans, the marine chemist is at a loss. Will the lead-tainted rains on the North Atlantic change its nature? What pollutants threaten the calcium balance in the ocean that governs carbon-dioxide levels in our air? Will DDT drastically alter the pattern of oceanic life?

"You're asking us to consider phenomena," Goldberg points out, "that occur on two thirds of the earth in which the time clocks generally are longer than human lives and in which the distances involved are very great."

Aside from the intrinsic difficulty of studying the oceans, there are some more mundane problems. Funding is one. Although a number of attempts have been made by Goldberg and others, there is no concerted effort underway or even in the hard planning stage to study ocean pollution. The scientists in the United States involved in marine-pollution studies are, according to Goldberg, a small number—a "handful"—and the funds available to them are still limited.

Money is available for the pressing problems—the best way to dump sewage at sea, for example—but tight for the marine chemist who wants to study, say, the cycle of the nutrient element phosphorus in ocean waters.

In addition, marine chemistry has only within the last few years begun to develop and use unique instruments needed to study the chemistry of the sea, whether from a ship or from calmer spots on land.

"There are two types of oceanography," says Ralph Horne. "In one case, in an Aristotelian kind of sense, when you are actually trying to describe what the ocean is doing, you've clearly got to look at the ocean. But then there's another enormous segment of oceanography concerned with the chemical-physical phenomena which go on, and the place to observe these is not at sea but in the laboratory, where you've got some control over conditions, including yourself."

The main reason we know more about the bottom of the oceans than the seawater over it is a deep-sea drilling expedition that has taken core samples of the bottom of the world's oceans and that has produced textbooks of new information on the nature and origin of ocean bottom. An intriguing bit of information that has dropped out of this work is that the bottoms of most oceans are *younger* than the waters over them. The reason is a phenomenon called sea-floor spreading, by which new ocean floor is constantly created, old floors shifted, and continents moved as a side effect.

Scientists who know and love the seas agonize over the fragility of its life. The seas provide a constant milieu, much as our blood gives us a constant *milieu intérieur*. The proportion of salts in any ocean is amazingly constant; temperatures change slowly and little with the seasons; the food cycle is rigid and invariable. The point is that because the seas have always been gentle with their life, tuna and plankton and oysters and so on have not learned to reject or adapt to the harsher conditions now being imposed by man. Marine life, almost uniquely and in still unknown ways, will concentrate toxic substances such as lead and mercury that animals on land reject; the largest amounts of DDT turn up in the fat of fishes; oil in a marine ecosystem can cripple it for years.

Fish and oysters and shrimp and other delicacies of the seas are nourished indirectly by the sun, whose energy is used photosynthetically by sea plants to create carbohydrates and oxygen from carbon dioxide and water. Sea plants divide into two types: algae, which are rooted to one spot, and the floating plants, or phytoplankton ("plant wanderer" in Greek). The latter constitute some 90 percent of ocean life, and it is largely their presence or absence near the surface that makes a particular part of sea fertile or infertile. Phytoplankton tend to be rather willy-nilly in their driftings but are concentrated in coastal waters, which is why most of our seafood comes from this area rather than the deep ocean, which has little phytoplankton and is largely infertile.

Phytoplankton are food for microscopic animals called zooplankton, which, in turn, are eaten by fishes of all sizes and by whales. There is overall a continual progression in size, bigger fishes eating little fishes, and so on. The efficiency of this food web is about 10 percent, which means that 1,000 pounds of phytoplankton will support 100 pounds of zooplankton, which supports 10 pounds of fish, etc.

Whatever phytoplankton take in or make with the sun's help tends to be passed up this food web. For instance, vitamins created by phytoplankton are passed upward until eventually they reach the larger fishes including the cod, which we value for their vitamin-rich oil.

But while vitamins are obviously good, such things as mercury, lead, and DDT which are also taken in by phytoplankton and passed up the food web are obviously bad. What compounds this unfortunate thriftiness is the ability of sea creatures to concentrate chemicals within their bodies to levels hundreds to thousands of times higher than the seawater in which they live.

Phytoplankton, marvelously uncomplicated creatures, are quite incredible chemists: they can concentrate lead 40,000 times higher, copper some 30,000 times. Pick almost any sea creature and it will display a talent (probably necessary for survival) for concentrating some particular chemical. The sea cucumber takes in vanadium; oysters gather in copper and zinc; lobsters and mussels are fond of cobalt; and so it goes.

The point of this excursion into marine biology is that while the oceans are vast, the structure of life within them—the interconnected food web and the abilities to hoard chemicals—assures us that what goes into the sea will come back in one fashion or another. Mercury and DDT, for example, are at relatively low levels in seawater and, in fact, have yet to be found in the open oceans, but are all too present in seafood—tuna, salmon, shellfish, etc.

It may be tempting to simply ask for a halt in feeding the seas toxic materials that can enter the food web. However, that ignores the interconnected nature of sea and land. Farmers began mixing common talc with DDT to simplify spraying after World War II. Within a year, the talc (and the DDT) reached the open ocean and glaciers of the Northern Hemisphere.

Dr. Goldberg's group cut through glacial columns and found that within months after talc was first used in DDT sprayings, it landed on glaciers thousands of miles away. Glaciers grow at predictable rates of several inches a year and trap whatever happens to fall on them within the growing ice column. Moreover, glaciers—more accurately, permanent snowfields—are found in every latitude and under every major wind system of the earth, making them perfect recorders of what goes into the oceans. Goldberg also has caught talc in the open ocean by using a sticky material—"flypaper traps." Obviously, pollutants, once in the air, can be expected to travel globally in a short time. Goldberg's work helps explain the worldwide ubiquity of DDT and chlorinated hydrocarbons, including polychlorinated biphenyls (PCBs), industrial chemicals that are now global pollutants, albeit on a lesser scale than DDT. The unfortunate point about chlorinated hydrocarbons is that they tend to be relatively intractable to sunlight, water, time, and other forces that normally break apart more fragile molecules. Hence, DDT not only reaches the remotest regions of the globe but also survives intact or only slightly changed, which is why it is found in the fat of Antarctic penguins and is crippling the reproduction of the Bermuda petrel.

The same concern over global travels of pollutants applies to lead and mercury. The lead going out of tailpipes, wafted through the atmosphere, is reaching both deep and coastal oceans. Dr. Tsaihwa J. Chow, a marine chemist, also at Scripps, has found high levels of lead both in San Diego rain and in the liver of fish caught offshore, both part of the chain from car exhaust to human blood and nerve tissue.

In a comparable study, Goldberg and Dr. D. H. Klein found mercury levels in marine life about La Jolla (about ten miles north of San Diego) at some five hundred times above the levels in seawater. One cowrie, or seashell, had gathered twenty-one parts per million of mercury; the World Health Organization puts the safe limit at one half part per million. High mercury levels have been found in life as diverse as algae and tuna by Canadian, Japanese, Swedish, and United States scientists.

Most of the mercury in the oceans is natural, contributed by the weathering of rocks and soil, which usually contain an extremely tiny amount of mercury. Overall, the mercury being dumped by man is small. Mercury levels measured in preserved specimens of tuna caught in the last century were the same as tuna taken today, indicating that the industrial use of mercury, which began this century, has not made a significant difference. Moreover, it is fair to argue that because fish such as tuna are notably heavy breathers, which means that they flush a great

Dr. Edward D. Goldberg of the Scripps Institution of Oceanography
measuring lead-isotope levels in samples taken from ocean bottoms.
Courtesy: Scripps Institution of Oceanography

Levels of lead in seawater being measured with mass spectrometer
by Dr. Tsaihwa J. Chow, research chemist at the Scripps Institution
of Oceanography. *Courtesy: Scripps Institution of Oceanography
(Photo by Glasheen Graphics)*

deal of water past their gills, the high mercury levels in these fishes is not due to man but marine biology.

However, that does not mean that man's wastes cannot have a significant and damaging effect on marine life, particularly in the coastal ocean and the estuaries where rivers mix with the sea. For example, Goldberg and Klein found that mercury levels went up the closer the fish swam to outfalls from sewers, a major source of mercury wastes. Moreover, many of the assumptions about mercury, lead, and other wastes in the oceans rest on the oceans' enormous ability to dilute dangerous levels to insignificant ones. This may be a delusion.

The oceans are compartmentalized, and what goes into one compartment may not necessarily seep into the next. The "walls" in the marine compartments are made up of many factors, one of the more substantial being the considerable increase in saltiness the deeper one goes. This means that surface water is lighter, less salty than deep water and that the two don't readily mix. Some researchers estimate that ocean water may "turn over" from top to bottom every 1,000 to 10,000 years.

More to the point, the fact that the oceans are stratified, or divided into layers, means that wastes such as lead raining on surface waters are not diluted by the entire ocean but are trapped in surface waters.

As a consequence, "the lead concentration in the upper layers of the oceans is now several times the average lead concentration in the total ocean," according to a report, "Wastes Management Concepts for the Coastal Zone," prepared jointly by the National Academy of Sciences and the National Academy of Engineering.

What applies to lead presumably applies to the other wastes, including chlorinated hydrocarbons and mercury, that can enter the oceans from the atmosphere. In any case, calculations or illustrations that take the whole ocean into account may be wildly, even dangerously, off the mark.

This may be as good a point as any to be reminded of the oceans' infinite capacity to surprise us. This is exactly what happened with mercury. For decades, industrial plants, farmers, and research scientists (even including such fierce environmentalists

as Barry Commoner) had made it a practice to dump mercury
freely into the open waters in the then-logical belief that it was
inert and that once on the marine bottom it would stay there.
In 1969 came the chilling report in *Nature* by two Swedish
scientists that "both mono and dimethyl mercury can be produced in bottom sediments and in rotten fish." Translated, it
meant that mercury metal in the sea has been transformed by
microbes into materials that could easily enter the marine food
web. Mercury was a menace. Of course, suspicions had been
sounded before, largely in Japan and Sweden, countries that
depend heavily on fishing and where "mercury incidents" have
occurred.

Although many details of the transformation of mercury by
microbes into methyl and dimethyl mercury (CH_3Hg + and
CH_3HgCH_3) are still unclear, it is apparent that the methyla-
tion reaction produces highly flexible mercury compounds that
can take several options in their return to man: they may be
soaked on to the surface of simple marine life, or may penetrate
the bodies of tuna and other fishes, either through the gills or
through the food chain.

It may be that the mercury problem will be with us for centuries, even though dumping has been sharply cut back. The
microbes that methylate mercury work slowly, and there is a
heavy "backlog" of mercury in the waters. We should be grateful that mercury is fairly expensive as industrial materials go
and that many companies did make a serious effort for economic
reasons to recover waste mercury rather than simply dump it.

Why was mercury overlooked for so long? There are many
reasons, some of a bureaucratic nature, but some technical.
Methyl and dimethyl mercury vaporize easily, and, because fish
tissue is usually heated as part of a chemical analysis, mercury
compounds were simply driven off and not detected.

Metals in the oceans are particularly worrisome to ocean
scientists because they are generally toxic and because they
are more-or-less permanent additions to the seawater, leaving
only after a residence of about 1,000 years. The actual effects of
metals such as lead and mercury on ocean life are unknown. In
humans, at high doses, both metals can cause serious damage
to the brain and eventually death.

The effects of low levels of DDT and similar chlorinated hydrocarbons can be more accurately cataloged. DDT can play havoc with the life cycle of any particular fish. For instance, it apparently may reduce the ability of the salmon to tolerate temperature changes, disorient it so it cannot return to the spawning stream, and in general cripple the "survival repertoire" —the mechanisms for avoiding hazards and for escape.

The ironic point about DDT, *Marine Pollution Bulletin* notes, is that the organisms in the sea "are often more sensitive to pesticides than are the pests they are used to control on land."

Crustaceans—shrimps, crabs, etc.—are quite vulnerable to low levels of DDT in the parts-per-billion range. Dungeness crabs, which help bring the tourists down to San Francisco's Fisherman's Wharf, are in decline, and DDT and other chlorinated hydrocarbons are being blamed. Tadpoles go into a tail-lashing frenzy in barely measurable levels of DDT, which may explain the decline of frogs in some areas.

In the laboratory, low levels of DDT interfere with the photosynthesis of phytoplankton. Whether that is true in the open sea is (typically) unknown, but, nevertheless, several scientists have pointed out that since a good deal of the world's oxygen comes from phytoplankton, DDT and other toxic pollutants pose a direct threat to our survival.

Many scientists are inclined to be doubtful. Dr. John H. Ryther of the Woods Hole Oceanographic Institution, writing in *Nature*, points out that even if photosynthesis in the oceans were to be completely cut off, "the total quantity of oxygen in the atmosphere could decrease by 10 per cent in no less than one million years." Moreover, as Ryther also points out, DDT seems to have a selective effect on phytoplankton, poisoning some species and having no effect on others. Thus, DDT "may influence the species composition of phytoplankton [rather] than eliminate them entirely."

DDT (and, again, the other chlorinated hydrocarbons) has several unfortunate properties that make it the perfect hazard. It is chemically very stable and may survive in the open oceans for decades. It does break down slightly through metabolism in animal bodies, but these metabolic products appear just as stable and toxic as their parent. DDT readily sticks to small particles, such as the talc Goldberg found in glaciers, which gives it its high mobility. This effect is compounded by the high evaporation of DDT from sprayed plants—60 percent according to one report. Most importantly, while DDT is not very soluble in water, it does dissolve easily in fatty, oily materials. In the oceans, that means DDT finds the fatty tissue of fish a more comfortable place than the seawater.

As with mercury, the problem of DDT and other persistent organic chemicals is quite likely to become worse even though several countries have or will severely limit its use. DDT has two uses: it controls agricultural pests, and it helps control the anopheles mosquito, which carries the parasite of malaria, a disease that contrary to popular belief is still a major killer in tropical countries. These countries, faced with a serious health problem and dependent on a cheap control such as DDT, are not inclined to worry over fish kill, poor bird reproduction, and suspected danger to humans. As a minister of health in Indonesia once put it at a meeting of the World Health Organization: "I would rather die of cancer in old age than of malaria in childhood."

The point here is that while Sweden, Hungary, Denmark, and other countries that don't have to cope with malaria have banned DDT and similar insecticides, other countries will continue to apply it enthusiastically.

"For example," says Edward Goldberg, "India may become one of the prime producers of DDT in the world, and the distribution of this chlorinated hydrocarbon for agriculture and public health may have a profound effect on marine life."

It is doubtful that India and other countries pressed by the basic need of survival will do any better in keeping DDT in bounds than we have. For example, it is believed that only about half of all DDT sprayed in the past ever reached the plants it was supposed to protect. About 240,000 metric tons a year eventually reaches the oceans.

The persistence of DDT in seawater means that it may continue to be a problem even in countries where its use is declining. Dr. James L. Cox of the Hopkins Marine Station in

Pacific Grove, California, reported in *Science* that DDT levels in phytoplankton have risen steadily from 1955 to 1969, even though this was a time when DDT use in the United States was going down. In effect, what is happening is that phytoplankton continue to soak up DDT that is already present in the water, accumulating in brick-by-brick fashion and doing it slowly enough so that the actual effects of declining use will not become apparent for years. As Cox put it, "a delay may be expected before the decline of domestic usage of DDT begins to be reflected in the components of these food chains."

While DDT and toxic metals are of greatest concern because of their persistence, the most dramatic and probably the most publicized oceanic pollutant is oil. But, again, its actual effects on both ocean and ocean life are uncertain. Crude oil is disposed of by natural processes. The "lighter fractions"—those portions that evaporate at low temperatures—are dispersed into the atmosphere. The heavier fractions spread out on the sea surface, forming a layer one or two molecules thick. This layer is attacked by microbes and oxygen, with the breakdown helped along by sea and sunlight.

But local oil spills in a bay, estuary, or channel can utterly destroy for many years the tight web of marine life. When, in March 1957, the oil tanker *Tampico Mara* went aground and spilled her load in a small, unpolluted cove on the coast of Baja California, Mexico, practically all life within the cove was destroyed; in about a year, all trace of the oil was gone, but it took two years before life in the cove came back to something approaching normalcy.

"Four years after the accident," reported Robert Holcomb in *Science,* "sea urchin and abalone populations were still greatly reduced, and, at the last observations in 1967, several species present ten years earlier had not returned."

Oil mixes quite nicely with DDT, and there is evidence that oil slicks at sea are considerably enriched in this pesticide. In effect, DDT is "packaged" and concentrated by the oil, setting a one-two trap for whatever form of life happens to encounter it. DDT and other pesticides are also concentrated by natural sea slicks formed from the decay of surface plankton. These slicks are quite common, especially in coastal waters, and often are several miles long.

Two scientists at the University of Miami, Drs. Eugene F. Corcoran and Douglas B. Seba, found that a natural slick contained thirteen parts per billion of DDT, while slickless water in the same area contained less than thirteen parts per *trillion*, or below the detection limits of their instruments.

The net effect, whether spilled oil or natural sea slicks do the concentrating, is to boost DDT from unmeasurable levels to amounts that can disrupt marine life. This kind of mutual self-help by pollutants is only beginning to be explored.

While several possible effects of low, nonkilling levels of oil on marine life have been suggested, ranging from slow poisoning of phytoplankton to higher rates of cancer among fishes, the actual effects are still uncertain. However, there is agreement that if oil is dangerous, the first victim may well be the Arctic Ocean. The most obvious reason is the cold. Oil is broken down more slowly in the colder waters of the North Atlantic because the microbes responsible for the breakdown prefer warmer temperatures. The best guess now is that oil in Arctic water may survive for fifty years or more.

Aside from the cold, it is the compression of life into a few short weeks when the sun is high and the ice has momentarily receded that makes the Arctic so vulnerable. "It is this greatly restricted season of plant production which is the true harshness of Arctic waters," comments I. McLaren in *Marine Life in Arctic Waters, the Unbelievable Land.*

The particular effects of oil on the Arctic ecology are unknown. Our knowledge of ecological cycles of the sea comes almost exclusively from the temperate oceans, particularly the North Atlantic and, to a lesser extent, the Pacific and Indian oceans. And what we know about these areas, according to *Marine Pollution Bulletin*, "is encyclopedic compared with what we know about the basic ecology of Arctic and tropical waters."

As with DDT and the toxic metals, the fact that we now know that oil can be a problem doesn't mean things are going to improve. For example, as United States oil reserves continue to decline, imports will increase, putting more oil on the high seas. Also, oil tankers now being built are so large, some having a greater draft than most aircraft carriers, that there is a very real danger that they will collide with the sea floor. Indeed a Japanese giant tanker, the *Idematsu Maru*, has already scraped the bottom of the Strait of Malacca, not because of navigation errors but because the ship was simply too large. Historically, there has always been a considerable margin for error between a ship's draft and the presumed depth of the waters being steamed through. Now, with increased economic pressures, that margin of safety is disappearing. As the *New Scientist* pointed out, an extra foot of draft on a modern tanker can mean another $70,000 to an oil company. The problem of giant size may be compounded by their reported lack of enough power to maneuver tankers quickly when needed.

Parenthetically, we do have the means now to make a very substantial dent in the amount of oil spilled on the oceans. This was pointed out by the Study of Critical Environmental Problems (SCEP), which emerged from a summer of work in 1970 in Williamstown, Massachusetts, with a splendid and very well-received report, *Man's Impact on the Global Environment*. SCEP noted that tankers cleaning out their tanks at sea after they have delivered their oil are the major source of oil pollution in the open ocean, pouring in some 530,000 metric tons a year. Some 500,000 tons of that, or 95 percent, comes from the 20 percent of the tankers that do not use the load-on-top (LOT) method of cleaning their tanks.

Tankers, after they have delivered their oil, use seawater as ballast for the return trip. The usual practice is to clean the tanks of residual oil and any debris by dumping it with the seawater before coming into port to pick up another cargo. In the LOT technique, before the ballast is poured out, the oil wastes are retained and dumped into a "sump tank" for later disposal. The LOT method is more expensive and less convenient, but it does cut oil pollution sharply.

For the tankers not using the LOT technique, the corrective is quite simple. As SCEP points out in understated fashion, "if the United States . . . were to ban tankers not using LOT from its ports, the resulting pressure to adopt LOT might be considerable."

The policing of the oil-pollution problem should improve.

NASA announced in 1971 that scientists at its Ames Research Center in Mountain View, California, have developed sensing devices that can find oil slicks from an aircraft and, eventually, a satellite. The oil is spotted by sharp differences from ordinary ocean water in the ultraviolet and infrared portions of the spectrum of sunlight reflected off the sea surface. This aerial reconnaissance not only makes it possible to follow the global travels of oil but also will enable researchers, by repeated flights and by comparing spectra, to actually measure the amount of oil spilled. In addition, methods are becoming available to identify the sources of oil slicks. One is neutron activation analysis (NAA), in which a slick is traced back to the suspected source by matching up "fingerprints" of trace elements between the slick and the source.

We do know a great deal about one pollutant that at times is beautifully controlled and indeed has taught us some basic facts about the oceans that may help assess the future effects of oil, metals, DDT, and so on.

This "helpful" pollutant is radioactivity—radioactive wastes from nuclear tests, power plants, and nuclear-fuel processing. While, as already pointed out, radioactive wastes are in every drop of ocean water, most (but not all) scientists familiar with the subject do not think them a danger, largely because of the tight control on radioactive wastes by most nuclear powers and our detailed knowledge of what radioactive wastes do in the open seas and where they go.

"We have more data on radioactive wastes in the oceans than anything else," says Dr. Vaughan T. Bowen of the Woods Hole Oceanographic Institution. Bowen should know; his laboratory helps gather about half the world's data on fallout.

The pioneer nuclear powers—the United States, Soviet Union, and Great Britain—have made a considerable effort to make sure their radioactive wastes don't leak into open waters. The British seem by common consent to have gone the furthest in making sure that their citizenry doesn't suffer from radioactive pollution. Their rewards have not only been a high degree of safety from radioactive hazards but a considerably better press for nuclear power plants than in the United States. Any new proposals for nuclear sites go through a filtering process of governmental and private agencies, including the British Society for Social Responsibility in Science, which can be as tough a watchdog as its name implies.

The elegance of the British approach to controlling radioactive wastes is testified by their concern for the laverbread eaters. Laverbread is a Welsh delicacy made from seaweed and sold in the market at Swansea and other towns in south Wales. It's actually made from a mixture of seaweeds, one of which is called *Porphyra umbilicalis* and grows offshore from the largest nuclear-fuel-processing plant in Britain, the Windscale plant on the Irish Sea. Windscale is operated by the United Kingdom Atomic Energy Authority and processes spent fuels from nuclear-power plants in England and Scotland. Included in the nuclear wastes put into the sea by Windscale is a radioactive form of ruthenium, ruthenium-106. Unfortunately, Porphyra has a talent for concentrating ruthenium to levels some one hundred times beyond its concentrations in seawater.

What the British have done is to make sure that the amount of ruthenium that goes into the Irish Sea is low enough so that even the most enthusiastic Welsh fancier of laverbread could stuff himself continually with laverbread made *exclusively* from Porphyra and still not take in damaging amounts of radioactive ruthenium.

While radioactive wastes do not appear to be a large-scale hazard at this time, studies of their distribution have pointed up serious gaps in what we know of the distribution and effects of other wastes in the oceans.

For example, Vaughan Bowen points out that because we don't really know the rain patterns in the open oceans, we can't easily tell where atmospheric pollutants in the rain—DDT, lead, etc.—are actually coming down. Also, the wastes that do fall on the oceans are stirred, or blended—"homogenized," Bowen says —at much lower rates than supposed. "Even after several years of stirring, the pot isn't mixed," Bowen says.

He and his colleagues have reported that strontium-90 fallout is much greater over the oceans than over land. An easy guess is because it rains more over the oceans. Whatever the reason, they point out that "an actual difference exists in the rate of transfer of stratospheric debris to the lower stratosphere."

So here are two facts that should make us wary of dismissing possible damage by toxic wastes to the oceans: more is likely to come down on the oceans than on land, and it will be homogenized, or diluted slowly, at rates measuring into years, meaning that a pollutant can build up in surface waters.

This is useful data, particularly to ocean scientists, who admittedly still lack the kind of knowledge about the natural ocean that can enable them to judge the effects of a particular pollutant such as mercury or lead or DDT or oil on ocean processes.

How desperate has the problem of waste disposal become? And why do the oceans look so attractive to sanitary engineers onshore, who have to face the daily disposal of hundreds of tons of sewage sludge and industrial and other wastes?

Unless the earth continually grows, which it doesn't, the old sea floor being pushed away by the newly created sediment must go somewhere, and it does at tectonic sinks, usually deep trenches in areas noted for their earthquake activity. These tectonic sinks, where old ocean floor disappears quite literally into the bowels of the earth, are located off the coastlines of the eastern and southern Pacific, the western and southern Atlantic, off North Africa, and elsewhere. Two researchers from the University of Washington in Seattle, Drs. R. C. Bostrom and M. A. Sherif, have suggested dumping wastes in tightly compressed containers heavy enough to go straight down into these tectonic sinks. They argue that the costs of transporting wastes in the United States (some $4.5 billion a year) are now so huge that their method might be cheaper—what *Marine Pollution Bulletin* calls a "natural whirlaway."

Until recently, we had no firm fix on what was actually being dumped into the oceans. Many of the specific wastes discussed (chlorinated hydrocarbons, metals, etc.) make up a significant portion. That we now have some proximate idea of what and how much is due to an already classical report prepared by the Dillingham Environmental Corporation, of La Jolla, California, under a contract from the United States Bureau of Solid Waste Management. In one year, according to the report issued in 1970, some 48 million tons of wastes were dumped into the oceans at a cost of $29 million. Most of that is dredge spoils carved out of the bottoms of rivers, estuaries, and the like by the United States Corps of Engineers as part of its responsibility for keeping navigation lanes cleared. What toxic wastes are in the dredge spoils is uncertain but probably substantial. Industrial and sewage wastes come next, then refuse and garbage, radioactive wastes, construction and demolition debris, and military and chemical warfare agents.

Each category gets different dumping treatment, the exact form depending on money available, the public relations aspects, and possible dangers. A guiding principle is (or should be) that if you dump into deep ocean water, then make sure it'll stay there; if you dump in near-shore, shallow water, then make sure it's quickly diluted and dispersed by currents.

What dumping can do is typified by the New York Bight, an area off Sandy Hook, New Jersey, where New York City has been dumping wastes for about forty years. The Bight is a desert. Continual dumping of fertilizing wastes—phosphates and nitrates—that, like fertilizers on land, spur plant growth (algae) and use up a necessary oxygen balance has stagnated the water. A ten-square-mile area of the Bight is covered by a blanket of wastes three feet thick. Whatever kind of life nature intended for the area has departed.

The important questions, however, are whether the wastes are moving beyond the dumping area and what are the consequences. So far, there is no hard evidence that any sizable movements are taking place. But again, conclusions are based more on what we don't know than what we do. How fast do wastes on the Bight bottom move? What sort of currents move over them, and in what directions? How fast do the wastes decompose? Is it possible to establish a balance sheet, matching the dumping rate with the Bight's ability to dispose of them?

Some notable attempts have been made to help the oceans in their self-protective dilution reaction to dumped wastes. For instance, Los Angeles and some other cities send their sewage sludge out through sea pipelines, some several miles long. These pipes come pierced at periodic intervals. If the depth and rate of seepage are correct, the sewage, rather than rising to the top, will billow out in a fine plume, becoming diluted to a point where the sea can easily assimilate it.

Much of the basic work on these colander pipes has been done by Professor Norman Brooks at the California Institute of Technology. The work takes advantage of the natural layers in the oceans formed by increasing saltiness with deeper waters. The denser layers of salt prevent the sewage from rising to the top.

Proposals have been made to cart solid wastes from garbage and refuse to sea and to incinerate them there. Obvious advantages are less urban air pollution and ready disposal. While the scheme is considered impractical so far, largely due to expense, it has produced some unique studies of the effects of dumping ashes into ocean waters. That work has been done by a group led by Dr. Melvin First, a sanitary engineer on the faculty of the Harvard School of Public Health in Boston. First's group looked at possible effects of incinerator residue on a spectrum of ocean life, from phytoplankton to flounder, and also examined possible effects along the ocean bottom. It is one of the most systematic studies of its kind ever done, and even includes a research submarine to watch underwater effects. First found that residues injected into what he calls "holes in the oceans"—valleys or depressions in the ocean bottom—will stay there. "What we also find," First says, "is that we must discharge the residue in waters that are at least two hundred feet deep in order to be assured that they will not spread around the ocean floor."

Their studies of the effects of dumped ashes on marine life were encouraging: while very heavy doses killed fish, as would ordinary clean sand, lethality was due to mechanical rather than chemical reasons. The gills of the fishes simply were plugged up by excess ashes. The effects of long-term but low-level residues on various marine life were tested on flounder and hardshell clams, which were penned up in a harbor. No untoward effects were found, and, in fact, the clams seemed to do better in the residue water. While some marine life—notably the sea scallop and the juvenile menhaden—were found to be sensitive to fairly low amounts of incinerator residue, the amounts used were equal to twenty-five years of daily disposal of five hundred tons over a square-mile area.

While cities have no plans to sail incinerators to sea, First's work indicates that wastes can be carried to sea and dumped with little harm to marine life if properly treated and judiciously rationed. But again the caveat! The sea has a way of surprising us, and even careful studies may miss a curve that the oceans will throw at us.

In the next few years, we will be forced to use the sea as tonnages of wastes—industrial and domestic—continue to rise steeply. Reports on ocean dumping, such as that issued in 1970 by the President's Council on Environmental Quality, call for virtually an across-the-board cut in ocean dumping and urge a turn to recycling wastes. That will come but not in the near future. Dr. M. Grant Gross, a research oceanographer at the State University of New York at Stony Brook, told a Senate Subcommittee on Air and Water Pollution in 1970 that "if the continental shelf is to be used for waste disposal, we must learn how to operate a 'sanitary landfill' at sea without seriously damaging the ocean, its life, or the adjacent shores. We have not done well in the past."

This plea of ignorance—the leitmotiv in any discussion of ocean pollution—begs the question of what do the scientists want to know? That itself can set off a squabble, but an excellent prescription for obtaining a base-line reading of the oceans' current state was offered by the Study of Critical Environmental Problems (SCEP). Essentially, it proposed a one-year program "to collect approximately 1,000 samples from the following components of the environment: oceans, organisms, rivers, glaciers, rain, and sediment."

SCEP suggested collecting samples at various depths and places from both the shallow and deep parts of the oceans. It suggested surface-film samples "spread generally over the ocean but with emphasis on the major zones of precipitation and evaporation, and on the major shipping routes (especially oil routes)."

SCEP urged the collection of 320 samples of oceanic life, primarily in the more fertile coastal areas; collection of water and bottom sediments from the major rivers, whose state is intimately tied to the state of the oceans; collection of glacier samples beginning at the present and cutting back into the historical ice column to 1800; collection of oceanic rain samples; and the sampling of deep ocean sediment such as ferromanganese nodules.

As this chapter, I hope, has made clear, there is a very real concern for the oceans, based not so much on hard fact but suggestive evidence: rising DDT levels, the quick global travels of lead and other pollutants, the fragility of the oceanic food chain, and other symptoms cataloged here. The SCEP survey is one approach to answering the question of whether and how the oceans can survive our culture.

A hard look at the oceans may help answer the question Edward Goldberg once asked: "When did progress end and ecological disaster begin?"

A

SELECTED

BIBLIOGRAPHY

CHAPTER 1: ATTACKING GENETIC MISTAKES

CARTER, C. O. *An ABC of Medical Genetics.* Boston: Little Brown and Company, 1969.

DAVIS, BERNARD D. "Prospects for Genetic Intervention in Man." *Science,* December 18, 1970, pp. 1279–83.

DEMARS, ROBERT, et al. "Lesch-Nyhan Mutation: Prenatal Detection with Amniotic Fluid Cells." *Science,* June 13, 1969, pp. 1303–5.

DOBZHANSKY, THEODOSIUS. *Mankind Evolving.* New Haven and London: Yale University Press, 1962.

HANDLER, PHILIP (ed.). *Biology and the Future of Man.* London: Oxford University Press, 1970, pp. 648–51.

LESCH, MICHAEL, and NYHAN, WILLIAM L. "A Familial Disorder of Uric Acid Metabolism and Central Nervous System Function." *American Journal of Medicine,* April 1964, pp. 561–70.

"Mass Screening Finds Infant Metabolic Defects." *Chemical & Engineering News,* March 8, 1971, pp. 50–51.

NYHAN, WILLIAM L. "Human Purine Metabolism and Behavior." *Engineering and Science* (published by the California Institute of Technology), April 1970, pp. 45–49.

ROGERS, STANFIELD. "Skills for Genetic Engineers." *New Scientist* (now *New Scientist and Science Journal*), January 29, 1971, pp. 194–96.

A comprehensive review of the work on the Lesch-Nyhan syndrome up to 1968 is found in *Federation Proceedings* (Vol. 27), July–August 1968, Federation of American Societies for Experimental Biology.

CHAPTER 2: DISSONANT HARMONY: THE RIDDLE OF AGING

BJORKSTEN, JOHAN. "Why Grow Old?" *Chemistry,* June 1964, pp. 6–11.

BULLOUGH, W. S. "Ageing of Mammals." *Nature,* February 26, 1971, pp. 608–10.

COMFORT, ALEX. *Ageing: The Biology of Senescence.* New York: Holt, Rinehart and Winston, 1964.

———. *The Process of Ageing.* New York: The New American Library, 1961.

"The Enigma of Human Aging" (two parts). *Chemical & Engineering News,* February 12 and February 19, 1962, pp. 138–46 and 104–10.

KOHN, ROBERT R. "Human Aging and Disease." *Journal of Chronic Diseases* 16, 1963, pp. 5–21.

SHOCK, NATHAN W. "Biological Concepts of Aging." *Psychiatric Research Report* No. 23, February 1968, pp. 1–25.

———. "The Physiology of Aging." *Scientific American,* January 1962, pp. 100–10.

SINEX, MAROTT F. "Biochemistry of Aging." *Perspectives in Biology and Medicine,* Winter 1966, pp. 208–24.

STREHLER, B. L. *Time, Cells, and Aging.* New York: Academic Press, 1962.

TAPPEL, A. L. "Will Antioxidant Nutrients Slow Aging Processes?" *Geriatrics,* October 1968, pp. 97–105.

VERZÁR, FREDERIC. "The Aging of Collagen." *Scientific American*, April 1963, pp. 104–14.

CHAPTER 3: SEEKING THE ORIGINS OF STARS AND LIFE

BUHL, DAVID, and SNYDER, LEWIS E. "From Radio Astronomy Towards Astrochemistry." *Technology Review*, April 1971, pp. 54–62.

DICKINSON, DALE F. "Radio Astronomy Opens Wider Windows on Space." *Smithsonian*, November 1970, pp. 56–63.

HOYLE, FRED. *The Black Cloud*. New York: Harper and Row, 1958.

———, and WICKRAMASINGHE, N. C. "Interstellar Grains." *Nature*, August 2, 1969, pp. 459–62.

MERRILL, PAUL W. *Space Chemistry*. Ann Arbor: University of Michigan Press, 1963.

MITTON, SIMON. "The Molecules of Space." *New Scientist* (now *New Scientist and Science Journal*), August 20, 1970, pp. 369–70.

"Tempo Quickens in Astrochemical Research." *Chemical & Engineering News*, April 14, 1969, pp. 38–39.

THADDEUS, PATRICK. "Molecules in Space." *Science Year* (1972), pp. 66–79.

THOMSEN, DIETRICK E. "Interstellar Clouds: A New Kind of Chemistry." *Science News*, August 8, 1970, pp. 124–25.

WICK, GERALD L. "Interstellar Molecules: Chemicals in the Sky." *Science*, October 9, 1970, pp. 149–50.

CHAPTER 4: THE SEARCH FOR SUPERHEAVY ELEMENTS

BHANDARI, N., et al. "Superheavy Elements in Extraterrestrial Samples." *Nature*, March 26, 1971, pp. 219–24.

KELLER, O. LEWIN, JR. "Predicted Properties of Elements 113 and 114." *Chemistry*, November 1970, pp. 8–11.

LEACHMAN, R. B. "Nuclear Fission." *Scientific American*, August 1965, pp. 49–59.

MARINOV, A., et al. "Evidence for the Possible Existence of a Superheavy Element with Atomic Number 112." *Nature*, February 12, 1971, pp. 464–67.

PEIRLS, R. E. "The Atomic Nucleus." *Scientific American*, January 1959, pp. 75–80.

SEABORG, GLENN T. "Elements Beyond 100, Present Status and Future Prospects." *Annual Review of Nuclear Science* (1968), pp. 53–151.

———, and BLOOM, JUSTIN L. "The Synthetic Elements: IV." *Scientific American*, April 1969, pp. 57–67.

CHAPTER 5: NEUTRINOS: HOW THE SUN SHINES

BAHCALL, JOHN N. "Neutrinos from the Sun." *Scientific American*, July 1969, pp. 29–37.

DAVIS, RAYMOND, JR. "Neutrino." *McGraw-Hill Yearbook of Science and Technology*, New York, 1969.

———, et al. "Search for Neutrinos from the Sun." *Physical Review Letters*, May 20, 1968, pp. 1205–09.

FOWLER, WILLIAM A. "The Origins of the Elements." *The Scientific Endeavor*. New York: Rockefeller University Press, pp. 10–46.

WICK, GERALD L. "Neutrino Astronomy: Probing the Sun's Interior." *Science*, September 10, 1971, pp. 1011–12.

Several past issues of *Sharp Bits*, published by the Homestake Mining Company, contain articles and pictures on the construction of the neutrino detector. For information, write to James B. Dunn, Homestake Mining Company, P.O. 887, Lead, South Dakota 57754.

CHAPTER 6: UNRAVELING THE MYSTERY OF ANCIENT GLASS

Application of Science in Examination of Works of Art. Boston: Museum of Fine Arts, 1966.

"Archaeology—A Growing Role for Chemistry." *Chemical & Engineering News*, September 30, 1968, pp. 36–39.

BRILL, R. H. "The Scientific Investigation of Ancient Glasses." *Proceedings of the Eighth International Congress on Glass* (1968), pp. 47–68.

———, and MOLL, SHELDON. "The Electron Beam Microanalysis of Ancient Glass," *Advances in Glass Technology* (Part 2) (1963), pp. 293–302.

BROTHWELL, DON R., and HIGGS, ERIC (ed.). *Science in Archaeology*. New York: Basic Books, 1963.

CALEY, EARLE R. "On the Application of Chemistry to Archaeology." *The Ohio Journal of Science*, January 1948, pp. 1–14.

SAYRE, EDWARD V., and SMITH, RAY W. "Some Materials of Glass Manufacturing in Antiquity." *Archaeological Chemistry: A Symposium,* (ed. Martin Levy). Philadelphia: University of Pennsylvania Press, 1967, pp. 279–311.

SCRANTON, ROBERT L. "Glass Pictures from the Sea." *Archaeology,* June 1967, pp. 163–73.

WERNER, A. E. A. "Analytical Methods in Archaeology." *Analytical Chemistry,* February 1968, pp. 28A–41A.

A very useful newsletter on the use of science in archaeology is published periodically by the Applied Science Center for Archaeology, University Museum, University of Pennsylvania, 33rd and Spruce Streets, Philadelphia, Pennsylvania 19104.

CHAPTER 7: ON THE TRAIL OF RIBONUCLEASE

BRAGG, LAWRENCE. "X-Ray Crystallography." *Scientific American,* July 1968, pp. 58–70.

DENKEWALTER, ROBERT G., and HIRSCHMANN, RALPH. "The Synthesis of an Enzyme." *American Scientist,* Winter 1969, pp. 389–409.

LOCKE, DAVID M. *Enzymes—The Agents of Life.* New York: Crown, 1969.

MERRIFIELD, R. B. "The Automatic Synthesis of Proteins." *Scientific American,* March 1968, pp. 56–74.

PERUTZ, M. F. "The Hemoglobin Molecule." *Scientific American,* November 1964, pp. 64–76.

STEIN, WILLIAM H., and MOORE, STANFORD. "The Chemical Structure of Proteins." *Scientific American,* February 1961, pp. 81–92.

CHAPTER 8: NITROGEN FIXATION: MORE PROTEINS FROM AN OLD PUZZLE

CARNAHAN, JAMES E., et al. "Nitrogen Fixation in Cell-Free Extracts of *Clostridium Pasteurianum.*" *Biochima et Biophysica Acta, 44,* pp. 520–35, 1960.

CHATT, J., et al. "Chemical Evidence Concerning the Function of Molybdenum in Nitrogenase." *Nature,* December 20, 1969, pp. 1201–02.

DELWICHE, C. C. "The Nitrogen Cycle." *Scientific American,* September 1970, pp. 136–46.

HARDY, R. W. F., and BURNS, R. C. "Biological Nitrogen Fixation." *Annual Review of Biochemistry*, 37 (1968), pp. 331–58.

POSTGATE, JOHN. *Microbes and Man.* Baltimore: Penguin Books, 1969.

———. "Biological Nitrogen Fixation." *Nature*, April 4, 1970, pp. 25–27.

VAN TAMELEN, EUGENE E. "Design and Development of an Organic-Inorganic System for the Chemical Modification of Molecular Nitrogen Under Mild Conditions." *Accounts of Chemical Research*, November 1970, pp. 361–67.

CHAPTER 9: INSECTS: A MOLECULAR LIFE

BLUM, MURRAY S. "Alarm Pheromones." *Annual Review of Entomology* (1969), pp. 57–80.

KARLSON, P., and BUTENANDT, A. "Pheromones (ectohormones) in Insects." *Annual Review of Entomology* (1959), pp. 39–58.

OHTAKI, TETSUYA; MILKMAN, ROGER D.; and WILLIAMS, CARROLL M. "Dynamics of Ecdysone Secretion and Action in the Flesh Fly Sarcophaga Peregrina." *The Biological Bulletin*, October 1968, pp. 322–34.

ROELOFS, WENDELL L., and ARN, HEINRICH. "Sex Attractant of the Red-Banded Leaf Roller Moth." *Nature*, August 3, 1968, p. 513.

———, and TETTE, JAMES P. "Sex Pheromone of the Oblique-Banded Leaf Roller Moth." *Nature*, June 20, 1970, p. 1172.

SCHNEIDER, DIETRICH. "Insect Olfaction: Deciphering System for Chemical Messages." *Science*, March 7, 1969, pp. 1031–37.

WILLIAMS, CARROLL M. "Third-Generation Pesticides." *Scientific American*, July 1967, pp. 13–17.

———. "The Juvenile Hormone of Insects." *Nature*, July 28, 1956, pp. 212–13.

WILSON, EDWARD O. "Chemical Communication in the Social Insects." *Science 49* (1965), pp. 1064–71.

CHAPTER 10: RUSSIAN WATER

CHRISTIAN, P. A., and BERKA, L. H. "Preparing Polywater and Other Anomalous Liquids." *Chemistry*, January 1971, pp. 25–28.

DERYAGUIN, B. V., "Superdense Water." *Scientific American*, November 1970, pp. 52–71.

EYRING, HENRY, et al. "The Liquid State." *International Science and Technology*, March 1963, pp. 56–66.

LEAR, JOHN. "The Water That Won't Freeze." *Saturday Review,* September 6, 1969, pp. 49–52 (also see articles by Frederick M. Fowkes and B. V. Deryaguin in same issue).

LIPPINCOTT, ELLIS R., et al. "Polywater." *Science,* June 27, 1969, pp. 1482–87.

ZIMAN, J. M. "Some Pathologies of the Scientific Life." *Nature,* September 5, 1970, pp. 996–97.

CHAPTER 11: THE POLLUTED OCEANS

Chlorinated Hydrocarbons in the Marine Environment. National Academy of Sciences, 1971.

GOLDBERG, E. D. "Chemical Description of the Oceans." *Technology Review,* June 1970, pp. 25–29.

———. "Chemical Invasion of Ocean by Man." *McGraw-Hill Yearbook of Science and Technology,* New York, 1970, pp. 64–73.

HAMMOND, ALLEN L. "Mercury in the Environment: Natural and Human Factors." *Science,* February 26, 1970, pp. 788–89.

JOSEPHS, M. J. "Chemistry and the Oceans." *Chemical & Engineering News,* June 1, 1964, pp. 3A–48A.

MACINTYRE, FERREN. "Why the Sea Is Salt." *Scientific American,* November 1970, pp. 104–15.

Man's Impact on the Global Environment. Report of the Study of Critical Environmental Problems (SCEP), Massachusetts Institute of Technology Press, 1970.

Ocean Dumping: A National Policy. Council on Environmental Quality, October 1970.

Wastes Management Concepts for the Coastal Zone. National Academy of Sciences/National Academy of Engineering, 1970.

In addition to the specific references given above, you may want to look at past issues of *Marine Pollution Bulletin,* a periodical published by Macmillan (Journals) Ltd., London.

To keep up with further progress in the eleven fields discussed, the following periodicals can be profitably consulted: *Chemical & Engineering News, Nature* (Friday edition), *New Scientist and Science Journal, Science, Science News, Scientific American,* and *Technology Review.*

INDEX

Italicized numbers indicate photographs

Accelerators. *See* Heavy-ion accelerators
Acetylene test, nitrogen fixation evaluation, 153
ACTH. *See* Adrenocorticotrophic hormone
Adenosine triphosphate, nitrogen fixation, 151, 157
Adrenocorticotrophic hormone, synthesis, 135
Aedes nigromaculis, 184
Age pigments, aging research, 34
Aging, 21–43
Air, interactions with seawater, 209; nitrogen source for ammonia, 145, 158
Alanine, ribonuclease structure analysis, 127; ribonuclease activity studies, 133
Albertino, Richard J., 15
Algae, marine life studies, 213
ALICE machine, 63
Alkali, glass composition, 102
Allantoin, 8
Allen, A. D., 156
Allen, Leland, 202
Allopurinol, gout treatment, 5
Alpha decay, superheavy elements, 67, 79
Alvarez, Luis, 92
Amenhotep II, glass samples, 106
Amines, production from atmospheric nitrogen, 157
Amino acids, detection in interstellar space, 60; nitrogen fixation, 147; protein production research, 38; protein structure determination, 127; ribonuclease structure, 120, 127
Ammonia, detection in interstellar space, 48; production by Haber process, 146; production by nitrogen fixation, 146, 148
Amniocentesis, Lesch-Nyhan syndrome test, 9
Anfinsen, Christian B., 129
Anomalous water, 187–206; distillation, 200; production, 189; production from heavy water, 201. *See also* Russian water
Antenna, insect olfaction studies, 170
Antimony, glass colorant, 107
Ants, slave-making weapons, 173
Apples, red-banded leaf roller moth attacks, 164
Archaeology, ancient glass. *See* Glass
Arctic Ocean, oil pollution, 222
Argon-37, solar neutrino detection, 92, 95

Arn, Heinrich, *165*
Arthritis. *See* Gouty arthritis
Ashes, ocean dumping, 228
Astrochemistry. *See* Molecular astronomy
Atomic number, 64
Atoms, detection in interstellar space, 48; nucleus models, 77
ATP. *See* Adenosine triphosphate
Autoimmune diseases, aging research, 42
Autoradiography, Lesch-Nyhan carrier detection, 12
Autosomes, 10
Azides, nitrogenase activity, 153

Bahcall, John N., 93, 99
Balloon flights, superheavy element detection, 72
Basal ganglia, 7
Beck, Curt, 118
Beechwood, magnesium source for glassmaking. 105
Bees, chemical communications, 175
Bello, Jake, 131
Bergersen, F. J., 161
Bergstrom, G., 174
Bernal, J. D., 121, 192
Beryllium, neutron production process, 93
Beryllium-8, solar neutrino detection, 98
Besborodov, M. A., 103
Beta decay, superheavy elements, 71, 79
Beth She'arim, glass slab, *104*
Bethe, Hans, 90
Bhandari, N., 76
BHT. *See* Butyl hydroxytoluene
Binding energies, 72
Binowski, Norbert J., 112
Bjorksten, Johan, 26
Black Cloud, The, 51
Blann, H. Marshall, 68
Blue-green algae, nitrogen fixers, 148
Blum, Murray S., 175
Board, Robert, 199
Bonds. *See* Hydrogen bonds
Boron, neutron production process, 93
Boron-8, solar neutrino detection, 98
Bostrom, R. C., 226
Bottom sediments, interactions with seawater, 209
Bowen, Vaughan T., 224
Bowman, Harry, 118
Bradykinin, synthesis, 138
Bragg, Lawrence, 121